Royall Tyler

Royall Tyler

G. *George* THOMAS TANSELLE

HARVARD UNIVERSITY PRESS

Cambridge, Massachusetts

1 9 6 7

TO MY

MOTHER AND FATHER

Preface

ROYALL TYLER once said of biographers, "I do not thank the author who pursues his hero into the recesses of domestic life, and exhibits the disgusting infirmities of our common nature." He also described, in verse, the scholar who looks on his musty manuscripts, "cites and quotes, / On illustration clear intent; / And in the margin gravely notes / A thousand meanings — never meant." [1] But perhaps he would pardon this intrusion on his privacy, however many unintended meanings it discloses, for the time has surely come, after a century and a half, when further abstinence would be a matter not of propriety but of neglect. If Tyler is not a major figure in the story of American literature, he is an important one historically, both in his accomplishments and in what he represents. He has long been accorded a line in literary histories for his play *The Contrast* (1787), the first native comedy professionally produced; but his efforts to encourage a truly American literature, in the formative years of the new republic, embraced fiction, poetry, and the essay as well, and his own productions in these areas, if less well-known, are equally significant. A study of Tyler not only encompasses nearly all the aspects of the literary world of his time but illustrates the dilemma faced by literary men of the young nation. Literature was not a profession, only a pastime; Tyler was a lawyer and man of affairs first, a writer second. But his dedication, in principle and in practice, to the idea of a native literature makes his story particularly worth record-

[1] *The Yankey in London* (New York, 1809), p. 53; *The Chestnut Tree* (North Montpelier, 1931), lines 625–628.

vii

ing; and it is that story which I have attempted to sketch here.

That this should be, only now, the first book on a man who has been called "one of the most interesting minds of his day" [2] is owing to a number of circumstances, chief among them the difficulty of gaining access to the Tyler papers. It is not, however, the result of a lack of interest in Tyler, for commentators have repeatedly remarked that he deserved closer study, almost from the time of his death in 1826. One obituary declared that "some of his fugitive productions were among the most animating effusions of the eventful days of the second, third, and fourth Presidents," and another said that his novel *The Algerine Captive*, "unquestionably one of the most original and brilliant productions of this generation, will forever secure him a high rank among American writers." [3] Three years later Samuel Kettell, in his *Specimens of American Poetry*, included six of Tyler's poems and a biographical sketch. [4] Then William Dunlap, in his pioneer *History of the American Theatre* (1832), gave a brief account of *The Contrast* and of Tyler, and Joseph T. Buckingham devoted eight pages of his *Specimens of Newspaper Literature* (1850) to the "Colon & Spondee" pieces. [5] Tyler's poetry was discussed in some detail by Pliny H. White, speaking before the Vermont Historical

[2] Alexander Cowie, *The Rise of the American Novel* (New York, 1948), p. 60.

[3] Boston *Columbian Centinel*, 23 August 1826; the second quotation is quoted by the *Centinel* from the Brattleboro *Messenger* (cf. *Northern Sentinel*, 8 September 1826). A contemporary estimate (though admittedly a conventional compliment) is found in James Elliot's *Poetical and Miscellaneous Works* (Greenfield, Mass., 1798), in the last four stanzas (16 lines) of his poem "The Autumnal Season, Addressed to Royal Tyler, Esq." (pp. 43–45): in Tyler he finds "the fruits of early knowledge shine" and "the graces and the virtues blend"; nature has given Tyler "Art, eloquence and taste, alike to grace / The bar, the senate or the studious shade," and Tyler deserves the "meed of genius and the poet's bays."

[4] Samuel Kettell, *Specimens of American Poetry* (Boston, 1829), II, 47–54.

[5] William Dunlap, *History of the American Theatre* (New York, 1832), pp. 71–74; Joseph T. Buckingham, *Specimens of Newspaper Literature* (Boston, 1850), II, 202–210.

Society on 18 October 1860,[6] and his newspaper columns were noticed by Andrew Peabody in 1889.[7] Those two large collections, the Duyckincks' *Cyclopaedia of American Literature* (1855) and Stedman and Hutchinson's *Library of American Literature* (1888), contained sections on Tyler, and the facts of his life were recounted in *Appleton's Cyclopaedia of American Biography* (1889) and in the *National Cyclopaedia* (1892).[8] The Duyckincks went so far as to say, "His life certainly deserves to be narrated with more particularity than it has yet received. His writings, too, should be collected and placed in an accessible form. American literature cannot be charged with poverty while it has such valuables uninvested in its forgotten repositories."

For several generations scholars have repeated essentially the same statement,[9] without producing either the biography or the "posthumous and elegant edition" (which one of Tyler's friends predicted in 1797).[10] A beginning was made by Thomas Pickman Tyler, who wrote a long memoir of his father, incorporating many letters and documents; though never published, it served as the basis for his paper before the

[6] Published as "Early Poets of Vermont" in the *Proceedings of the Vermont Historical Society, 1917–1918* (1920), pp. 93–125 (pp. 108–119 on Tyler).

[7] In an article on the *Farmer's Weekly Museum* in the *Proceedings of the American Antiquarian Society*, n.s. VI (1889), 106–129 (see pp. 115–116).

[8] Evert A. and George L. Duyckinck, *Cyclopaedia of American Literature* (Philadelphia, 1855), I, 432–437; E. C. Stedman and E. M. Hutchinson, *A Library of American Literature* (New York, 1888), IV, 92–106; *Appleton's Cyclopaedia of American Biography*, VI (New York, 1889), 201; *National Cyclopaedia of American Biography*, VI (New York, 1892), 39.

[9] A contrary point of view is represented by William P. Trent, who described Tyler, in his *History of American Literature* (New York, 1903), as "a versatile American who deserves to be respected, though hardly to have his works republished" (pp. 200–202); and George O. Seilhamer, in his *History of the American Theatre* (New York, 1888–1891), had said that Tyler's works were "deservedly forgotten" (II, 239).

[10] William Coleman to Tyler, 24 September 1797, in Tyler memoir (cf. Chapter 1, note 4, below), p. 103.

Vermont Bar Association on 20 October 1879 and for Henry
Burnham's extensive account of Tyler in his book on Brattleboro (1880).[11] A mark of this renewed and serious interest
was Thomas J. McKee's edition of *The Contrast* in 1887 (its
first printing since 1790), as the first publication of the Dunlap Society. Since that time the fortunes of Tyler have been
in the hands of a few devoted researchers with either a family or a Vermont connection. Helen Tyler Brown, Tyler's
great-granddaughter, spent much of her life doing an enor-
mous amount of genealogical and historical research on the
family and had ambitious plans for a full-scale biography and
edition. She worked closely with Professor Frederick Tupper
of the University of Vermont, and together they edited the
reminiscences of Tyler's wife, published in 1925 as *Grandmother Tyler's Book*. Also she contributed an introduction
to James B. Wilbur's elegant limited edition of *The Contrast*
in 1920, and Tupper read a general paper on Tyler before the
Vermont Historical Society on 7 July 1927.[12] Walter J.
Coates, with his Driftwind Press of North Montpelier, took
an interest in Tyler, published his long poem *The Chestnut
Tree* in a limited edition in 1931, included a checklist in
Driftwind in 1932, and edited several anthologies of Vermont
verse which contained Tyler poems.[13] Four years later Arthur
Hobson Quinn wrote, for the *Dictionary of American Biography*, the most scholarly biographical account that had appeared. Next came two scholars from Norwich University
in Northfield, Vermont — Arthur W. Peach and George F.
Newbrough. In 1941 they edited from the Tyler Papers four
unpublished plays for the Princeton series of "America's Lost

[11] Tyler, "Royall Tyler," *Proceedings of the Vermont Bar Association,*
I (1878–1881), 44–62; Burnham, *Brattleboro, Windham County, Vermont*
(Brattleboro, 1880), pp. 83–101.
[12] *Proceedings of the Vermont Historical Society*, IV (1928), 65–101.
[13] *Favorite Vermont Poems, Series One* (North Montpelier, 1928), pp.
5–9; *Series Five* (1934), pp. 18–19; and, with Tupper, *Vermont Verse: An
Anthology* (Brattleboro, 1932), pp. 25–27.

Plays"; but their plans, announced in that volume, for a complete edition and a definitive biography did not reach fruition. One of Tupper's graduate students, Bertrand W. Chapman, wrote a master's thesis on Tyler's "nativism" in 1933; and in 1962 Marius B. Péladeau prepared an edition of Tyler's poetry for his Georgetown master's degree. Beyond this, there has been virtually no work on Tyler, other than a few popular magazine articles (usually on *The Contrast*) and brief accounts in standard surveys. Arthur Peach wrote in 1936, "It is an interesting, if not a somewhat tragic fact, that the literary history of America has been lacking in any adequate consideration of the work of the writer of the first American comedy, acted in professional theaters, and the author of the first American novel to be republished in England." [14]

There is no doubt that much of Tyler's work is difficult to come by — scattered anonymous pieces in scarce newspapers or editions of which only a few copies survive — but this situation is equally true of certain of Tyler's contemporaries, like Joseph Dennie and Thomas Green Fessenden, who were the subjects of biographies fifty years ago. The main reason for Tyler's neglect has been the peculiar, but not altogether unusual, situation surrounding the family papers. Because the family had a strong sense of its heritage, various members have hoped to write their own accounts before the materials were released to outsiders. Helen Tyler Brown, attempting to carry on the work of Thomas Pickman Tyler, did allow certain scholars — particularly Tupper and Peach — to work with her, but she wanted to produce an "official" family biography of Royall Tyler. As time passed, and the quantity of research notes increased, she began to deposit them (through the early 1930's) in the Vermont Historical Society, but with the understanding that they be closed to the public until her

[14] "The Royall Tyler Collection," *Proceedings of the Vermont Historical Society*, n.s. IV (1936), 3-4.

biography was completed. Before her death in 1935, she appointed three trustees (Tupper, Henry S. Wardner, and Mary R. Cabot, later replaced by Peach), who would have exclusive use of the papers until a biography and an edition could be published. They managed to get out the *Four Plays*, but nothing else, before they died (within a few years of each other), leaving no instructions about who was to continue the work. The Vermont Historical Society was thus left with a legal problem; scholars asked to see the papers, but the Society, acting under the terms of Helen Tyler Brown's will, was not free to admit them. The papers remained inaccessible for twenty years, until the Society, working with Judge Beatrice J. Brown of the Marlboro District Probate Court and the heirs, was finally able, in May 1964, to open them to qualified scholars.[15] The good intentions of Helen Tyler Brown had the effect, in the end, of turning scholarly attention away from her great-grandfather — even of stimulating wild speculations, as the repeated contemporary references to his youthful indiscretions, followed by a descendant who closely guards the family papers, were bound to do.

The Tyler Papers should be of great usefulness to the historian, the economist, and the genealogist of nineteenth-century New England, for the ten large boxes of material are fullest in the accumulations of notebooks, letters, and sermons of Tyler's children and grandchildren and in material relating to Helen Tyler Brown's research. The papers of Tyler himself are unfortunately few in number, and many exist only in later typed copies; but what there is can now be examined, and a major impediment to research has been re-

[15] The text of the agreement between the heirs and the Society, opening the papers to scholarly use, is in the Vermont Historical Society *News and Notes*, XV (July 1964), 84–86. For other information about the Tyler Papers, see *Proceedings of the Vermont Historical Society*, n.s. IV (1936), 3–4, 22, 27, 29, 35, 39, 43; V (1937), 44.

moved. It is time to sift the remains and to complete the task begun over a century ago by Thomas Pickman Tyler. If a definitive edition and biography of Royall Tyler could appear in a 1952 list of the desiderata for scholarship in English and American literature,[16] they would still be on the list. I have tried to assemble some of the facts about Tyler and to assess his literary career, not to produce the authorized account Helen Tyler Brown hoped for, but to provide a starting point for the further research which she knew was justified.[17]

G.T.T.

Madison, Wisconsin
Lebanon, Indiana
   June 1965

[16] Chauncey Sanders, *An Introduction to Research in English Literary History* (New York, 1952), p. 124.

[17] I wish to express my gratitude to the Graduate School of the University of Wisconsin for providing the grants necessary to carry out part of the research for this book.

Contents

Illustrations

A photograph showing some of the material in the Tyler Papers, as displayed in 1929, is reproduced in *The Earliest Diary of John Adams*, ed. L. H. Butterfield *et al.* (Cambridge: Harvard University Press, 1966), facing p. 43. Portraits of other members of the Tyler family are reproduced in *Grandmother Tyler's Book*.

Royall Tyler

❊ I ❊

Lawyer and Wit

B OSTON in the middle of the eighteenth century was a bustling settlement of something less than fifteen thousand inhabitants, a commercial center that exuded the atmosphere of being at the heart of important events. It was to become an even more exciting place in the next two decades, though the Bostonians who followed the activities of Braddock, Shirley, and Montcalm in the 1750's could not know that the steps leading to a break with England would occur virtually in their front yards only a few years later. The Stamp Act in 1765 brought about the organized resistance of the Sons of Liberty and the Boston merchants, who again voiced their protest, in 1767, to the Townshend Acts; the next year Boston customs officials were attacked when they tried to collect duty on the cargo of the *Liberty*, and the merchants agreed on a firmer policy of nonimportation. There followed the quartering of troops in Boston, continual skirmishes with these soldiers leading to the "Boston Massacre," Sam Adams' organization of "committees of correspondence," the Boston Tea Party, and eventually the battles at Lexington and Concord.

If the air everywhere was full of whispered conversations and secret plans, it was especially so in the center of Boston. Among the successful merchants there, who profited from war contracts and who met with Sam Adams and the patriots of the "Long Room Club" over Edes & Gill's printing office, was Royall Tyler, Sr. He lived in Ann Street, in the shadow

I

of Faneuil Hall, and operated his importing business from an adjacent storeroom that faced the wharf. Ambitious in politics, he was called "Pug Sly" and was well versed in the art of giving elaborate dinners and in all the hypocrisies of gaining public favor (the fine points of which he taught to his Harvard classmate James Otis). He served on innumerable town committees and worked his way up, through Justice of the Peace and Overseer of the Poor, to a seat in the House of Representatives (1759–1764) and then to a position on the King's Council, which he held from 1764 until his death in 1771. Fond of the limelight, he found himself there frequently — as, in 1754, when he refused to testify upon being questioned about a pamphlet ridiculing the House (he even sued Speaker Hubbard for imagining that he could be connected with it); or when, in 1768, he led the committee which demanded the withdrawal of the British fleet from the harbor and the troops from the city; or when, at a meeting after the Boston Massacre, he spoke so rashly about driving out the British soldiers that he turned his fellow Whigs against him.[1]

This active figure was a member of an established Boston family, settled there in 1680 by his grandfather, Captain Thomas Tyler, son of a Devonshire merchant-ship captain. One of Thomas' four sons, William (born 15 March 1688), had married Sarah Royall on 7 December 1710; and the patriot Royall, born on 8 September 1724, was one of their ten children. Rejecting the practice of law after his graduation from Harvard in 1743 to take over his father's business, he had married Mary Steele, daughter of Captain John Steele, on 24 December 1747, and the couple had four children.[2] One can imagine no more exciting place for a child to grow up than in Boston's Ann Street of the 1760's, where the happenings in the harbor could be clearly viewed. It is perhaps not surprising that one of these children, who could watch his father and other patriots in daily activities that led to revolution and who had roots in Boston going back four generations, would be among the first to use native American materials in works of literature and to express his patriotism as naturally in belles-lettres as in more direct service to his government.

College, War, and Love

The youngest child of Royall and Mary Steele Tyler was born on 18 July 1757, ten years after their marriage. He was named William Clark, but following his father's death the name was changed by an act of the General Court, at his mother's request, to Royall.[3] We are told that he was "more studious and thoughtful" as a child than his brother, John Steele[4] (there were two older daughters, Mary and Jane), and in 1765 he entered the South Latin School in Boston (under Tory principal John Lovell). One can picture him walking to school from Ann Street, by Faneuil Hall, along the thoroughfare of Cornhill, past the State House, to the Latin School on School Street near King's Chapel. On this route he must have witnessed hurried conferences between patriots and occasional fights when the British troops arrived, and he must have spent many after-school hours watching the activities in the harbor or listening to the bells that announced the Boston Massacre or the repeal of the Stamp Act,[5] although he was to make very little reference to Revolutionary events in his later writings. But the Boston of his childhood did furnish material for certain passages in "The Bay Boy," especially his description of a typical Boston street scene on a Saturday and Sunday, with the street cleaners replaced by the church crowds. No doubt he had sat through many a Sunday afternoon service, in which "every pew exhibited drowsiness in all its dozing attitudes" — the "witty maiden," for example, sleeping "serenely under the covert of her hat or bonnet unconscious that her waving plumes by their abrupt noddings betrayed the secret she so artfully attempted to conceal."

3

And perhaps, like the hero of "The Bay Boy," he kept his eyes on one such maiden at church and found that his "heart thumped like a bass drum."

Just before his fifteenth birthday, Tyler finished the usual seven years' work at Latin School and was ready to enter Harvard, which he did on 15 July 1772. Harvard in these years was just as much a center of revolutionary activity as Ann Street, and Tyler found that his brief journey across the Charles did not take him to a secluded retreat. The student body was anxious to express its patriotism: one way was to abstain from tea (as the seniors had voted to do four years before Tyler's entrance), but a more direct way was to join the student military company, the Marti-Mercurian Band (formed in 1769–70), which had been furnished with weapons only the year before Tyler's arrival. The presence of the General Court meetings in Cambridge (until March 1773) further aroused student feeling, so that by the end of Tyler's freshman year agitation was beginning to mount rapidly. It was not until the end of his second year, however, that British troops occupied Boston to enforce the Boston Port Act and thousands of armed patriots converged in Cambridge, preparatory to besieging Boston. In the midst of such unsettled conditions, college authorities decided not to hold a public commencement that year — nor, as it turned out, was another held until 1781. Students occasionally went into Boston to watch the British drills, but in the spring of 1775, Tyler's junior year, they had an opportunity to see British soldiers in Cambridge, when Lord Percy marched through on his way to give support to the troops at Lexington. As the patriot forces gained strength, the problem of housing them in Cambridge became increasingly acute, despite the availability of the vacated mansions on "Tory Row." The Committee of Safety sent the students home early that year, on 1 May, and the Provincial Congress appropriated the college buildings; even so, tents had to be

4

pitched all over town, and, as winter approached, temporary barracks were constructed in the college Yard and the Common. The college obviously could not operate in Cambridge, and Concord was eventually selected as the place where classes would resume on 4 October 1775. Tyler spent his senior year there, until 21 June 1776, when the depleted student body (probably fewer than one hundred students) returned to Cambridge.[6]

Tyler attended Harvard in the years just after certain important changes in policy were made. In 1766, for instance, the practice of having separate tutors for each subject was instituted (instead of one tutor who taught all subjects to each class); and at the beginning of Tyler's stay, under the administration of Samuel Locke, the ranking of students according to social and financial standing was changed to a listing in alphabetical order. The revised 1767 laws stipulated that "No one shall be admitted, unless he can translate the Greek and Latin Authors in common use, . . . understands the Rules of Grammar, can write Latin correctly, and hath a good moral Character." The Latin School had furnished Tyler with these accomplishments, and the moral character presumably was to be perpetuated by the required morning and evening chapel. A more interesting article in the laws, considering the direction of Tyler's later achievement, read, "If any Undergraduate shall presume to be an Actor in, a Spectator at, or any Ways concerned in any Stage Plays, Interludes or Theatrical Entertainments in the Town of Cambridge or elsewhere, he shall for the first Offence be degraded — & for any repeated Offence shall be rusticated or expelled." [7] Public speaking, on the other hand, was allowed, and both the Speaking Club (formed by Samuel Phillips in 1770) and the Mercurian Club (guided by Fisher Ames of the class of 1774) were in operation during Tyler's first year — with the Speaking Club, at any rate, more interested in literary than political subjects. The two clubs merged in 1773 but became less active as war approached; the group was revived, however, by some of Tyler's classmates and friends, such as Christopher Gore and Rufus King, and Tyler (though not a member) may well have begun at this time to practice the oratory for which he was to become known in the courtroom.

Nineteen years old, Tyler received his degree in July of 1776, just after the Declaration of Independence, in a class that included Gore (later Governor of Massachusetts and a United States Senator) and Samuel Sewall and George Thacher (later Justices of the Massachusetts Supreme Court); for his academic achievement he was also awarded a B.A. from Yale *ad eundem*.[8] Directly before and during Tyler's college years, several events took place in his family: in 1771 his sister Mary died at the age of eighteen; his father died on 20 May of the same year (aged forty-six) and was buried at King's Chapel with elaborate rites befitting his prominence — or notoriety; on 11 October 1772, his mother remarried (again a merchant, William Whitwell) and moved to Jamaica Plain; during the spring of 1775 (Tyler's junior year) this second husband died; and that June Tyler's brother John married their stepsister, Sarah Whitwell. Tyler's father had been successful as a merchant, and, whatever the precise amount of the estate, Tyler's inheritance was large enough to prevent his having any financial worries at this time; it is probable that he spent money with some freedom during his college years and those immediately following.[9] The only incident which family tradition records for Tyler's college career involves his rustication to Maine with his roommate Gore, but not for spending money. It seems that their room was above the door to their building; one day, when they had thrown down a hook and line to catch a pig from among the litter in the yard, they became so engrossed that they did not notice Samuel Langdon (the ineffectual President who had succeeded

6

Locke in 1774) heading for the door under them, and the hook inevitably caught in his wig.[10] Given Tyler's disposition as revealed in his later writing, his possession of some money, and the general atmosphere (discipline had been notoriously slack under President Locke, and many students boarded in taverns during the Concord period), it is unlikely that all Tyler's escapades were as mild as this one.

After graduation, Tyler began the study of law with Francis Dana of Cambridge, who had just returned from a year and a half in England, having concluded that a peaceful settlement was impossible; when Dana left to attend the Continental Congress in 1777, Tyler continued his legal preparation with Benjamin Hichborn of Boston and perhaps with Oakes Angier, a prominent lawyer who had formerly been a student of John Adams.[11] Whatever reputation for wit and brilliance Tyler had achieved during his Harvard years increased through his association with a group of talented and promising young men who gathered in the rooms of the painter John Trumbull, at what was later 5–9 Scollay Square (previously occupied by John Smibert). Trumbull, of the class of 1773, commented in his autobiography (1841) on this "club . . . of young men fresh from college" (mostly from the classes of 1776 and 1777), which included, besides Tyler, William Eustis (later a member of Congress and minister to Holland), Aaron Dexter (later a Harvard professor of medicine), Rufus King (later a Senator and minister to England), Thomas Dawes (a lawyer), and Christopher Gore. These men, says Trumbull, "regaled themselves with a cup of tea instead of wine, and discussed subjects of literature, politics and war," [12] although their activities were not always so restrained. On 20 October 1777, for example, Tyler, Sewall, and King created a drunken disturbance in Cambridge ("horrid Profanity, riotous & Tumultuous Noises, & breaking of Windows at College") and were summoned before a faculty meeting.

According to the faculty records, Tyler responded, "Pray Gentlemen! What right have you to call me before you? I am surprized you should be ingaged in such Business! What Punishment can you inflict upon me? What do I care for a little paltry Degree which may be bought at any time for twenty shillings. If honor in this Country consists in Degrees, you are very welcome Gentlemen to deprive me of yours, for I have two others already." [13] Jeremiah Mason recalls that Tyler (with his "brilliant wit," "amusing conversation," and "natural talents") "entered at once, with great zeal and zest, into the dissipated habits and manners which at that time characterized the young men of Boston." [14] It has been suggested also that Tyler was the father of Royal Morse (born in 1779) by a well-known college "character," the cleaning woman Katharine Morse.[15] Whether or not this particular report is true, Tyler did later refer to these years as his period of "dissipation," and the general tone of the combined testimony is undoubtedly accurate.

Perhaps it was as a result of some of the discussions at Trumbull's "club" during the winter of 1777–78 (the same winter when Burgoyne's surrendered troops were quartered in Cambridge, contributing — in the historian Mercy Warren's view — to the atmosphere of idleness and dissipation) [16] that several of the men joined the Independent Company of soldiers then forming in Boston under Colonel John Hancock. Tyler, as well as King and Trumbull himself, enlisted; Tyler's preceptor Hichborn was the third officer and his brother John Steele the fifth.[17] By late summer of 1778 General John Sullivan had assumed control of the attack on the British at Newport, and Tyler was made an aide to Sullivan, with the rank of major. In August, Sullivan had under his command at Providence a force of ten thousand men and was ready to proceed toward Newport and make a combined attack with the French fleet under d'Estaing. But the French fleet arrived first and, after a skirmish with Howe and the damages of a storm, decided to sail to Boston for repairs, leaving Sullivan's militia without support. Sullivan began to retreat on 28 August; the Battle of Rhode Island (or of Quaker Hill) on 29 August demonstrated that the British were still in control of Newport and ended Sullivan's ill-fated expedition. During the confused retreat, even before the battle, the troops became separated, and it happened (according to the family story) that Tyler and a soldier named Daggett found themselves sharing a barn the night before the combat. They discussed, among other things, the best part of the body in which to receive a bullet; the next day, with a bullet in his lungs, Daggett said, "Ah, Rial, you see I did not have my choice." [18] Such is the extent of Tyler's participation in the war.

Following this interlude, Tyler returned to his legal studies, presumably under Benjamin Hichborn, was granted a master's degree from Harvard in 1779 (after apologizing for his conduct in 1777), and was admitted to the bar (the Inferior Court) on 19 August 1780.[19] Because business in Boston was at a low ebb during this part of the Revolution and commerce was forced to go to Maine, he decided to begin his legal career in Falmouth (now Portland), which was just beginning to recover from a British burning. Although no record of the extent of Tyler's practice at Falmouth survives, one episode is traditionally told: accompanied by the sheriff, he boarded a privateer in the harbor to serve a writ, whereupon the privateer sailed away, pausing only long enough to put Tyler and the sheriff off at Booth Bay.[20] Whether such experiences or the generally more optimistic outlook in Boston was responsible — or whether, as Abigail Adams later said, "his ambition & genious could not brook a retirement like that" [21] — Tyler moved back to the Boston area in the spring of 1782, after less than two years at Falmouth.

He took lodgings in Braintree with the family of Richard and Mary Cranch, and opened an office in their house as well. There were two Cranch daughters of eligible age, and it is not to be wondered that a handsome young lawyer, of high promise and great wit, with his scarlet coat and ruffled shirt, should have caused some excitement in the household; indeed, his arrival seems to have been discussed by all the young ladies of the village. Possibly for the very reason that Betsy Cranch and the others invited his attention, he had little interest in them, but an equally cogent reason was that his eye had quickly been caught by the Cranches' niece, seventeen-year-old Nabby Adams, daughter of John Adams, the future President. Mary (Smith) Cranch was a sister of Abigail Adams, and the relationship between the house in Braintree and that in Quincy was an intimate one. During the summer and fall of 1782 Tyler's acquaintance with Abigail and her daughter grew increasingly close, and he found excuses for calling on them — for example, when he had a particularly difficult writ to draw, he would ask if he could borrow a book of forms from Adams' library. By winter he was spending many evenings with them, and the mother, at least, was charmed by him. She could see that he was falling in love with Nabby (as the young Abigail was generally called by her family) and felt somewhat guilty about not having mentioned the situation in her letters to her husband, who had been in Europe since early 1780 negotiating the peace treaty.

Accordingly, on 23 December 1782 she wrote him in detail about this young man with "a sprightly fancy, a warm imagination and an agreable person." Although she felt obliged to mention the fact that there had been a period of dissipation in his life, when he was "rather negligent" in pursuing his professional career, she emphasized the fact that he had now reformed completely. "I am not acquainted with any young Gentleman whose attainments in literature are equal to his, who judges with greater accuracy or discovers a more delicate and refined taste." After commenting on her daughter's reserved nature, which seemed only to attract him the more, she continued, "I know not a young fellow upon the stage whose language is so pure or whose natural disposition is more agreeable — his days are devoted to his office, his Evenings of late to my fire side — his attachment is too obvious to escape notice. I do not think the Lady wholly indifferent; yet her reserve & apparent coldness is such that I know he is in miserable doubt." [22] Exactly a week later Abigail wrote her husband another long letter about Tyler, describing his previous legal career and reporting that he had been conducting his Braintree office with "great steadiness and application," which had "gained the esteem and business of the Town." She found his disposition "exceedingly amiable" and his "attractions perhaps too powerful even to a young Lady possesst with as much apparent coldness and indifference as ever you saw in one character" — with the result that his attention "daily becomes more pleasing" to Nabby.[23] In a third letter, on 10 January 1783, Abigail again alluded to the matter: "I see, what I scarcely believe in my power to prevent without doing violence to Hearts which I hope are honest and good. . . . I wish for your advice and counsel." [24]

John Adams' advice, in no equivocal terms, was prompt in coming, for by 22 January he had received the first of Abigail's letters on the affair and replied, "I confess I dont like the Subject at all. My Child is too young for such Thoughts, and I dont like your word 'Dissipation' at all." Nabby was a "Model," he felt, not to be given to "any, even reformed Rake"; while a lawyer would be his choice, "it must be a Lawyer who spends his Midnights as well as Evenings at his Age over his Books not at any Lady's Fire Side. . . . A youth who has been giddy enough to spend his Fortune or half his Fortune in Gaieties is not the youth for me, let his Person,

Family, Connections and Taste for Poetry be what they will. I am not looking out for a Poet, nor a Professor of belle Letters." Tyler's brother in Europe, according to Adams, was "a detestible Specimen"; Tyler's father, on the other hand, was "an Honourable Man," although he "had not all those nice sentiments which I wish." Finally, Adams criticized Abigail for allowing the matter to have advanced so far and for implying disapproval of Nabby's reserve ("her greatest Glory"); "I dont like," he added, "this Method of Courting Mothers." His letters throughout the winter and spring continued to take up the subject — indeed, to belabor it. On 29 January he warned Nabby not to be impressed by superficial accomplishments; on 4 February he said of Tyler, "That Frivolity of Mind, which breaks out into such Errors in Youth, never gets out of the Man but shews itself in some mean Shape or other through Life"; and on 28 March he summed up his feelings:

My dear Daughters happiness employs my Thought night and Day. Dont let her form any Connections with any one, who is not devoted entirely to Study and to Business, — to honour & Virtue. — If there is a Trait of Frivolity and Dissipation left, I pray that she may renounce it, forever. I ask not Fortune nor Favour for mine, but Prudence, Talents, and Labour. She may go with my Consent wherever she can find enough of these.

He was willing to admit, however, that Tyler seemed to be a promising young man, except for one "Trait in his Character, his gaiety" — which made him "but a Prodigal Son." [25]

Even before she received these letters, Abigail had concluded that it would be prudent "to put a present period . . . to the Idea of a connection," [26] and Nabby went to Boston in January to spend the rest of the winter there — though not, as Abigail assured her husband, because "any of those Qualities you justly dread have appeared in this gentleman since his residence in this Town," for "his conduct has been regular, and his manners pure, nor has he discovered any Love of Gaiety inconsistent even with your Ideas." She admitted "a partiality in his favour," but was happy to be able to report that the affair "is now so far laid aside as gives me reason to think it will never again be renewed." [27] That this conclusion was premature became clear after Nabby had returned from Boston, for Abigail then reported that Tyler "now visits in this family with the freedom of an acquaintance, tho' not with the intimacy of a nearer connection," and she again spoke on his behalf: "he is regular in his liveing, keeps no company with Gay companions, seeks no amusement but in the society of two or 3 families in Town, never goes to Boston but when business calls him there." [28] By July 1783 Tyler had been sworn in as an attorney of the Supreme Judicial Court; [29] by October he had a young schoolmaster named Perkins studying law under him; and by December he had purchased the excellent 108-acre Borland farm [30] — all three facts indicative of his seriousness and desire to settle down, and duly recorded by Abigail. In fact, her confidence in him was great enough that she turned over Adams' account books to him, in case he could collect some of the accounts that had become delinquent since Adams' departure.[31]

Adams, anxious to be reunited with Abigail after their long separation, decided that a trip to Europe for both mother and daughter would not only accomplish the purpose of bringing them all together but perhaps end the connection with Tyler. He set forth this plan once on 14 October: "The Lady comes to Europe with you. — If the Parties preserve their Regard untill they meet again and continue to behave as they ought, they will be still young enough." [32] But by late January 1784 he was more temperate about forcing Nabby to accompany her mother:

if Miss Nabby is attached, to Braintree, and you think, upon advising with your Friends, her object worthy, marry her if you will and leave her with her Companion in your own House, Office, Furniture, Farm & all. His Profession is, the very one I wish. — His Connections are respectable and if he has sown his wild Oats and will study, and mind his Business, he is all I want. . . . I can scarcely think it possible for me to disapprove of her final Judgment formed with deliberation, upon any Thing which so deeply concerns her whole Happiness.[33]

Nevertheless both Abigail and her daughter did sail for England, on board the *Active*, on 20 June 1784. One can imagine the parting scene, as Abigail recounted it: "I have great satisfaction in the behaviour of my daughter. The Struggle of her mind was great, her passions strong, never before calld into opposition; the parting of two persons strongly attached to each other is only to be felt; discription fails."[34] Tyler returned to his room crying, "She is gone! I shall never see her more!" and threw himself upon the couch and wept.[35]

Before this break, Tyler had written to Adams only once, five months before, on 13 January:

I will not presume . . . that my attentions to your Daughter are unknown to you: If you demand why an affair of so much importance to your Domestic Concerns was not communicated by me sooner — I hope that my youth, the early progress of my professional career, and the continued expectation of your daily return to your Family will be accepted as a sufficient Apology. . . . I do not think myself entitled to your Consent to an immediate union yet I cannot suffer this separation without requesting your permission to expect it when ever she shall return to Her native country.

The letter was enclosed in one from Richard Cranch, who commented on Tyler: "he has boarded at our House for near two years past, and, from my acquaintance with him, he appears to me to be possessed of Politeness, Genious, Learning and Virtue; and I think he will make a very respectable Figure in his Profession of the Law. His Business in that Department increases daily." [36] Adams did not receive Tyler's letter until early April but replied immediately in a friendly tone:

Your Connections and Education are too respectable for me to entertain any objections to them: Your Profession is that for which I have the greatest respect and Veneration. The Testimonials I have received of your personal Character and Conduct are such as ought to remove all Scruples upon that head.

He praised Tyler's purchase of land and offered Tyler the use of his library. "But" he added significantly, "the Lady is coming to Europe with her Mother. It would be inconvenient to you to make a Voyage to Europe perhaps." Nevertheless, "you and the young Lady have my Consent to arrange your Plans according to your own Judgments." [37] Two days after receiving this letter, on 27 August, Tyler replied, expressing "all those returns of gratitude, which, a man of Ingenuity may be supposed to render to the person, to whom he shall have been Indebted in a High Degree, for the Principal Enjoyments of his Life." It would have been overly selfish, he piously continued, to have married Nabby before the trip because her filial duties in accompanying her mother across the Atlantic were more important. And he concluded in proper style, "We — I venture to speak for your Daughter — shall chearfully submit to your Inspection and advice, and I hope that our union will afford you and your Lady, that Enviable Satisfaction, which Parents experience when they Perceive their children, Usefull, Worthy, Respectable and Happy." [38]

For a time all was well. Tyler had written two letters to Abigail by 6 November, and she replied at great length on 4 January 1785, describing the daily routine in London and addressing Tyler as "the person to whose care & protection I shall one day resign a beloved and only daughter." Letters from the Cranches in the fall of 1784 refer to the letters Tyler was receiving from Nabby and the picture she had sent; and in January, Mary Cranch could still allude to Tyler with satisfaction: "His business I think increases & as far as I can judge he attends it with steadiness. He has his share at this court." [39] But by June her letters to Abigail contained rumblings that Tyler was not behaving as he should. For one thing, he was not delivering the letters which Nabby had sent to her friends in his care ("She must never wonder why she does not receive answers to her Letters till she is sure they are received. . . . It is one of his whims not to deliver Letters for a long time after he has recv'd them").[40] In addition, Tyler was apparently not writing to Nabby and did not even answer her May letter asking why he had not written. The vague rumors of Tyler's instability, combined with his seeming lack of attention and with the attractive presence in London of Adams' secretary of legation, Colonel William Stephens Smith, caused Nabby to decide (doubtless with some parental prompting)[41] to break off the match with Tyler. In the late summer of 1785 she wrote him: "Herewith you receive your letters and miniature with my desire that you would return mine to my Uncle Cranch, and my hopes that you are well satisfied with the affair as is / A.A." [42] Ten months later, on 12 June 1786, she and Smith were married.

The standard accounts of this whole episode, certainly one of the most celebrated in Tyler's life,[43] vary according to the conflicting traditions which have grown up in the two families. From the Adams point of view, Tyler had behaved dishonorably, both in his activities in Braintree and in his failure to write to Nabby; from the other side, Tyler was seen as the victim of malicious gossip circulated by Mary Cranch in her jealousy over the fact that Tyler did not court one of her daughters.[44] The truth no doubt lies in between, for there was some justification for dissatisfaction on both sides: it is evident, from Tyler's own admission, that he wrote very few letters to the Adamses in Europe, and it is equally clear, from

Mary Cranch's surviving letters, that she lost no opportunity of putting Tyler in an unfavorable light. In the middle of October 1785, before he had received Nabby's cold note of dismissal, Tyler had managed to write two long and friendly letters, one to John Adams and one to Abigail, full of current news, praise of John Quincy Adams (who had attended the opening of the Supreme Court in Boston with Tyler), and an explanation:

It has not been without anxiety, that I have refrained from addressing a Letter to you for some months past. But . . . there was but one Subject upon which I could write to you liberally: and I intended to have Desisted from that, until the Completion of my Arrangements should enable me to Discuss it to our mutual Satisfaction. But I am apprehensive, that you may impute to some less pleasing motive, what really originated in Respect: I Reassume my Pen.[45]

Meanwhile Mary Cranch was beginning her long series of letters to Abigail, each letter going into more detail than the last about Tyler's disgraceful behavior. On 8 November she reported that his office had been closed for five weeks, that he was ostentatiously showing Nabby's letters to everyone, and that he was even boasting about the fact that he had received six letters from Nabby before she could have had one from him; on 10 December she accused him of lying about putting letters aboard every ship; on 9 February 1786 she described his refusal to give up Nabby's letters and his announcement that Nabby's dismissal of him was only a misunderstanding created by unfriendly relatives; on 2 April she remarked disapprovingly that Tyler left the Cranch house each day after breakfast and did not return until the family was in bed at night, and that he planned to sail to Europe soon to straighten everything out. And through all these detailed accounts ran protestations that she had given Tyler no reason to be angry with her.[46]

However much credence may be given to Mary Cranch's letters, they were effective, and the general sentiment which prevailed among the Adams relatives, upon the announcement of Nabby's marriage to Smith, was one of relief that an unfortunate connection had been avoided. John Quincy Adams wrote to this effect on 28 December 1785, even though he and Tyler had been on friendly terms for several months before that time; [47] Eliza Shaw, another sister of Abigail's, pitied Tyler but granted that everyone felt the break to be for the best; [48] and Mary Cranch outdid herself in reporting Tyler's dejection:

I most heartily congratulate you all, not only upon your acquisition but upon your escape. — Can he after this delude another Family — must another unsuspecting fair one fall a victim to his vanity. — I have no pity to bestow upon him unless for his folly. He means to brave it I see — he puts on such an air of indifference & gaiety as plainly shows how much he is mortified. . . . How much more pleasure do you feel by introducing a man of such a universally good character into your Family than one exactly opposite to it.[49]

Two months later she could still describe him as "*dismally* mortified," and added, "I cannot help pitying him a little although he has told so many Fibs about me." [50] But the following fall she continued to recount unfavorable stories about Tyler, until Abigail finally asked her not to mention the subject again.[51] Despite the remarkably full documentation available, it is not possible to know the complete story nor to assign the shares of blame accurately; but at least one may say that neither side was wholly blameless — and surely John Adams was pleased that his original plan for avoiding the Tyler connection had worked so well.

Tyler's dejection found one outlet in physical activity, for he worked at improving the Borland farmhouse and even constructed a windmill in the spring of 1786 — which turned out by July to be a fiasco because (according to Mary Cranch) he did not listen to advice.[52] From the spring of 1785 on he had spent an increasingly smaller part of his time at the Cranch establishment, partly because of his suspicions of Mary Cranch's role in the split with the Adamses and partly because lodgings in Boston were more convenient when the court was in session there. While still keeping his room and office at the Cranches', he took another room with the Joseph Palmer family on Beacon Street. Among the lodgers there in the fall of 1785 was the blind Henry Moyes, who was delivering a series of lectures on "natural history" (particularly electricity), and family tradition has it that Tyler assisted him.[53] At any rate, Tyler was scarcely in Braintree at all during October and November. Through the spring of 1786 he generally returned to the Cranch house only to sleep, and by May he was not going there at all, even though he was still serving on some local committees. Early in July, after the word had spread all over town that he had lost Nabby, he stopped in to pick up some of his belongings and left in low spirits for his mother's place in Jamaica Plain.[54] By fall he had returned to his practice in Boston and to the Palmer household; but the work he was having done on his Braintree property was putting him in debt,[55] and he was ready to welcome almost any opportunity which would take him away from these scenes of unpleasant events. Such a chance for escape offered itself the following winter.

Throughout the fall of 1786, there had been agitation among the farmers in the western part of the state as a result of the depression which was especially severe in the rural areas. By January 1787 a group of these discontented men, organized under Daniel Shays, decided that it was useless to expect a peaceful settlement of their grievances, and they planned an attack on the federal arsenal at Springfield. General Benjamin Lincoln, who had conducted an unfortunate campaign in

South Carolina during the Revolution, was appointed leader of the state troops for an expedition against Shays. Tyler joined this force and was made aide-de-camp with the rank of major. In the midst of a severe New England winter, the troops set out to protect the arsenal. Though Shays had intended to meet Luke Day, in charge of another group of insurgents, and make a joint attack, he arrived first, attacked alone, and was defeated by Major General William Shepard's militia (already stationed there) before Lincoln arrived. Lincoln then proceeded against Day, scattered that band, and pursued Shays, who had retreated with some of his followers to Amherst. By the end of January he promised to recommend for pardon any rebels who would surrender, but he had no authority to grant amnesty, as Shays demanded; he therefore continued after Shays and, on 2 February, made his famous surprise attack at Petersham, by marching through a snowstorm at night, and captured many of Shays's remaining men.[56] On one occasion during these maneuvers in the deep Berkshire snows, Tyler, in charge of a troop of cavalry, came upon a number of rebels piously listening to a discourse in a meetinghouse on Sunday — a diatribe about the tyranny of the government. Since the men had left their weapons outside with only one guard, it was a simple task to surround the building and take the entire group prisoners. According to legend, however, Tyler waited until the speaker had finished, marched to the pulpit, and addressed his literally captive audience on the benefits to be derived from allegiance to the government. If it is an overstatement to say, with one nineteenth-century chronicler, that the result was "the instant conversion of the whole band into good citizens," the force of Tyler's eloquence does appear to have swayed the insurgents.[57]

Though the Petersham attack effectually ended the rebellion, certain of the ringleaders had escaped, Shays himself into Vermont. Lincoln asked Tyler to accept the important mission of pursuing these men, a particularly delicate matter, since the governments of the surrounding states were not always sympathetic to the rather autocratic Governor Bowdoin of Massachusetts, and one further complicated by the fact that New York still claimed jurisdiction over the so-called "New Hampshire Grants" in Vermont territory (though Vermont had declared itself independent in 1777). The official request came from Lincoln on 14 February 1787: "I have therefore to solicit, sir, that you would pursue & apprehend these delinquents. And all such farther powers as you may need in executing this commission, You will please to apply to the Governors of the neighboring States for them. To whose countenance you are particularly recommended as a Gentleman to whom the most perfect respect and confidence is due." [58] Tyler set out the next day and made arrangements at Williamstown for Colonel Fay to have his five hundred men ready to move at a minute's notice. On arriving in Bennington, Tyler found the Vermont council (to whom his petition was presented on 17 February) opposed to issuing any warrants for the arrest of the rebels, and Ethan Allen expressed the view that persons fleeing Massachusetts for safety should not be seized. The tact with which Tyler could handle such difficult situations was illustrated soon after his arrival. A number of the leaders in the Vermont government "seemed to feel mortified," as he put it, that the governor of Massachusetts had not formally written to the governor of Vermont about this matter; Tyler then explained that Massachusetts law did indeed require such action, and they "amicably resolved that his Excellency's dispatches must have been intercepted by the rebels." [59]

The nature of Tyler's activities at this time is conveniently summed up in one of his letters to the Palmers, written from Bennington:

My good Friends: How I wish you could look in upon me, and

see your old friend the center, the mainspring of movements, that he once thought would have crazed his brain — this minute, haranguing the governor and Council, and House of Representatives; the next, driving 40 miles into the State of New York, at the head of a party to apprehend Shays: back again in 20 hours: now, closing the passes to Canada: next, writing orders to the frontiers — as thus: "Mr. Officer! have 200 men in readiness." "Messrs. Selectmen! provide sleighs to transport them at a moment's warning." "Pray, where is your Honor going?" — "To Major Tyler. The Commissioners levy!" Will not this make you laugh? — I hope to be home, and bring Shays with me. If the command of a pocket full of money, and 500 choice men will do it; and if this State are not blind to their own interest, I shall do it.[60]

Nevertheless, Tyler's mission was not a success; he captured only Abram Wheeler, who was then rescued by a band of men from New York. But he had spoken so persuasively that, after he left Bennington on 27 February, the Vermont government, following a long debate, issued the very proclamation against aiding fugtives that he had been arguing for. Still, in his official "Memorial" to the Massachusetts legislature on 6 March, he pointed out that "Proclamations . . . can never Coerce the General Sentiment of the People" and that "the Bulk of the People in Vermont are for affording protection to the Rebels." [61] Lincoln wrote to Tyler, "You have done a great deal; we cannot command success; to deserve it has the same merit." [62] Because Tyler had capably conducted the Vermont business, he was asked to pursue several further negotiations in regard to the Shays affair. After reporting to Lincoln at Pittsfield, he was sent to Stockbridge to ascertain the facts of the final rebel attack, which had taken place on 27 February; he then proceeded to Boston, arriving early on the morning of 5 March, sent dispatches to Governor James Bowdoin and Judge Theodore Sedgwick, talked to the Governor the next day, and was asked by the Council to take on another mission, this time to the authorities in New York.[63]

Setting out on 8 March, he arrived in New York City on 12 March and, with the cooperation of the state government, accomplished his mission. The insurgents asked for pardon, and later in the year amnesty was granted (to all but a few leaders, who were pardoned in 1788). It may have been affairs of state which drew Tyler to New York City, but this man who was too gay and frivolous for John Adams was not one to limit himself to such business. He had not been in New York before, and undoubtedly he was determined to take advantage of the various opportunities for amusement which the city offered — notably, of course, the theater. Such is the background for the most famous moment in Tyler's life. Five weeks after his arrival in New York, he had written a comedy with a native setting and had seen it performed: *The Contrast*, given at the John Street Theatre on 16 April 1787, has the distinction of being the first American comedy produced commercially. Little more than a month later, on 19 May, another work of his was put on the stage, a comic opera called *May Day in Town*. Although Tyler had read widely in English literature and (as we know from the Adams letters and his participation in the Trumbull gatherings) had exhibited some literary inclinations, he had not before been a "literary figure" — a position which he was now enjoying to the full. According to tradition, the handsome young lawyer and Major who could dash off popular plays was, during those two months or so, "petted, caressed, feasted and toasted." [64]

After this triumph it is all the more difficult to understand why Tyler should have fallen into a state of depression and left New York. In fact, almost nothing is known of this period in his life, but he returned to his mother's home in Jamaica Plain for a while, before he resumed his legal practice in Boston, boarding again with the Palmers. Almost the only incident of this time recorded in family tradition, though perhaps apocryphal, at least shows Tyler's interest in protecting the family property on Ann Street and is suggestive of his general impulsiveness: when city officials, over his protests, attempted to move a small building into an alley on the Tyler land, he seized an axe and cut the rope by which several men were pulling the building, causing them to fall abruptly on top of each other.[65] If Tyler seems to have been simply marking time during this period, the course of his future was beginning to take shape. For if he had lost Abigail Adams, he still had little Mary Palmer, eighteen years younger than he, right there in the house where he was boarding. He had first admired her as a child of eight or nine when he took her on his knee and called her "my little wife"; and Mary herself recalled that, "if ever a life-long love was commenced at first sight, it was then done on my part." A new phase of Tyler's life was about to begin.

Mary Palmer and Vermont

The Palmers were not as old a Boston family as the Tylers, but they were an extraordinarily interesting one. Young Mary Palmer's grandfather, Joseph Palmer of Devonshire (1716–1788), came to America in 1746 with his wife, Mary Cranch, and his brother-in-law, Richard Cranch (who later married John Adams' sister-in-law, Mary Smith). The two men, settling in the Germantown part of Braintree, had built by the mid-1750's various factories — notably a glassworks, but also chocolate mills and spermacetti- and saltworks. Palmer, as the overlord of all this activity, constructed an elaborate house, Friendship Hall, in which, it is said, he lived "more like an old fashioned English country gentleman, than any one beside has ever done amongst us." [66] He was gregarious and philanthropic; the Braintree town records reveal him as active in civic affairs from 1755 on and generous in contributing funds to pay the local militia in 1780; and his name appears frequently in the annals of pre-Revolutionary agitation, since he was elected (in early 1775) the Braintree representative to the Massachusetts Provincial Congress and was on the committee of safety. As Brigadier-General of the 1777 Rhode Island expedition, he received a great deal of blame for its failure, but was acquitted in a court-martial held in November of that year. His spirits dashed and his finances depleted, he died before he could put into operation his schemes for rebuilding his fortunes.[67] John Adams wrote in general of both the Palmers and the Cranches, "Those 2 families well deserve the Character they hold of friendly, sensible, and Social. The Men, Women and Children, are all sensible and obliging." [68]

The unusual prominence of the Palmers, however, extends beyond Joseph Palmer and the connection with the Adamses. Palmer had three children, two daughters and a son, Joseph Pearse Palmer (1750–1797), who like his father participated in Revolutionary events, as a secretary of the committee of safety and an "Indian" in the Boston Tea Party. This son married (after parental objections were quieted) Elizabeth Hunt (1755–1838), one of the five daughters of John Hunt of Watertown, who were celebrated for their beauty. Mary Hunt Palmer (1775–1866), whom Tyler eventually married, was one of the nine offspring of this union, but three of her sisters produced distinguished families as well. Elizabeth Palmer married Nathaniel Peabody and thus became the mother of the famous Peabody sisters (Elizabeth Palmer Peabody, the educationalist; Mary, the wife of Horace Mann; Sophia, the wife of Nathaniel Hawthorne); Amelia Palmer gained as a son-in-law the editor and writer Park Benjamin; and Catherine Palmer married Henry Putnam and became the mother of the publisher George Palmer Putnam.[69]

It was into this family that Tyler found himself more and more intimately drawn through the 1780's. He first met the Palmers while he was boarding with the Cranches in Braintree in the winter of 1783–84, and he began to make frequent visits to the house at Germantown. Joseph Pearse Palmer became one of his closest friends; Mary Palmer recalled that the two were "twin souls," and that Tyler was repeatedly their "friend in time of need." General Palmer had returned from the war in financial difficulty, and a quarrel with John Hancock about the depreciation of the currency seemingly caused more pressure to be exerted on him, so that he was forced to give up the Germantown estate; from then on the Palmers occupied a succession of rooming houses in Boston, and Tyler not only paid them rent but at times paid their creditors as well.[70] For several years at the end of the decade and at the beginning of the 1790's, Mary Palmer and Tyler saw little of each other. For one thing, Mary spent the spring and summer of 1789 in New York taking care of the children in the family of Elbridge Gerry — during which time she not only witnessed the inauguration of Washington but also discovered, according to her account, that *The Contrast* was a frequent topic of conversation, as a result of its revival on 10 June 1789.[71] After her return, the Palmers, dissatisfied with their Boston existence, gladly accepted the opportunity of moving to the Hunt farm at Framingham.[72]

At the same time, Tyler had also resolved on a move away from Boston. In the summer of 1790 he stopped at the Palmer house in Framingham and announced that he was on his way to Vermont, which, according to Mary Palmer, was "then considered the outskirts of creation by many, and [an area] where all the rogues and runaways congregated, and for that reason considered a good place for lawyers." [73] It is true that Vermont offered such advantages as cheap land and low taxes, and that statehood and an influx of population were immediate prospects. Even so, it is difficult to fathom Tyler's reasons for leaving an established practice and friends in Boston for the Vermont frontier — or, indeed, for any of his abrupt changes of location and fits of depression. Idle speculation is pointless;

all one can do is to observe that in 1787 he had suddenly abandoned the gaiety of New York social life for his mother's
place at Jamaica Plain and that in 1790 he relinquished his
Boston life, turned the family property over to his mother,
left his brother John Steele to look after her, and set out to
begin again in Vermont. There is no doubt that an altercation
with his mother was partly responsible, for she objected to
his interest in Mary Palmer; and as Mary later said, he "had
ever been a spoiled child, and unused to being thwarted in his
inclinations." [74] He was always depressed after seeing his
mother and refused ever to discuss these visits with Mary.
What lay behind his mother's objections, and what other factors were involved, it is now impossible to say.

In any event, Tyler must have remembered from his earlier
visit to Vermont in the Shays affair where the best opportunities might lie, for in early 1791 he established himself in Guilford. With 2432 inhabitants [75] (many attracted there by the
town's rebelliousness in previously throwing off the yoke of
both New Hampshire and Vermont), Guilford was the largest settlement in the state, boasting of two merchants and two
doctors, but no other lawyer. Tyler's account book for 1791
shows that his practice flourished and that he was given cases
and attended courts in several neighboring counties. He took
pride in the fact that he settled some cases which had been
dragging on inconclusively before he arrived, and his increasing reputation was evidenced by the eighty-four cases he
handled in the June and November terms of 1793.[76]

During these years, between terms, Tyler made periodic
trips south to visit the Palmers. He had offered, when he
stopped there in 1790 on his way to Vermont, to look for a
position for Mary's father, possibly as a teacher, and he wrote
to the family on this subject during the winter. In the summer
of 1792, after the adjournment of the court at Bennington, he
visited Judge Sedgwick at Stockbridge, Massachusetts, and pro-

ceeded to New Lebanon, New York, where Mary was staying with her uncle, Ephraim Hunt. Mary was overjoyed at
Tyler's surprise visit, after an absence of two years, but she
found that considerable explanation was required before her
aunt and uncle "could be quite pleased with me for welcom-
ing him in such an extraordinary manner." When they learned
who Tyler was, though, they were favorably disposed, since
Uncle Ephraim's only reading besides the newspapers was
his printed copy of *The Contrast*, which he inflicted on his
wife each evening until she had it nearly memorized. Tyler
gave Mary the material for a dress on that visit, and his sub-
sequent visits, which became more frequent, were always
accompanied by presents, such as a bracelet with two hearts
and the motto, "True as steel." [77]

It was probably in the winter of 1793–94, when Mary was
eighteen, that Tyler formally proposed marriage and explained that he was about to buy a house, which would be
ready for her the following spring.[78] Since he had been elected
State's Attorney for Windham County, he had to return to
Vermont immediately, but he took Mary's father with him,
for he had found employment for Palmer in Windsor, about
sixty miles from Guilford. In May 1794 Tyler, after a dis-
turbing visit with his mother, returned to Framingham and
asked Mary if she would consent to a secret marriage, not to
be announced until the following winter when the snow
would make possible a sleigh journey with luggage to Vermont. Mary's own account of this marriage and the ensuing
months emphasizes the mysteriousness of Tyler's behavior
and the difficulties of her own position, innocent of the
reasons for secrecy and forced to reveal the marriage sooner
than Tyler intended because of the premature birth in December of their child. Explanations suggest themselves but
they must remain mere speculation, for there is no other
source of evidence. Whether or not Mary's story is distorted

by more than the simple passage of time, all one can d(
recite the facts as she gives them. Tyler returned, she says,
in February 1795, hoping he could finally take her and the
baby to Vermont, but sufficient snow did not fall and she
had to wait another year. Understandably this period was
difficult, and she describes, in her devoutly religious way, the
considerable soul-searching which she went through. Her
picture of Tyler stresses his unfailing kindness (in providing
the poverty-stricken Palmers with supplies or presenting
Mary with such gifts as monogrammed teaspoons) and accepts unquestioningly his peculiar behavior as partly the result of his disagreements with his mother and partly the
natural eccentricity of a literary man.

In February of 1796 heavy snow fell at last, so that Tyler
could go to Framingham and bring back Mary and fourteen-
month-old Royall. Accompanied by Mary's young brother
Hampden, now a law student with Tyler, and driven by
Tyler's team of horses, Crock and Smut, they entered
Guilford after a three-day journey, passing the houses of Dr.
Stevens, Major Field, and Dr. Hyde, and descending the hill
into the village and their home, where Tyler's housekeeper
Molly Clough had all in readiness.[79] Thus began the five years
of married life which the Tylers spent in Guilford, years that
saw the birth of three more children and the death of Mary's
father and her young brother Edward (both in 1797, just
a week apart) and, in 1800, of Tyler's mother.[80] Tyler and
his mother were never reconciled (though she sent Mary a
tablecloth and dishes in 1796 and wrote her a letter), and he
was not informed of her death, learning about it only in a
newspaper obituary after she was already buried.

If the rhythm of their lives in Guilford was set by births
and deaths, by weekly social gatherings at friends' houses,
and by Tyler's periodic departures for legal sessions, there
was still time enough for occasional writing and the art of

conversation. Soon after his move to Vermont, Tyler had met Joseph Dennie at Charlestown, New Hampshire, and was drawn into a group of intelligent and witty young men, many of them lawyers, who indulged their appetite for literary activity. Out of this association in 1794 came the partnership of "Colon & Spondee" — that is, Dennie and Tyler — which produced a large number of amusing and satiric essays, sketches, and verses appearing in the *Eagle, or Dartmouth Centinel,* then in the *Farmer's Weekly Museum* (published by David Carlisle and Isaiah Thomas in Walpole, New Hampshire), and later in Dennie's *Port Folio.* Tyler had not given up playwriting, either, and knew something of the Boston theater world through his brother, who was managing the Federal Street Theatre. At this time he wrote a comedy called *The Georgia Spec,* produced in Boston on 30 October 1797 and later that year in New York; his other comedies — *The Farm House, The Doctor in Spite of Himself,* and *The Island of Barrataria* — may also have been performed at this period, though no record of their production survives. In addition, Tyler found enough leisure to turn out a novel on the timely subject of the Barbary pirates, published pseudonymously in two volumes in the fall of 1797 by Carlisle in Walpole.

After his mother's death, Tyler went to New York to settle the estate and returned with three thousand dollars. Out of this money he purchased, with Mary's encouragement, the Micah Townsend farm in Brattleboro and moved his family on 3 March 1801 to the town which would be his location for the rest of his life. With 1867 inhabitants, this "little collection of houses" (as Timothy Dwight called it) was somewhat smaller than Guilford and was not to grow rapidly, increasing by only 274 in the next three decades. The farm consisted of 150 acres, with several orchards, fields of wheat and rye, a number of cattle, hogs, sheep, chickens, and turkeys, and fruit and vegetable gardens around the house. Situated on the hill where the first meetinghouse in town had been, the farmhouse contained seven rooms downstairs, including an office with an outside door. In a long letter written soon after the family moved in, Tyler noted that the "house is entirely secluded from a view of any neighbors; though on the crown of a hill it is yet in a hollow, but the necessary buildings around it give it the air of being a little neighborhood. . . . I think this place may be made comfortable and even pleasing." [81] That first summer the Tylers held a large dinner party for their new neighbors, and under Mary's skillful management the house was apparently as pleasing as Tyler had predicted. They lived on the farm until 1815, when they moved into town, and, according to Mary's diary, the years passed by in great happiness. Although that diary, written between 1858 and 1863, long after Tyler's death, may romanticize certain hardships of the past, this remarkable and courageous document is fitting testimony of Mary's strength of character and devotion. Throughout the Brattleboro years, she continued to bear and educate children (seven more) and to manage the house with kindness and efficiency. [82]

Mary Tyler was an author, as well as a mother and wife, and *Grandmother Tyler's Book* was not her first effort. No one knew the trials of motherhood better than she, and by June of 1810 she had written her experiences and advice into a book of 291 pages, published anonymously in the fall of 1811 by the New York publisher Isaac Riley, with whom her husband had been dealing. [83] Taking as its motto the dubious maxim, "Every Mother her Child's best Physician," the book is well described by its title page: *The Maternal Physician: A Treatise on the Nurture and Management of Infants, from the Birth until Two Years Old. Being the Result of Sixteen Years' Experience in the Nursery. Illustrated by Extracts from the Most Approved Medical Authors. By an*

American Matron. It went into a second edition in Philadelphia in 1818 (published by Lewis Adams), and James Thacher, in his *American Modern Practice* (1826), referred to its author both as a "sensible writer" and as "a fascinating American writer," and praised the book as "a production replete with interesting matter, and worthy the attention of every nursing family." [84]

The six chapters of the book comprise the early care of infants, education in the use of hands and feet, weaning and discipline, diseases, medicinal plants, and a conclusion. For measles — to take one example of her remedies — she recommends a mixture of rhubarb, cinnamon water, and orange peel. Tyler's influence perhaps shows in her use of literary epigraphs and quotations throughout, but these often create a ludicrous effect. Thus, when she begins to discuss the treatment of children younger than four months, Pope's *Essay on Man* (slightly misquoted) supplies her with "For thee health gushes from a thousand springs" (p. 20); or, in stressing the value of the mother's own milk, she exclaims, "O what a blissful moment to a fond mother! when 'The starting beverage meets the thirsty lip, / 'Tis joy to yield it, and 'tis joy to sip'" (p. 31); or she chooses an epigraph from Drayton's *Idea* sonnets when she gives directions about weaning: "Since there's no help, come let us kiss and part" (p. 140). It is unkind to imagine that Tyler's sense of humor could have led him intentionally to suggest to his wife such misapplications; it is more likely that he accepted the quotations as legitimate embellishments to a highly sentimental and flowery mode of writing.

The cultural and social milieu in which the Tylers lived was one which would tolerate Mary's description of her subject as "the all-important and delightful task of nursing those sweet pledges of connubial love, over whom every good mother watches with tremulous anxiety, and almost painful affection" (p. 6), or as "the preservation of this lovely and interesting portion of society" (p. 100). Her dedication to her mother represents this tradition at its nadir:

Madam,

That helpless babe which reposed on your affrighted bosom when you fled the vicinity of Boston, on the day of the ever memorable battle of Lexington, now a wife, a mother, and near the meridian of life, as a small tribute for all your maternal cares, most respectfully addresses this little volume to your perusal; candidly confessing that all which is valuable in it she derived from you.

For the nurture of my infancy I am *most grateful* — but for my education, and, above all, for the sublime lesson you taught me, *"that the best pleasures of a woman's life are found in the faithful discharge of her maternal duties,"* I owe you more than gratitude.

May you find an ample recompense in the assurance that from your grandchildren I receive that filial love and respect which has ever been rendered you by

> Your Daughter
> MARY.

Another passage gives a glimpse of the Tylers' home life (and shows Tyler in a more indulgent mood than he often appears in Mary's memoir):

I was here almost tempted to address a word or two of advice to *fathers*; but my own good man, who sits laughing on the sofa, whilst his favourite little Joseph is drawing his watch tied to a string round the carpet for a plaything, and who just now *looked* as if he thought me cruel for refusing the dear enchanting little innocent my ink-standish for a go-cart, might esteem it *too presuming*. (p. 170)

If Mary's writing deserves little attention, at least the fact of her writing is noteworthy, as well as the totality of her experience, encompassing both the Revolution and the Civil War.[85] Her story, especially as she tells it, illustrates the kind of integrity and stability that Tyler was continually holding up as goals for the people of the new republic.

Royall Tyler

Law and Poverty

During these years Tyler was pursuing his vocation and was becoming in the process a celebrated and successful lawyer. He had young men studying under him from time to time[86] and devoted considerable effort to improving his own legal knowledge as well as to handling cases all over the state. For most of the Guilford years, from 1794 until 1801, he served as State's Attorney for Windham County, a position which brought him in touch with many prominent figures. As a result, on 12 October 1801, he was elected one of the three judges of the Vermont Supreme Court. He and Stephen Jacob, a good friend from Windsor, were Assistant Judges; the Chief Justice was Jonathan Robinson, earlier somewhat hostile to Tyler's Federalism and his satiric comments on Republicanism in the *Farmer's Museum*, but after their association on the bench quite friendly and cooperative. On 14 October 1807, after Robinson was elected to the United States Senate, Tyler was made Chief Justice (the ninth in Vermont history). His Federalism seems to have become so mild that he could take office amidst a general Republican victory, but for the same reason could not survive the Federalist victory of 1813.[87] Even so, he served twelve years, longer than any other Supreme Court judge in Vermont prior to Charles K. Williams (whose term began in 1822). He also ran for the United States Senate in 1812, but was defeated by Dudley Chase, 110 votes to 94.[88] Overlapping his court tenure was his service to the University of Vermont: he wrote to his wife on 20 January 1802 that he had accepted appointment as a trustee of the University (a position he held until 1813), and from 1811 to 1814 he was Professor of Jurisprudence there (with a master's degree from Vermont *ad eundem*).[89]

Tyler's success in law was no doubt partly due to his skill in public speaking, and several anecdotes about his oratory

34

survive, such as the story of his meetinghouse speech to the captured men during the Shays pursuit. A similar incident occurred during one of his first winters in Vermont. In Charlestown on legal business, he was asked to serve as lay reader at church one Sunday, in the absence of the minister; he not only read from the prayer book but delivered a sermon of his own composition, based on Luke 2:13–14. The members of the congregation, which included several lawyers in town for the court session, were so enthusiastic about his performance that they requested him to give the Christmas sermon also. After this experience he seriously considered entering the clergy. His wife recalled his comment on the episode: "And in truth it would have been a rest to my soul at that time had I dared [become a preacher], but a consciousness of having lived too gay a life in my youth made me tremble lest I should bring in some way disgrace upon the sacred cause!" [90] This remark, authentic or not, is an indication of Tyler's basically religious nature and another of those persistent allusions to his "dissipated" early behavior. Despite Tyler's enthusiasm as a lawyer, his wife's statement that he "never ceased to regret his decision" (to remain in law rather than take up the ministry) must carry some weight.[91]

Another of Mary Tyler's undoubtedly biased observations is that "few were the audiences who could resist his eloquence. I always thought his power consisted greatly in the remarkably melodious intonation of his voice aided by as remarkable insight into human nature." [92] Tyler himself described his effect on an audience, though the occasion was not a characteristic one; on 22 February 1800 he delivered an oration on the death of George Washington, which had occurred two months before. "The spectators," he wrote to Mary, "were numerous, and my success — was what you might wish. I shall only say here, that the austere Democracy, who came resolved to be displeased; down whose hard unmeaning faces ne'er stole the pitying tear, wept. I never more earnestly wished your presence." His remarks were so highly admired that Governor Tichenor requested their publication, and a sixteen-page pamphlet duly appeared in March, printed by David Carlisle at Walpole for Isaiah Thomas. That Tyler could pronounce such an oration and that his name would be allowed to appear on its title page are further indications of the general taste of the time and the attitude toward literature; for the speech is in the same ornate style as the *Maternal Physician* and, as a useful public discourse, carried enough respectability to be claimed by a professional man. For that matter, there was a professional motive behind it, and the flowery rhetoric may indicate only that Tyler knew what would move the public: "One great inducement I had to deliver this Oration was the hopes of making myself more known in this vicinity; and giving the people a sample of my speaking powers. I have found the good effects of my plan already. In one hour after I left the meeting house, I was engaged in three important causes; and I am told that I shall be in more." [93]

The *Oration*, of about 2500 words, begins with some reflections on human mortality, then asks "ye children of our political father" to "hear the instructive lesson of your parent's life" (p. 4). In a series of parallel rhetorical questions the virtues of Washington — "vigour of mind," "martial courage," equanimity, modesty, and so on — are enumerated as models for emulation: "He taught us how to live" (p. 5). This discussion constitutes the bulk of the oration, but, when Tyler comes to the virtue of "conjugal excellence," he elaborates on the grief which Washington's widow must feel:

Oh! at those solitary moments, when busy, meddling memory, in barbarous succession, musters up the fond endearments of your tender heart; at those cheerless moments when you recollect pressing the clay cold hand of a dying husband, wiping the clammy sweat from his forehead, while his fixed eye balls gave the last look of affection upon you, and closed forever; when you remember that heart rending hour, when you thought all happiness flown from you forever, and you felt yourself alone, and the world was a blank before you; then, while your agonized bosoms throb with anguish at your own loss; think on the pangs of her who mourns a WASHINGTON. (pp. 10–11)

Obviously Tyler had mastered all the techniques of the melodramatic oratory of the time. The speech is full of emotional appeals and balanced constructions: "Such was the man whom we lament; and such was the man whom the world applauds" (p. 11). In the last few pages he emphasizes national unity as one of Washington's fondest hopes: "Thus united in affliction, let us be united in love; and at this moment, while we recline over his bier, let us resolve never more to separate; but to inhabit the goodly heritage, which God has given us, like a band of brothers" (p. 16). The performance is a competent, even skillful, example of the funeral eulogy in this tradition, and it illustrates the quality of Tyler's rhetoric, if not of his thought.[94]

Another trait which stood Tyler in good stead as a lawyer, and especially as a judge, was his human compassion. Writing to Tyler from Washington in 1810, Justice Robinson provides an insight into this aspect of Tyler's nature:

Dear Sir: — You speak well of Bro. Fay, as a judge. I had never any doubt either of his honesty, clearness of perception, legal knowledge or patience, so essential for a judge, but feared he might be too legal, in other words, might give too great weight to technical precision, although useful, yet not wholly essential in administering impartial justice to ignorant but honest suitors. But I knew you and Bro. Herrington would stand as a check. I was always pleased with you more than I ever expressed on that account, because it is a bright gem in the character of a court lawyer, not to lay too much stress on the manner of action or pleading. When we come to be judged for our judgments, my friend, the question will not be whether we pursued legal forms or technical niceties, but have you heard the cry of the poor and relieved them from their oppressors. But I hope that the philanthropy of Bro. Fay and yourself will prevent all unpleasant results because he does not carry the Hopkinsian doctrine to that lofty pinnacle of revelation and philosophy to which you so justly and rationally aspire.

Robinson further characterizes Tyler two years later, in a postscript describing how his own letter would be received among the judges:

Bro. Tyler filled his pipe and said, "Come, Brethren, let us see what Bro. Robinson has to say." Reads. Bro. Fay spits and says, "Bro. Robinson is as cross as the devil." "Well," says Bro. Herrington, "I feel easy about it, it is a pack for their backs, not mine." Bro. Tyler smiled, and filled his second pipe.[95]

These were the qualities which had already been recognized, as early as 1797, by John A. Graham, who published in London his observations on Vermont and included a comment on Tyler:

Mr. *R. Tylor* (formerly of *Boston, Massachusetts*), lives in *Ryegate*; he also was bred to the Law: he possesses a fine turn for poetry, and unites to it the most humane disposition, and a most benevolent heart. — Does misery need an advocate? Mr. *Tylor* eagerly steps forth, its unpurchased champion. Does guilt (when not atrocious) sink down heart-broken and desponding? in Mr. *Tylor* it finds a man, who (though his own morals are irreproachable) feels for the errors of others, pities their vices, and compassionates their wants. How commanding is his oratory when pleading in their behalf! with what resistless power does it assail the hearers! he rouses every sympathizing passion of their souls, attacks them in every vulnerable part; awes, soothes, softens, and finally prevails. Such a character can seldom fail of being considered with due respect. Mr. *Tylor* is looked up to with admiration, affection, and esteem.[96]

Also to Tyler's advantage were his handsome appearance and his ready wit. His sense of humor frequently entered the courtroom. Once, earlier in his Vermont career, he found himself defending a man who, when his lease was up, wanted to remove a barn he had built on rented land. Tyler guessed, from the way the opposing lawyer read his Latin quotations, that he did not really understand them, and he knew that the farmer-judge did not; therefore Tyler cited as his authority the line, "Cujus est solum ejus est usque ad coelum," and translated it for the court as "Who builds a barn on hired land has a right to move it off again." [97] The constant puncturing of pretentiousness found in his writings was a part of his life as well.

Tyler's position as Chief Justice made his name widely known for a time, but a more lasting legal fame resulted from his publication of reports of Vermont Supreme Court cases. Soon after Tyler became Chief Justice, Isaac Riley in New York began communicating with various state courts about the possibility of publishing reports of their cases (eventually bringing out those for Connecticut, Maryland, New York, and Virginia). Tyler, on 8 November 1808, replied, "I can merely state, that, ever since I have been upon the bench, now nine years, I have been collecting reports of decisions of my official labors, to prepare them for the press." He estimated that his material would fill three volumes of six hundred pages each and that he could have one volume ready by the following August. So he set to work, using his spare time and vacations for the extensive revisions necessary, and sent batches of the manuscript to Riley as he got them finished. For every hundred printed pages, he was to receive one hundred twenty dollars plus fifty dollars' worth of books and stationery. Volume I was completed by mid-summer of 1809 and was published late in the year; by the end of 1810 a second volume appeared.[98] Both carried Tyler's name on their title pages, making them his only major work not published anonymously.

The *Reports of Cases Argued and Determined in the Su-*

preme Court of Judicature of the State of Vermont cover, in the two volumes, the cases between January 1800 and February 1803. Though no more were published, Tyler's *Reports* are the only record of Vermont cases in the interval between 1797 and 1813. The legal reports, of all states, were chaotically published during the early years of the republic — and were not published at all except when someone like Tyler had the energy to prepare them. In Vermont, one earlier judge, Nathaniel Chipman, had compiled *Reports* to cover the years 1789–1791; but after Tyler there were no published reports until those of William Brayton (for 1815–1819) and Daniel Chipman (who filled in some cases for 1797 and 1813–1815, before he proceeded with those for 1824, the beginning of the series unbroken to the present). Tyler's *Reports* give evidence of careful compilation, and they provide adequate indexes and marginal headings. Their initial reception seems to have been favorable, if the reaction reported by William A. Palmer, in a letter of 21 July 1810, is typical. Writing to ask Tyler for a copy of the *Reports*, he went on to say, "They are generally spoken highly of; and your *enemies* do you the justice to say that they are not only *accurately*, but *elegantly* reported." Later that summer R. C. Mallory wrote that Vermont jurisprudence had often been ridiculed in the past; "Your Honor, therefore," he continued, "claims the highest esteem for boldly standing forth in defense of its reputation, and lending your talents and influence to rescue it from unmerited reproach." [99] But aspersions continued to be cast, for Chief Justice John Savage of New York remarked in 1825 that "Tyler's Reports are not considered good authority, even in his own state." [100] Other than a vague distrust of Vermont courts on Savage's part, it is difficult to find any basis for this statement. If Tyler took occasional liberties with the transcription of an opinion, he was doing no more than other state reporters of the day. There can be no doubt that his *Reports* were of great usefulness at a time when records of American precedents were sparse, and one can have only praise for the efforts of those few scholarly men dedicated enough to attempt the publication of their cases.

Of the one hundred twenty-five cases in Tyler's two volumes, Tyler himself delivered the opinion or made a statement in eight of them (Robinson was Chief Justice during these years and handed down a majority of the opinions), and is recorded as dissenting or hesitating in five.[101] In some of his statements he expresses his personal opinion about what *should* be true, as "I have long considered that some general rule ought to be adopted . . ." or "it would be desirable that . . ."; in others, he allows himself digressions and irony, as when he points out that James II "had unhappily imbibed opinions of the royal prerogative, which were held by the nation totally incompatible with that portion of liberty which ought to be enjoyed in a limited monarchy." [102] Many of the cases dealt with actions of ejectment and trespass or with promissory notes and debts. In Robbins v. Windover and Hopkins (July 1802), Tyler set forth the rule that, in applications for a new trial, the affidavit of a panel member cannot be used to reveal what passed in the jury room. In Harris v. Huntington *et al.* (May 1802), he expressed the view, in a long and orderly opinion citing numerous precedents, that statements made by a citizen in a petition to the General Assembly are not actionable for libel — "a question of greater magnitude, and more interesting to the people of *Vermont*," he believed, "than any which has been hitherto agitated in this Court."

But Tyler's most important decision occurred in Selectmen v. Jacob (August 1802). Stephen Jacob (one of the Assistant Justices) had brought a slave into the state in 1783, and she worked many years for the town of Windsor; the town was now bringing action to demand that Jacob assume part of the expense of her support in old age. Tyler pointed out that the issue was whether or not the defendant's bill of sale was valid in Vermont; since the Vermont constitution provided that no inhabitant could hold a slave, Tyler reasoned that when a person brings a slave into the state "his bill of sale ceases to operate here." This is true, he said, because the United States Constitution is not involved, and the ruling can be a local one; but he hoped that the people of Vermont would "submit with cheerfulness to the national constitution and laws, which, if we may in some particular wish more congenial to our modes of thinking, yet we must be sensible are productive of numerous and rich blessings to us as individuals, and to the State as an integral of the Union." [103]

Perhaps the other most celebrated case over which Tyler presided was the *Black Snake* affair in the late summer of 1808. The Embargo Act of 1807 had resulted in a flourishing smuggling trade on Lake Champlain, and clashes between customs officials and smugglers occurred repeatedly. One ship, the *Black Snake*, which had been smuggling potash, was captured at Joy's Landing on the Winooski River near Burlington on 3 August, but only after three government men were killed. The crew was indicted for murder, and Tyler, as Chief Justice, was in charge of the grand jury trials held in a special session of the court at Burlington, beginning 23 August. His main apprehension was that strong partisan feelings might triumph over justice; in his charge to the jury, therefore, he addressed himself to that subject, and his remarks are said to have achieved a wide contemporary reputation:

The awful and melancholy occasion of our present meeting must be a subject of deep and lasting regret to every upright and feeling mind: it is so considered by this Court; we doubt not it is so viewed by you. We officially learn, by the verdict of the Jury of inquest, that three of our peaceable, unoffending citizens have been wilfully murdered: that our once peaceful and happy land has been polluted with human gore; and the voice of the blood of our brethren crieth from the ground. . . . In a word, if you are assailed by hatred or malice; by fear, favor, affection, or hope of reward, repair to your oath. Remember it is not merely your guide now, but can be your only justification to your consciences hereafter.

A verdict of guilty was returned in the case of eight men, but only one of them, Cyrus B. Dean, was executed (on 11 November 1808); the others were sentenced to prison terms. Tyler worked over the records of these trials to prepare them for publication and late in 1808 Samuel Mills of Burlington brought out *The Trial of Cyrus B. Dean for the Murder of Jonathan Ormsby and Asa Marsh.* Though the 48-page pamphlet does not include the jury charge, it does provide a good sample of Tyler's sustained legal argument, in his denial on 16 September of the appeal made by Dean's counsel. At the end, after discussing states' rights and state citizenship, he must have been thinking of his own life when he said that "this state is emphatically a land of emigrants, the language of our constitution is inviting to all to come and fertilize our soil." [104]

If legal affairs had always caused Tyler to be away from home a great deal, his tenure on the Supreme Court kept him away even more. A typical year (such as 1802) found him in both Chittenden and Addison counties for the January and June terms, in Rutland County in February and July, in Bennington in February and May, in Windham and Windsor in August, and in Orange and Caledonia in September; [105] every year he twice made the circuit up the Connecticut River and down the west side of the state with his horse and sulky. Mary was left with the main responsibility for household affairs and rearing the children (five were born during these twelve years). Tyler wrote to her frequently, in letters full of affectionate yearnings for home and family. On one occasion, during the February term of 1802 in Rutland, he saw a man from Guilford in the audience and wondered if the man had brought letters from Mary; he could hardly wait until court was adjourned, at which time he "leapt from the bench," he says, "with a skip and a jump, rather inconsistent with the gravity of a Judge," to ask for news from home. His letter of 8 February 1802 is characteristic:

My dearest Friend: I have just returned from spending an hour with Mrs. Blake, to whom I have delivered a hasty line for you; but I cannot go to bed before I write a few more lines, though I have nothing to communicate, but the evidence that I have the wish to convince you that I am not content with merely writing because it is proper, but that I take a pleasure in conversing with you. Indeed, amidst the hurry of business, when I can get a moment to you, it seems to be a refreshing retirement from the world, and brings you, and home, and the children, and happiness nearer to me. Do you consider that it is but a few weeks, and this tedious circuit will be ended, and we shall have two whole months to be together; and, what though the weather may be cloudy and the roads deep, shall we not have all the joys of our fireside to comfort us; all the pleasures of our children to gratify; and all the blessings of our affection to bless us? And what shall we want more? And when the miry season's over, we can mount our horses, and go a visiting; and stroll the fields, and inhale the breath of spring.

Many letters report purchases for Mary — silk for a cloak, a new bonnet, and "some good furs for your tippit." The theme is always the pleasures of home versus the duties of business: "Do not think, my love, that I forget you, or home, or the children one moment. I think always of you, and frequently catch myself in audible ejaculations for your health, happiness and safety; but if I think too much on the subject, I cannot perform these public duties." [106]

The public duties ended for him (at the age of fifty-six) with the October elections of 1813, and, within a year or two, Tyler found his private practice, though not lucrative, more profitable than his thousand-dollar annual salary as Chief

Justice.[107] During his time on the bench he had begun to suffer from a skin cancer which was developing on the left side of his nose near the eye; he now decided to wear a black silk patch on his face to hide the spot. An instance of his undaunted spirit and his flair for courtroom drama concerns this patch. It was a jury trial in the Newfane court, with a Mr. Richardson as his client. The opposing lawyer suggested that Tyler would never have brought the case to court if he had been in good health and that the court must overlook Tyler's actions in his present condition. When Tyler's turn came to address the jury, he began by saying, "Richardson! go home! there is no use of your staying here! I thought you had a good case." He then summed up all the points of the case and concluded, "But I was mistaken in supposing you had any rights that could be maintained. It appears you have no case because my faculties are failing, and what is worse, you have no case at all, because I have this patch on my nose. Go home! go home! I can't be expected to say a word to the jury under such circumstances." The other lawyers were astounded at his performance, and Richardson gained a favorable verdict.[108]

During all Tyler's main years of legal activity, however, he did not neglect his writing, and the *Reports* were not his only publication. Simultaneously with the first volume of reports he worked on a book of essays about English customs, supposedly written by an American visiting England; it was published anonymously by Riley in 1809 as *A Yankey in London*. Even earlier, in one of his first Vermont years, 1793, he published (anonymously) a poem called *The Origin of Evil*, and a *Christmas Hymn* was issued in broadside the same year. At the turn of the century he had the idea of writing a work to be called "Moral Tales for American Youth" and also a comic grammar; he did actually write substantial parts of them, but publishing plans seemed never to develop. In

1810 he wrote to Riley that he would like to do an "American Law Dictionary," which would be "entirely original, excepting as to the definitions of some English law terms"; he estimated its size as "two quarto volumes," but "much remains to be done to complete it for the press." [109] It was never completed, for his cancer made writing increasingly difficult. In 1817 he worked on *The Touchstone, or A Humble Modest Inquiry into the Nature of Religious Intolerance*, but only a part of it was ever printed. His three religious plays may be products of these later years, and he was preparing "The Bay Boy," a semi-autobiographical narrative, for the press when he died. One cannot estimate how important these unfulfilled projects might have been, but they bear testimony to a continuously active mind.

The last two of Tyler's eleven children were born in the years after his retirement from the bench, in 1815 and 1818. The oldest of his children, Royall, Jr. (1794–1813), and the second oldest, John Steele (1796–1876), approached university age during Tyler's last years as Chief Justice, but his salary would not permit him to send both to college; John Steele accordingly went to Boston in 1810 and entered the business of his uncle, George Palmer, while Royall, Jr., in the fall of 1811, became a freshman at the University in Burlington. He was a promising student and followed his father in writing a poem ("The Present Age") and a play ("Quackery" or "The Dumb Gent," performed at the college in 1812), but he died of typhoid fever at the beginning of his junior year. The youngest child, Abiel Winship (1818–1832), also died in his teens, but most of the other children lived long and active lives: Mary Whitwell (1798–1874), kindergarten teacher; Edward Royall (1800–1848), Yale graduate, minister, and editor of the *New Englander*; William Clark (1802–1882), Boston merchant; Joseph Dennie (1804–1852), Yale graduate, Episcopal clergyman, and head of the Virginia Deaf and Dumb

Asylum; Amelia Sophia (1807–1878), dedicated teacher. trained by Elizabeth Palmer Peabody; George Palmer (1809–1896), graduate of Yale and Union Theological Seminary, and Congregational pastor; Royall [Charles] (1812–1896), Harvard graduate and Vermont lawyer; Thomas Pickman (1815–1892), Trinity (Hartford) graduate and Episcopal pastor.[110]

Perhaps the most depressing period in Tyler's life was the fall of 1813, when, in sudden succession, he lost his judgeship, learned of his oldest son's death, and returned home to find creditors clamoring for his property (since his steady source of income was now stopped). It was some time before he recovered from this triple blow: he raised some money by selling the farm and moving into town, and, through the kindness of Judge Gilbert Denison,[111] he was made Register of Probate for Windham County (beginning in December 1815) and managed to reestablish his private practice. Nevertheless, the ensuing years were not easy, and the children, particularly John, contributed to their parents' support; it was John who established them in a house on Putney Street in Brattleboro in 1821.[112] Soon afterward, the severity of Tyler's cancer began to prevent his attending to probate duties, and in December of 1822 he was removed from that position. Earlier the same year John's business in Boston had failed, and the Brattleboro property had to be signed over to other hands. From that time, the Tylers became objects of public charity.

Mary Tyler began keeping a journal in 1821, and its entries through 1826 tell a story of unrelieved poverty and sickness.[113] The children would make visits and contribute what they could afford; anonymous letters enclosing five dollars would arrive; friends would join together and donate fifty dollars; and neighbors would supply butter, rice, sugar, turkeys, and other food. Tyler's cancer eventually reached into his eye,[114] and he sat with the window shades drawn while Mary read to him from the Bible, Cooper, Scott, Maria Edgeworth, Byron, Cellini, Josephus, and many others. Pathetically he still held the hope of publishing more of his own writings. Mary records that, in 1822, he wrote "several beautiful little poems" and that, by late 1824, he was in the midst of revising *The Algerine Captive*; he also wrote a play, "Five Pumpkins," for the children of a local school, and, as late as April 1825, sent the manuscript of his collection of tales for children, "Utile Dulci," to New York.

The theme of Mary's journal is expressed in her entry for 28 May 1822: "Support us O God! under this and every dispensation of thy providence!" Doctors and friends struggled vainly to suggest remedies that would at least ease the pain, and Tyler tried them all in turn — copperas curd, yellow dock root, pokeberry salve, rhubarb, and magnesia. Only opium and laudanum gave much relief, and on some days he took between seventy and eighty drops of laudanum. Mary's entry of 20 July 1826 presages the end: "This day as a last resort my afflicted husband consented after much persuasion to try injections, which relieved him but kept him uneasy and restless the chief of the night." Finally, on 26 August 1826, she wrote: "On Wednesday the 16th my husband was released from his sufferings. . . . My husband died with perfect composure and resignation and surely he passed from Death into Life! . . . May I be enabled to do my duty in my new situation." He was buried in Prospect Hill Cemetery, in the east village of Brattleboro, under this epitaph: "ROYALL TYLER / Reip. V. Mont. Cur. Sup. Jurid., / Princ. / Mortem Obiit / Die XVI. Aug. Anno Domini / MDCCCXXVI / Etatis Suae / LXVIII / Uxor et liberi / ejus / Hoc saxum ponendum. / Curaverunt." [115] As in life, he was officially known for his judicial services, while his literary productions, unannounced, continued to attract attention.

⁂ II ⁂

Dramatist: The Contrast

WHEN Tyler, after his unsuccessful pursuit of Shays in
Vermont, was sent to New York by Governor Bowdoin in
the spring of 1787, just two months before the opening of the
Constitutional Convention in Philadelphia, he had probably
never had an opportunity to witness a professional dramatic
performance. Before the Revolution — in fact, as early as 1749
— professional troupes had appeared in such cities as Philadelphia, New York, Williamsburg, and Charleston; but the
religious climate (influenced partly by a view of the Restoration stage, linking it with dissipation, but particularly by the
Puritan heritage) was hostile to the theater, and laws were
passed in some colonies prohibiting, or restricting, such entertainment. In the Boston of Tyler's youth the prejudice
against the theater was particularly strong, reflected in the
Harvard regulations and in Tyler's own description of the
conditions under which Boston amateur groups had to struggle:

The front door of the store was closed and every crack and key-
hole carefully stopped with paper or cotton that no glimmering
light might alarm the passing watchman; the entrance was through
a bye lane into a door in the backyard, and such was the caution
observed that but one person was admitted at a time, while two,
one at each end of the lane, were on the watch to see if the person
to be admitted had been noticed. No knocking was permitted,
but a slight scratch announced the approach of the initiated. . . .
A Panic seized the whole assembly [upon the approach of the

watchman;] . . . the lights were extinguished or put under a bushel, but the voice of the watchman as he chanted his midnight ditty distancing as he passed on, we took new courage and the play proceeded.[1]

Any progress which the drama had made in America, despite such difficulties, was halted on 20 October 1774, when, in view of the impending war, a resolution of the Continental Congress banned all plays and public entertainments. At that time only one play by an American had been produced.

It was inevitable, however, that playwriting would begin to flourish, despite the ban, for a period of revolution and national crisis always stimulates the corrective of satire. Writers like Mercy Warren turned out plays on patriotic or national themes, printed when they could not be produced. By August of 1785, about two years before Tyler's arrival in New York, the American Company under Lewis Hallam had reopened the John Street Theatre, though the restrictions were not to be relinquished in some cities for another decade. The kind of theater which Tyler encountered in 1787 was different from the pre-Revolutionary one: attended by all classes of people, it was a force for national unity and, with its plays on political subjects, has been called "spoken journalism." [2] But the principal fare was still imported drama, and in the first few weeks after his arrival Tyler could have attended productions of *Much Ado About Nothing, Cymbeline, Richard III, The Clandestine Marriage, The Jealous Wife, She Stoops to Conquer*, and, most important, *The School for Scandal* (on 21 March). Whether or not he saw these plays, he was able to construct, by 16 April, a work of his own which treated a native subject, for the first time, in a comedy produced on the stage and which helped to demonstrate, in so doing, a value and a future for the drama in America.

Dramatist: The Contrast

Misconceptions and Disagreements

Because of its early position among American plays, *The Contrast* has received much comment over the years, particularly at the hands of anthologists and literary historians who wish to fill in the background with a few hurried sentences. A tradition quickly becomes established, each writer making the same points without bothering to check on their authenticity. If, then, one is to approach the play with a clear mind, one must be aware of several misconceptions that have become established in this way. Though it may not be possible to ascertain the truth in every instance, one should at least realize that certain points have not been resolved.

The largest of these muddled areas has to do with the dating of the play and its relative position in American drama. Because William Dunlap, in his pioneer *History of the American Theatre* (1832), made an unfortunate error in recording the date of the first performance, many nineteenth-century commentaries place it on 16 April 1786.[3] Thomas P. Tyler, doing research on his father's life, believed that this date was in error but argued that the correct date was 16 April 1789 and the place the Park Street Theatre.[4] The play was actually performed, as Joseph Ireland had recognized as early as 1866, on 16 April 1787 at the John Street Theatre in New York.[5] The accuracy of this date is clear from numerous contemporary advertisements and references. The New York *Daily Advertiser*, on 14 and 16 April 1787, announced a comedy, "Never [before] Performed," by "a Citizen of the United States," entitled *The Contrast*, to be acted on Monday, 16 April, along with "the English Burletta, Called *Midas*"; it was reviewed at length in the same paper on 18 April.[6] On the 17th and 18th the advertisements were repeated, for a second performance on the 18th; both performances were mentioned in the review in the *Worcester Magazine*, which did not appear until the first week of May. Then on 1 May the play was announced for a third performance on Wednesday, 2 May — this one reviewed on 5 May in the *Independent Journal*. Finally, on 12 May, came a benefit performance, "at the particular request of the Author," to help those suffering from the Boston fire.[7]

It is not necessary to say that the play enjoyed a "run," as some writers do, in order to emphasize its success. Four performances within a month was a record which no other American play had thus far attained, and it would have been unusual even for the most popular of the English plays. Baltimore was next to see *The Contrast*, on 12 August 1787, and on 10 December Thomas Wignell (the comedian of the American Company who made a hit as Jonathan in New York) gave a reading of it in Philadelphia; it was repeated in Baltimore on 19 August 1788 and then in New York, soon after Washington's inauguration, on 10 June 1789. Next came Philadelphia (on 7 July 1790), where a newspaper referred to the "curiosity which has everywhere been expressed respecting this first dramatic production of American genius." [8] It may not be too much to say, therefore, that *The Contrast* was the first commercially successful American play. The question of "firsts," however, which always attracts such zealous interest, is a tricky one, despite the assertion in its dedication that *The Contrast* is "the First Essay of *American* Genius in the Dramatic Art." There should be no doubt on certain points: the play is certainly not the first ever produced in America (it came 125 years too late for that), and it is just as clearly not the first by an American to be produced (a distinction generally assigned to Thomas Godfrey's *The Prince of Parthia*, a full twenty years earlier), nor the first with a native subject (Robert Rogers' *Ponteach*, 1766), nor the first printed in America (Robert Hunter's *Androboros*, 1714).[9] Yet one writer in 1880 entitled an article about *The*

Contrast "The First American Play," and another in 1889 called it "the first play of American authorship that ever appeared on any stage"; as late as 1916 a portrait of Tyler, accompanying an article by Montrose Moses, bore a caption describing him as the author of "the first play to be written by an American," and in 1961 he was referred to as "the first American playwright." [10] Other writers, searching for a safer way to state the case, have used such complicated phrases as "the first American play . . . got up on a regular stage, by a regular company of comedians," "the first public performance in a regular theatre of a play written by a citizen of America," [11] and so on, until it is difficult to see precisely how it has any priority at all. Put most simply, *The Contrast* is the first native comedy to be professionally produced.

Another myth connected with the chronology of the play concerns the date and circumstances of its composition. The extraordinary success of an untutored genius is an appealing concept which, in this case, has been transformed into the legend that Tyler, with no knowledge whatsoever of the theater, wrote in less than three weeks (or, in some versions, a matter of days) a strikingly successful play. It must be admitted that this tradition derives from a source close to Tyler, for Wignell, in the "Advertisement" to the published version of the play, reported that "it was written by one, who never critically studied the rules of the drama, and, indeed, had seen but few of the exhibitions of the stage; it was undertaken and finished in the course of three weeks." Though intended to gain favor for the play by emphasizing the remarkable facts in its composition, this statement is mild compared to some of its later embroiderings, and some recent writers have declared that Tyler "dashed off" his play.[12] This he may have done, but the general tenor of the legend is almost certainly not true. Neither is there evidence to support the idea that Tyler wrote the play during his military service and had it finished when he went to New York.[13] We shall probably never know exactly how many plays Tyler had seen nor exactly when he began to write *The Contrast*. But we do know that he arrived in New York for the first time on 12 March, little more than a month before *The Contrast* was performed, and that *The School for Scandal* was given on 21 March. That Jonathan's famous description of "The School for Scandalization" in the third act of *The Contrast* may be a fictionalized account of Tyler's own first visit to a theater is suggested not only by the Sheridan title but by the reference to "Wig — Wag — Wag-all, Darby Wag-all," since Wignell, for whom Tyler created Jonathan, had taken Darby's role in *The Poor Soldier*, the other play on the same bill. Even so, there is no reason to suppose that Tyler was entirely unacquainted with drama, for amateur or private performances had been given in Boston before that time, and, judging from the breadth of his allusions to English literature in other works, he may well have had a wide reading knowledge of plays. In any event, the play is so overflowing with the devices and themes of eighteenth-century British drama that one may reasonably assume on Tyler's part a more extensive familiarity with theatrical literature than is usually conveyed by accounts of his hurried composition.[14]

One further misconception relating to the circumstances under which the play first appeared has to do with contemporary knowledge of Tyler's authorship. It is all very well for Frederick Tupper to say that Tyler assigned the copyright to Wignell because he did not dare to "link his patrician name with the experiment." [15] That writing was a pastime for Tyler and that he generally published his literary works anonymously is true, but one should not infer that his authorship was thereby concealed. The advertising, to be sure, did not reveal his name, and the title page of the published work three years later, in the spring of 1790, was still maintaining that the author was simply "A Citizen of the United States." But it must have been a very open secret, for the *Independent Journal* review of the 2 May performance took Tyler's authorship for granted, referred casually in the opening sentence to "the new Comedy, written by ROYAL TYLER, Esq.," and concluded with a eulogy that Tyler could hardly have looked upon with disfavor:

America has long boasted successful adventurers in the various walks of literature, the Drama excepted, that path had hitherto remained unexplored — and it must give sincere satisfaction to every lover of his country to find that this, the most difficult of all the works of human genius, has been attempted with such abundant success, and that it is likely from the abilities of this Gentleman, if his other avocations will permit him to cultivate his talent in this species of writing, that America may one day rank a *Tyler* in the Dramatic Line as she already does a *Franklin* and a *West* in those of Philosophy and the Fine Arts.

Similarly the review in the *Worcester Magazine* named "ROYAL TYLER, Esq.; of Boston, *Attorney at Law*, and late *Aid de Camp* to the Hon. Major General Lincoln" as the "author of the truly sentimental entertainment," going on about how he had "just left the active field of MARS" and "was in this city, on business that could not occupy his whole time." When proposals for printing the play were issued, it was called "A *Comedy* written by *Major Tyler*," and by 1797 one of his later plays was openly advertised as "by R. TYLER, Esq. Author of the Contrast, &c." [16] He enjoyed, in other words, a high literary reputation, and his squeamishness about its effect on his legal reputation has sometimes been overemphasized; if recognition could come without his resorting to the ungentlemanly device of appearing to ask for it by signing his work, one may imagine that he was certainly not averse to gathering in the accolades.

A second area in which there is room for disagreement concerns the relative importance of the character Jonathan, the provincial Yankee servingman in *The Contrast*. It has become traditional, following Dunlap, the Duyckincks, Odell, and many others, to point to Jonathan as Tyler's "distinctive contribution to drama" (in the words of Oral Coad) and to speak of that character as the first in a long line of stage Yankees, or "Jonathan-figures." [17] One even hears the suggestion that Tyler's Jonathan was the prototype for Uncle Sam. To attribute much of the success of the play to Jonathan, as Arthur Hornblow does, is an entirely different matter, for it is surely true that, with the popular Thomas Wignell playing the part, this comic role must have been the main attraction in the piece.[18] And there is no question that the stage Yankee became one of the most popular types in American drama, portrayed on the nineteenth-century stage by James H. Hackett and George Hill in a large number of plays, in some of which the character was even named Jonathan (as in Woodworth's *The Forest Rose* of 1825 or Dunlap's *A Trip to Niagara* of 1829). One student of the subject has said that "no satisfactory Yankee characters" appeared in American drama before 1787, but immediately following *The Contrast* came the Yankee servant in Dunlap's *The Modest Soldier* (1787) and the housemaid in his *The Father* (1788), Dolly the country girl in Samuel Low's *The Politician Out-Witted* (1788), and Yorick the Yankee Federalist in *The Better Sort* (1789).[19]

One can, with some justification, think of *The Contrast* as standing at the head of a tradition, but to point to it as the ultimate source of the Jonathan character (or of native characters speaking idiomatic American speech) is to oversimplify, and thus misunderstand, a complex process. For one thing, more than half of the approximately forty native plays written before 1787 contained attempts at realistic American characters, including at least one homespun farmer like Jonathan (Simple in *The Blockheads*, 1776). Further, when one observes that the figure dropped to about a third after that time,[20] one sees not only that Tyler did not stimulate a tradition of native characters but also that the presence of such figures in plays is partly a reflection of nonliterary factors, in this case the nationalistic feelings surrounding the Revolution. In addition, the term "brother Jonathan" had been used pejoratively by Tories even before the Revolution as a synonym for "Yankee," and affectionately later by patriots.[21] It was well enough known that a retired British Army captain, Joseph Atkinson, who had served in the United States during the war, could use the name Jonathen for the Yankee servant of an army officer in his play *A Match for a Widow*, performed in Dublin almost exactly a year before *The Contrast*, on 17 April 1786, and published in 1788. Atkinson's play, based on Joseph Patrat's *L'Heureuse Erreur* (1783), contained a Yankee whose talk resembles Tyler's Jonathan and whose function of showing up affectation by provincialism was similar; and Atkinson declared in his preface that he had, "for the first time, attempted the introduction of a *Yankee* character on the European stage." [22] While Tyler may have heard reports of this play, it was probably not an important source for him since it was not printed until after his own play had been performed; anyhow, it is patently untrue to give Tyler credit for being the first to employ a stage Yankee. In view of these facts, it seems more sensible to think of *The Contrast* as the culmination, not the inauguration, of a tradition; and, for that very reason, it could embody satisfactorily and concretely certain attitudes of Americans toward themselves (previously unformulated and subconscious), so that it served to solidify the type if not to create the symbol, and to stand as a model for later representations.[23] Leaving aside these points, it is unfair to stress Jonathan as the sole important contribution of a play which, unlike most of its American predecessors, is still actable today.

A final source of disagreement is provided by the two songs

in the play. "Yankee Doodle," which Jonathan attempts to sing in Act III, causes little difficulty; though it would be rash to say that no one has ever nominated Tyler the originator of it, there is general agreement that his use of the song popularized the most familiar and traditional version, which was not otherwise printed until much later. The tune, which goes back to the time of Charles I, was first heard in an American play twenty years earlier, in Thomas Forrest's *The Disappointment* (1767);[24] whether or not one wishes to say that Tyler made the first dramatic use of the *text* in America depends on how hard one is straining to find Tyler firsts. The important point is that Tyler saw the dramatic value, both for his characterization of Jonathan and for his nationalistic theme, of including an authentic popular song, sung by the troops and civilians alike, which had accumulated a patriotic emotional charge.

The other song, which the disconsolate Maria is singing as the second scene opens, is a sentimental lyric on the nobility of a dying Indian. The first of its four stanzas illustrates its rhyme and sound patterns and its mood:

> The sun sets in night, and the stars shun the day;
> But glory remains when their lights fade away!
> Begin, ye tormentors! your threats are in vain,
> For the son of Alknomook shall never complain.

The fourth line, with slight variations, becomes a refrain closing each stanza and explains why the song is referred to as "Alknomook." It is perhaps the best surviving example of what is almost a genre in itself, the Indian death song emphasizing the heroic endurance, or simple integrity, of the primitive warrior.[25] The story of its numerous publications, in differing versions, is a complicated one, but the gist of the matter is it has been variously attributed to three different authors, one of them Tyler. Thomas J. McKee, in 1887, wrote, "After considerable research, I have become convinced that

Alknomook is the offspring of Tyler's genius"; and Arthur Hobson Quinn, thirty-six years later, said, "I see no reason to attribute it to anyone else." [26] The poem appeared anonymously, however, three months before *The Contrast*, in the January 1787 issue of the *American Museum*, the third edition of which (in 1790) assigned it to "P. Freneau." Though Freneau never claimed the poem, others have given it to him; F. L. Pattee, for example, included it in the Princeton edition of Freneau's poetry in 1903. [27] The third candidate is a British poetess, Mrs. Anne Home Hunter, who included the words among her *Poems* in 1802; her right to them was not questioned in a contemporary review nor in her obituary in 1821. Since the first appearance of the poem was in a 1783 British song collection and since the British sheet music of about the same date credited the words to "a Lady," Mrs. Hunter seems to have the strongest claim. Although the printing of the music with *The Contrast* may suggest that the song was not universally known, it was nevertheless extremely popular in both England and America; there is no reason to suppose that Tyler was any more responsible for its composition than he was for "Yankee Doodle." He, like Ann Julia Hatton in *Tammany* (1794), was simply making use of a current lyric — one which contributed to a sentimental characterization and foreshadowed, through that character's own analysis of the words, her later admiration for an equally noble, if superficially different, soldier. [28]

Dramatic Technique

If there is little documentary evidence about Tyler's preparation as a dramatist, one glance at *The Contrast* reveals his familiarity with dramatic conventions. The plot, though less involved, is otherwise reminiscent of eighteenth-century British drama, with its hypocritical rake, gossiping young ladies, and domineering parent. Mr. Van Rough has arranged a marriage for his sentimental daughter Maria, against her wishes; meanwhile, her betrothed, Billy Dimple, equally displeased with the match, pays his respects simultaneously to two of Maria's more sprightly friends, Charlotte and Letitia. When Charlotte's brother, the patriotic Colonel Manly, enters the scene, he and Maria are instantly drawn to one another; and the impediments to their engagement are removed when all of Dimple's treachery is exposed — not only his behavior to Charlotte and Letitia (who, at the end, are also repentant for having encouraged him) but his profligacy (which is the decisive factor for Maria's father). Tyler's lack of experience is shown perhaps in the fact that this basic plot is not elaborated upon; instead, the time is filled with conversations about fashions or patriotism and with scenes involving the servants (which do not, however, constitute a subplot, for there is no intrigue in these scenes — nor do they cause complications in the main plot). The result is a play with a great deal of talk and little action; but, given such a plot, Tyler shows in other ways his awareness of various tricks of the craft.

The play is held together, to an even larger extent than usual, by contrasts and comparisons, and the theme is the contrast of the title, between the polished but hollow and insincere Dimple, with his British affectations, and the forthright, honest Manly, who may have fewer social graces but is a loyal son of liberty. It is only an adaptation, to fit the circumstances of a young republic, of the perennial concern of social comedy — the differentiation of hypocrisy and sincerity, of surface show and inner worth — and the construction of the play is based on these contrasts. The word "contrast" is used twice to make explicit this structure, once in reference to Dimple and Manly and once to their servants, Jessamy and Jonathan. At the end of act II, Jessamy muses, "How sweet will the contrast be, between the blundering Jonathan, and the courtly and accomplished Jessamy!" [29]

Royall Tyler

Mary Hunt Palmer Tyler

Frontispiece to *The Contrast*

THE

C O N T R A S T,

A

C O M E D Y;

IN FIVE ACTS:

WRITTEN BY A

CITIZEN OF THE *UNITED STATES;*

Performed with Applause at the Theatres in NEW-YORK,
PHILADELPHIA, and MARYLAND;

AND PUBLISHED *(under an Assignment of the Copy-Right)* BY

T H O M A S   W I G N E L L.

Primus ego in patriam
Aonio——deduxi vertice Musas.
VIRGIL.
(Imitated.)

First on our shores I try THALIA's powers,
And bid the *laughing, useful* Maid be ours.

P H I L A D E L P H I A:

FROM THE PRESS OF *PRICHARD & HALL,* IN MARKET STREET,
BETWEEN SECOND AND FRONT STREETS.

M. DCC. XC.

Title Page of *The Contrast*

THE

ALGERINE CAPTIVE;

OR, THE

LIFE AND ADVENTURES

OF

DOCTOR *UPDIKE UNDERHILL:*

SIX YEARS A PRISONER AMONG THE ALGE-
RINES.

————————By your patience,
I will a round unvarnished tale deliver
Of my whole course.————————

SHAKESPEARE.

by Royal Tyler.

VOLUME I.

Published according to ACT *of* CONGRESS.

PRINTED AT *WALPOLE,* NEWHAMPSHIRE,
BY DAVID CARLISLE, JUN.
AND SOLD AT HIS BOOKSTORE.

1797.

Title Page of *The Algerine Captive*

Dimple, in a parallel speech near the end of the play, makes the point even more directly: "Ladies and gentlemen, I take my leave; and you will please to observe, in the case of my deportment, the contrast between a gentleman, who has read Chesterfield and received the polish of Europe, and an unpolished, untravelled American."

One need not be told, either in the title or these speeches, that the play is built on contrasts, for the fact is obvious enough in the methodical balancing of scenes. Tyler not only submitted to the conventional five-act pattern; but, unlike his British models, he divided each act into two roughly equal scenes. The two scenes of act I introduce the three ladies: in the first Charlotte and Letitia are discussing fashions and Dimple; in the second Maria is lamenting the match her father has made for her. Act II begins like act I, with Charlotte and Letitia again discussing fashions, after their return from the shopping trip on which they were just embarking at the end of the first scene; but where Charlotte, in the opening scene, had revealed (in an aside) her attraction to Dimple, Letitia in this scene does the same. We also meet three men in this act: Manly, just arrived in town, enters to greet his sister in the first of the two scenes; and in the second the two servants, Jessamy and Jonathan, having met on the mall, converse about etiquette. The only major character who has not yet appeared is Dimple, so act III opens with him and his servant Jessamy; but Dimple soon leaves, and Jenny (Dimple's maid) and Jonathan enter, making this another scene devoted to the servants. Since the second scene finds Manly and Dimple together in the mall, the structure of act III reverses that of act II, in which the two servants had met on the mall in the second scene. It also illustrates the parallelism of Tyler's method, for we are shown the first meetings of the principal contrasting characters on the mall in the second scenes of two consecutive acts.

Although the first and third, and the fourth and sixth, of these six scenes may be balanced, it cannot be said that there has been much direction to the play thus far. These scenes have served as an uneconomical way of introducing the characters and presenting discussions on certain topics; the only hint of any plot has come in three asides or soliloquies — Charlotte's and Letitia's expressions of interest in a man supposedly engaged (Dimple), and Dimple's exclamation of displeasure upon learning that Manly is Charlotte's brother. Only the last two acts have any plot in the usual sense. Act IV, scene i, brings together for the first time the three ladies and the two gentlemen, and intrigue results not only from Dimple's setting a rendezvous with both Letitia and Charlotte for the same evening but from Maria's recognizing Manly as the person she fell in love with at first sight when he accidentally stepped into her apartment that morning. Tyler's attention to continuity of action is demonstrated in the next two scenes. In IV.ii Maria's father is agitated over the revelations of the banker (whom he was just preparing to see at the end of I.ii); and V.i begins with Jonathan and Jessamy talking over Jonathan's attempt to make love to Jenny in III.i. The banker's information about Dimple's monetary extravagances predisposes Maria's father favorably toward any substitute, and, after the other disclosures of V.ii about Dimple's behavior, no further obstacles stand in the way of Maria and Manly's happiness.

If the plot (which thus exists almost exclusively in two scenes, IV.i and V.ii) is not handled very adroitly, it is clear that Tyler was making an attempt to use various dramatic techniques which had come to his attention. The concern with continuity of time and action, the balancing of scenes, the alternation of scenes on different social levels, the distribution of key speeches among several roles, and the pattern of confrontations among characters are evidence of this. Fur-

ther, *The School for Scandal* (if not numerous other plays)
taught him the usefulness of concealed characters who overhear conversations, and this device occurs three times in the
last three scenes. In IV.ii Van Rough retires to a closet so that
he can hear what kind of sentiments Manly expresses to his
daughter Maria, and in V.ii Manly first conceals himself in
the closet and then Letitia listens at the door. Manly is able
to hear Dimple profess his love to Letitia and call Charlotte
"that trifling, gay, flighty, coquet, that disagreeable —"; then
both Manly and Letitia overhear him making advances to
Charlotte, referring to Letitia as "that insipid, wry-mouthed,
ugly creature." Also, whether or not Tyler was familiar with
his Congreve, he had learned the value of well-timed en-
trances, for, just as Dimple is pronouncing his disparaging
description of Charlotte, it is Charlotte herself who enters, and
Dimple abruptly changes his tone: "My dear Miss Manly, I
rejoice to see you; there is a charm in your conversation, that
always marks your entrance into company as fortunate."

The theater, too, which so frequently enters in an important way into English eighteenth-century plays, has its role
here. Any play which deals with fashions and hypocrisies,
with appearance and reality, finds the metaphor of the theater
useful for illustrating a distortion of values and for comparing
the acting on-stage with the acting off-stage; in addition,
fashions and etiquette are naturally on display at the theater,
and the playwright is able to bring his point home all the better
because it will be an actual theatrical audience listening to
his remarks about the theater. The state of the American theater in 1787 and Tyler's own recent introduction to the stage
combine to make any theatrical allusions in *The Contrast* of
special interest. A few brief references show that the society
we are concerned with took the theater for granted, at least
enough to use it metaphorically in conversation, as when
Charlotte, commenting on her brother's high-flown language,

compares him to "a player run mad," his head "filled with old scraps of tragedy" (II.i). Later in the same scene she describes satirically the behavior of a group of ladies who often share a box at the theater, in a passage which surely is not entirely literary in origin and must in part reflect Tyler's acuteness of observation of the post-Revolutionary American theater:

Every thing is conducted with such decorum, — first we bow round to the company in general, then to each one in particular, then we have so many inquiries after each other's health, and we are so happy to meet each other, and it is so many ages since we last had that pleasure, 'and, if a married lady is in company, we have such a sweet dissertation upon her son Bobby's chin-cough;' then the curtain rises, then our sensibility is all awake, and then by the mere force of apprehension, we torture some harmless expression into a double meaning, which the poor author never dreamt of, and then we have recourse to our fans, and then we blush, and then the gentlemen jog one another, peep under the fan, and make the prettiest remarks; and then we giggle and they simper, and they giggle and we simper, and then the curtain drops, and then for nuts and oranges, and then we bow, and it's pray Ma'am take it, and pray Sir keep it, and, oh! not for the world Sir; and then the curtain rises again, and then we blush, and giggle, and simper, and bow, all over again. Oh! the sentimental charms of a side-box conversation!

Then Dimple, in IV.i, comments on American provinciality by referring to the "miserable mummers, whom you call actors," that "murder comedy, and make a farce of tragedy"; he pointedly declares that, the one time he was "tortured" at an American theater, he sat with his back to the stage, "admiring a much better actress than any there; — a lady who played the fine woman to perfection."

But the most elaborate use of the theatrical metaphor is Jonathan's description of his accidental attendance at the theater (III.i), the most famous scene of the play and by all odds the one most frequently anthologized. Jonathan, reflecting the puritanical prejudice against the theater, asserts that he will never be caught in the "devil's drawing-room" where "the devil hangs out the vanities of the world, upon the tenter-hooks of temptation." He then proceeds to describe his disappointment the night before when, after buying a ticket to see the *"hocus pocus* man," he finds nothing but a "great green cloth" which was presently lifted, allowing the audience to "look right into the next neighbour's house"; he wonders if many houses in New York are made in that way, and he judges the family to be "pretty much like other families; — there was a poor, good natured, curse of a husband, and a sad rantipole of a wife." His description of what takes place, as well as his reference to the "School for Scandalization," makes clear what play he was viewing; and his mention of "Darby Wag-all" as the actor's name is a pun the contemporary audiences would have enjoyed, since Wignell himself played Jonathan. The entire scene is not only good comedy — the comedy of naïveté — but an integral and effective part of several larger concerns of the play. For one thing, it enables Tyler unobtrusively to ridicule the absurdity of religious attacks on the theater. The very fact that Jonathan is unable to distinguish the "wicked players" from an ordinary family emphasizes not merely the innocuousness of the theater but, at the same time, the great amount of acting in real life. Even Jonathan is able to make the application on an elementry level, for "Mr. Joseph," in the play, "talked as sober and as pious as a minister; but like some ministers that I know, he was a sly tike in his heart for all that." Furthermore, the naïve viewpoint is an advantage in contrasting common sense with excesses of convention, and the patriotic aspect of the contrast is evident in Jonathan's criticism of Darby's fear of firearms: "Now, I'm a true born Yankee American son of liberty, and I never was afraid of a gun yet in all my life." The Jonathan scenes may not be an essential part of the intrigue, but they form an indispensable foundation for the contrast theme.

Another mark of Tyler's awareness of dramatic technique is his use of asides and soliloquies. Such speeches — as well as disguises (which Tyler does not use) and eavesdropping — are easy ways for the dramatist to reveal hypocrisy in his characters, but their ease can lead to excessive dependence on them. Tyler was familiar with the tradition of asides in Renaissance and Restoration drama, but, just as he relied on hidden characters for the elaboration of his plot, his inexperience as a dramatist resulted in an awkward use of asides. In the opening scene Charlotte delivers an aside of thirty-eight words, which amounts to nothing more than a direct exposition to the audience, explaining how "Letitia little thinks" that Dimple is making himself disagreeable to Maria "in order that she may leave him at liberty to address me." This interpretation is not quite accurate, and it does fit Charlotte's character — but the fact remains that the speech is an interior thought made objective in a framework otherwise composed of externals and that it is a short cut to exposition purchased at the cost of a change of method. The rivalry between Charlotte and Letitia and their desire for Dimple continue to be expressed in asides — Charlotte unnecessarily explains, " 'I'll endeavour to excite her [Maria] to discharge him' " (IV.i), and Letitia later says of Charlotte, "So anxious to get me out! but I'll watch you" (V.ii). A similar kind of awkward exposition occurs when a character is alone on the stage: Maria's exclamation, "Ha! my father's voice," or her long speech about "How deplorable is my situation" (I.ii).[30] It is true that the soliloquies of Maria and Letitia (II.i), at the ends of two consecutive scenes, reinforce the balanced structure and that those of Jessamy and Jonathan, at the ends of the next two scenes (II.ii, III.i), emphasize the contrast theme; but when Dimple closes the following scene (III.ii) in the same way, talking about Manly, one begins to feel that the device is being overworked.

66

Jonathan's asides, however, are more successful, as are those of Jessamy and Jenny in the scenes with him, because they are more appropriate to the dramatic context and are not the exclusive source of information. That is to say, these speeches are often merely exclamations of a kind that such characters might be expected to make under their breaths, and the information imparted supports what the audience has learned about these characters in other ways. So when Jessamy admires his own choice of a word, asserts that Jonathan ("horrid brute") cannot have read Chesterfield, or admonishes himself for being "guilty of a vile proverb" (II.ii), he is simply reinforcing the traits of affectation he has already demonstrated and is not providing essential exposition. Similarly, Jenny's exclamations of "stupid creature" about Jonathan or Jonathan's confessions of social inadequacy (III.i) are at least harmless, and usually a source of humor, if not actually constructive. There are a few other asides of this kind in the play: Dimple's expressions of self-satisfaction ("I have hit the Bumkin off very tolerably," III.ii), displeasure ("The devil she is! . . . Plague on him!," III.ii), conceit ("an affair of this sort can never prejudice me among the ladies," V.ii), or amused admiration ("How he awes me by the superiority of his sentiments," III.ii); Charlotte's comments on Maria's love for Manly ("some folks . . . can praise a gentleman," "Oh! ho! is that the case," and "A lucky thought," IV.i); and Maria's reactions to a conversation about Manly ("Oh! my heart!" and "His family! But what is it to me," IV.i). The best that can be said of these asides is that they are not objectionable. In *The Contrast* asides are either innocuous exclamations of emotion or awkward announcements of plot; they are not successful in serving the more subtle purpose of revealing complexities of character.

This failure, in any case, is a function of the characterization, for there are few complexities of character to be revealed.

Details of character can be filled in by the audience once the type is known, and Tyler's assemblage of types shows once again his acquaintance with the post-Restoration tradition. There is the unscrupulous rake (Dimple), whose affectation and hypocrisy are an integral part of his double dealings with women; and there are the scheming women (Charlotte and Letitia), full of gossip and ready to exploit their closest friends in order to gain the attentions of a man. Present, too, are their opposites, Manly and Maria, the gallant and serious-minded male and the helpless and unprotected female. Maria states the familiar dilemma succinctly in a soliloquy: "How distressing for a daughter to find her heart militating with her filial duty!" (I.ii). She has the usual intolerant father who is sure that the match he has arranged is best for her, and she makes the usual protestations of helplessness ("Who is it that considers the helpless situation of our sex, that does not see we each moment stand in need of a protector"). Finally, there are servants who reflect certain qualities of their masters and illustrate the theme on another social level.

Manly and Maria are the two most exaggerated character types. Maria's sentimental view of the world is ridiculed not only by the extravagance of speech which the author gives to her but by the other characters as well. Early in the play Charlotte exclaims, "A fig for sentiment" (I.i), and later says to Letitia, "I hope you are not going to turn sentimentalist" (II.i); she refers to "the grave Maria, and her sentimental circle" (I.i) and to the "flow of sentiment meandering through [her and Manly's] conversation like purling streams in modern poetry" (II.i). As in *The School for Scandal*, literature is held partly to blame. Letitia describes how Maria "read Sir Charles Grandison, Clarissa Harlow, Shenstone, and the Sentimental Journey" (I.i) and came to see that, "according to every rule of romance," she should reject a suitor forced on her by a parent. Later Charlotte, speaking to Maria, mocks the sentimental approach: "Why, I should be shut up in my chamber [if I were to be married in a few days]; and my head would so run upon — upon — upon the solemn ceremony that I was to pass through! — I declare it would take me above two hours merely to learn that little monosyllable — *Yes*" (IV.i). Though Maria recognizes this as "raillery," it does not prevent her from saying, " 'Oh! how sweet it is, when the heart is borne down with misfortune, to recline and repose on the bosom of friendship!,' " nor from admiring Manly because "he spoke the language of sentiment."

Manly's language is certainly an extreme and comes in for its share of criticism. His sister likens his conversation to " 'old fashioned brocade' ": " 'it will stand alone; every sentence is a sentiment' " (II.i); she describes his constant lecturing which makes her " 'as melancholy as if I had been at church.' " One is inclined to think her judgment too charitable when Manly enters to pronounce his first words:

My dear Charlotte, I am happy that I once more enfold you within the arms of fraternal affection. I know you are going to ask (amiable impatience!) how our parents do, — the venerable pair transmit you their blessing by me — they totter on the verge of a well-spent life, and wish only to see their children settled in the world, to depart in peace. (II.i)

He continues in the same vein throughout the play, pointing out that "nothing can compensate for the loss of a parent's affection" (IV.ii), emphasizing patriotically that in America "affections are not sacrificed to riches," and, most amusingly, advises Maria to obey her father: "we may be assured, that if we are not happy, we shall, at least, deserve to be so. Adieu! I dare not trust myself longer with you." The sentimentalism of these two characters, though overdone, is functional, because there is a depth of feeling, good sense, and sincerity on their part, brought out by contrast with the usually jeering but superficial Charlotte in her move toward sentiment at the end. When she talks of her "practice of the meanest arts," her violation of "the most sacred rights of friendship," and the "littleness" of her past conduct (V.ii), it becomes evident that there are contrasts to be made in sentiment as in everything else.[31]

That the characters are essentially stock varieties is further supported by Tyler's use of the easy, and widespread, device of naming them suggestively. The choice of "Manly" for the solid American is obvious, but Tyler does not deny himself the occasion for a reinforcing pun and has Maria describe him as "so manly and noble" (IV.i). Manly's opposite, the affected Anglophile, is accordingly "Dimple" (his father is "Van Dumpling"), and Maria's stern father is "Van Rough." But it is for characters who are only alluded to, where a capsule characterization is especially convenient, that these names are applied most profusely: a milliner named Mrs. Catgut, a "rich Carolinian" Mr. Indigo, a matched couple in Miss Lovely and Bob Affable, the fashion-conscious girls Miss Blouze, Sally Slender, and Nancy Brilliant, the gossipy Miss Wasp, the sallow Miss Wan, the bankers Mr. Transfer and Mr. Van Cash, the loan shark John Hazard, the noblemen Colonel Piquet, Lord Lurcher, and Sir Harry Rook — to say nothing of a theater party consisting of Billy Simper, Jack Chassé, Colonel Van Titter, Miss Promonade, and the two Miss Tambours.[32] As with other simple devices, Tyler abuses this one, but the contrast he is making gains force when we observe (though a different principle of suggestiveness is involved) that the girls Jonathan knows are named Tabitha Wymen and Jemima Cawley.

This interest in puns and names is one aspect of a prevading concern with the resources of language. The characters are differentiated by their use of language, from Van Rough's "mind the main chance" to Jonathan's "dogs." But Van Rough's continual repetition of one phrase (four times in one speech in IV.ii) is merely a mechanical use of a hackneyed device — the "tag" line so common in the Restoration and post-Restoration theater[33] — whereas Jonathan's expressions represent, not an imitation of locutions from English drama, but an attempt to create an authentic Yankee. It is true that Jonathan's inventiveness in oaths may partly result from Tyler's possible familiarity with Sheridan's Bob Acres, but one must admit that the oaths, set against Dimple's affectations, give the desired effect. Jonathan will swear "by the living jingo" or simply "swear"; he will say "dang it all," "tarnation," "mercy on my soul," "what the rattle," "smite my timbers," "maple-log seize it," or "swamp it"; he is fond of "what the dogs" or "the dogs a bit"; and, for adjectival oaths, he turns to "cursed," "tarnal," and even "damn'd" (but only to apply to a Tory). He cannot utter a sentence without one of these expressions or a cliché: "the bag to hold," "a burning shame," "kicking up a cursed dust," "every mother's son of us," "as thick as mustard," "pretty dumb rich," "a month's mind," "chock full," or "all that." His speech may be ungrammatical, but his repeated admiration of the "true blue son of liberty," the "true blue Bunker-hill sons of liberty," or the "true born Yankee American son of liberty" is sincere.[34] That a man who says "buss" for "kiss" and "counted" for "thought" is at the same time honest, unassuming, and candid epitomizes the contrast of the entire play between inelegant goodness and polished deceit.

The linguistic basis of this contrast is at times one of the most subtle features of a play not generally known for quiet effects, and it shows that Tyler's perennial attention to the colloquial idiom had already begun. When Jessamy asks if Jonathan blackens his master's boots, Jonathan replies, "Yes; I do grease them a bit sometimes" (II.ii). The shift to "grease," like Jonathan's inability to understand "kiss" or his interpretation of "gallantry" as "girl huntry," is the verbal expression of a more basic lack of communication between the two. Jessamy himself comments on Jonathan's "indelicacy of diction" when he remembers that Jonathan was going to "stretch his legs upon the Mall" (III.i), but we know what Jessamy means by elegant speech, for he has already observed Jonathan's "most prodigious effect upon [his] risibility." His mind has fewer thoughts than Jonathan's, for he avoids clichés only because Lord Chesterfield disapproves of them, and he has no ideas to express anyway except those he parrots. Tyler has given us, then, a sophisticated inversion of the usual situation, to enforce his point — clichés here carry more thought, because used instinctively, than speech which eschews them only out of affectation. Of course Jonathan's language is a principal ingredient of the comedy of the play, but when we observe him speaking nonsense in an attempt to imitate Jessamy (as when he says "cherubim consequences" for Jessamy's "cherub of a consequence"), the comedy is springing from a deep, and serious, source.

Evidence of still other verbal experimentation abounds, from the use of grammatical errors for comic effects (Jonathan says "with I") to the presence of foreign phrases as a suggestion of affectation (Jessamy makes a vain effort to impress Jonathan with his French). Malapropism is practically unavoidable in such a play, and one is surprised not to find more of it — at any rate Jonathan does say "sturgeons" for "insurgents" and "hystrikes" for "hysterics." Unusual words, like "rantipole" (III.i) and "penseroso" (IV.i),[35] as well as enduring colloquialisms like "henpeck" (I.ii), reveal Tyler's delight with language, further displayed in passages of witty repartee and verbal sparring (as when Charlotte assures Manly she will introduce him "to two or three ladies of my acquaintance," and Letitia remarks, "And that will make him acquainted with thirty or forty beaux," II.i). The balancing of lines and sentences is another manifestation of this interest. In the first scene of act II there is a passage of ten short lines spoken alternately by Charlotte and Letitia, a kind of sticho-mythia in which each line plays on the preceding one; and in the opening scene Letitia consciously produces a parallel construction in casual conversation: "the wickedness of Love-lace without his wit, and the politeness of Sir Charles Grandi-son without his generosity." Figurative language appears, too, but chiefly as a means of characterizing Charlotte, who feels, in the first scene, "the rage of simile" upon her and re-marks later that Manly's tours in "the fields of conversation" always end in "the temple of gravity" (IV.i). It is not neces-sary to overemphasize these matters to see that Tyler does have an interest in them, which he goes on to develop more overtly in certain chapters of *The Algerine Captive* and *The Yankey in London.*

The central theme of the play, involving not just the con-trast between affectation and plainness, but also between city and country, hypocrisy and sincerity, can accommodate with ease an emphasis on patriotism and native worth — and it is here that the originality of the play lies. Otherwise its theme strikes one as little different from countless Restoration and eighteenth-century plays, and no less distinguished in execu-tion, despite its stiffness, than many of them. When one comes across a discussion of gossip (with Charlotte saying, "I take care never to report any thing of my acquaintance, especially if it is to their credit, — *discredit*, I mean," I.i), or satire of fashion (Charlotte buys clothing which "will never sit be-comingly" on her only because it is fashionable, II.i), or asides which reveal hypocrisy, or a situation of conflict between parental commands and natural inclinations in love, and so on — when one encounters these in *The Contrast*, one feels comfortably within the familiar English tradition.

Tyler, however, was doing something more. The Revolu-tion had emphasized the perennial problem of artistic independence, and the concomitant heights of patriotic fervor demanded the use of native materials. If he was not able to avoid being imitative in form, he at least was acutely aware of the problem (as his later preface to *The Algerine Captive* shows) and was successful in fitting an American subject into the ready-made framework. Patriotism crops up everywhere, from Charlotte's remark on her brother's constant desire to do "a gallant act in the service of his country" (II.i) and Jonathan's repetitive "true blue son of liberty" to comments on "our illustrious Washington" and on "those inestimable blessings that we now enjoy, our liberty and independence" (III.ii). One may feel that this insistence on patriotism is rather oppressive at times, as when Manly comes on stage to deliver about four hundred words on the theme, "Luxury is surely the bane of a nation." And he takes the ancient Greek states as his principal example of a country ruined by luxury:

They exhibited to the world a noble spectacle, — a number of independent states united by a similarity of language, sentiment, manners, common interest, and common consent, in one grand mutual league of protection. — And, thus united, long might they have continued the cherishers of arts and sciences, the protectors of the oppressed, the scourge of tyrants, and the safe asylum of liberty: But when foreign gold, and still more pernicious, foreign luxury, had crept among them, they sapped the vitals of their virtue. (III.ii)

As if the parallel were not obvious enough, he goes on to explain the dangers of division and concludes, "Oh! that America! Oh! that my country, would in this her day, learn the things which belong to her peace!"

It is evident that Manly is addressing this advice directly to the audience. The important point, though, is not that this element of the play turns the work into a tract or piece of propaganda; rather it is, perhaps surprisingly, the degree to which such a speech (admittedly too long) is dramatically appropriate in the context. We have come to expect Manly to speak in a solemn, didactic, self-righteous way; and it is precisely the "pernicious" "foreign luxury" of which he talks that we have seen operating in the play in contrast to his own stiffly forthright conduct. The speech is not a set piece that intrudes itself, relevant only in terms of historical events external to the play, but it grows directly out of the character and situation. Thus the usual dichotomies take on one further ingredient: surface polish, affectation, and hypocrisy equal the British; honesty, sincerity, but lack of social finish equal the Americans.[36] Everything else falls into place accordingly. The city–country theme becomes the sophistication of Europe versus the provinciality of America, with Jessamy finding the mall wanting in comparison with Ranelagh and Vauxhall (II.ii) and Dimple disparaging the "two or three squeaking fiddles" that New Yorkers consider music and the actors that "make a farce of tragedy" (IV.i). When Dimple predicts that Manly, after visiting the attractions of Europe, "will learn to despise the amusements of this country," Manly replies, "Therefore I do not wish to see them; for I can never esteem that knowledge valuable, which tends to give me a distaste for my native country." He explains that partiality to one's country is "laudable" because it adds to one's happiness without hurting others and leads to "the noble principle of patriotism." Even the question of fashion in clothing can be turned to account, for when Charlotte criticizes Manly's attire, he springs to the defense of his "regimental coat," which he had worn in the service of his country, and reaches the nearly blasphemous extreme of professing that "it is of little consequence to me of what shape my coat is" (II.i).

This statement is shocking, in a world of affectation, for the very reason that it denies the importance of surface appearances. The deceptiveness of surfaces is continually associated with the English–American contrast in the play, as when Jonathan is surprised that Jessamy calls himself a "servant," for, as he says, "you look so topping, I took you for one of the agents to Congress" (II.ii). The word "servant" is, in itself, repugnant to Jonathan, and Manly, too, disapproves of class consciousness based on superficial factors — he says proudly, when wooing Maria, "In our country, the affections are not sacrificed to riches, or family aggrandizement" (IV.i). Both Dimple and Jessamy take Lord Chesterfield as their ideal and regard departures from his sacred words as unworthy of a cilivized being. Jessamy believes that Jonathan "never can have been in a room with a volume of the divine Chesterfield" (II.ii), and Dimple cannot read him without pausing after each sentence to say, "Very true, my lord" (III.i). The result is that they live only by the book: Jenny is criticized because there is "something so execrably natural in her laugh" (III.i), and Jonathan because he laughed at the wrong places in the play he attended (V.i). When he asks, "don't I laugh natural?," Jessamy replies, "That's the very fault." It does not occur to Jessamy and Dimple that in their efforts to become cultivated human beings, they have ceased to be rational beings.

Obviously Tyler knew the English tradition. If his play is to be criticized as the work of a novice, the fault is not that he was unaware of conventions but that he was trying too hard to get them all in. Despite this essential imitativeness, the play can be called original. Tyler found that American characters, speech, settings, and issues would fit the old framework, and he made an important stride forward in the use of native materials for art. Significant as this step was, he had the greater insight of understanding that the patriotic theme grew directly out of the long-repeated themes of English comedy and that, though he was adding something, he was not destroying an organic whole. Questions of personal integrity and of national integrity are inevitably connected; and if what Tyler had to say about the individual in society was particularly cogent and salutary for an audience of the early republic, it has not lost its relevance with the years. Few would say that the play is an unqualified success, but, strangely enough (on second thought, understandably enough), it is limited and dated most by the very elements borrowed or imitated rather stiffly from the British tradition. At the same time, Tyler could not have found a way to express himself with such integrity and coherence if he had not been provided with the accumulated and patterned experience of a convention. His achievements and his limitations are testimony to the nature of the dilemma faced, and the triumph occasionally attained, by the "colonial" (if not "provincial") artist.

Reputation

Contemporary comments on *The Contrast* were, by the standards of 1787, quite full, and the three known reviews show that the main question, from the very beginning, was one of disentangling a consideration of the play's intrinsic merits from a recognition of its historical importance. "Candour," in the *Daily Advertiser*, after providing detailed criticism, said that "the piece, particularly when considered as the first performance does the greatest credit to the author." "Philo. Dramaticus," in the *Independent Journal*, was more specific when he referred to "the partial ardour of [the play's] friends, who have hitherto applauded the novelty of the attempt, in this country, without strictly weighing the merits of its execution," but went on to conclude that, considering the difficulties under which it was produced, "candour must allow its being an extraordinary effort of genius." The *Worcester Magazine* struggled with the same duality most aphoristically: "An American comick production, is a novelty —

therefore it was pleasing . . . this is not the whole truth — the piece has merit, and it will not be denied, that *merit* with *novelty*, forces applause, whereas *novelty* without *merit*, simply attains it." A review of the Baltimore performance, a few months later, declared that the comedy is a "specimen in proof that these new climes are particularly favorable to the cultivation of arts and sciences" and that it "rivals the most celebrated productions of the British muse in elegance of invention, correctness and splendor of diction." [37]

The *Daily Advertiser* had much more to say, to the extent of about nine hundred words. The "greatest defect," according to the reviewer, was "the want of interest and plot," which might have been alleviated by "a scene between Dimple and Maria," an interesting suggestion intended to make Maria's love for Manly seem more believable. Realism, in fact, lay behind most of this critic's comments. After praising the "sentiments" of the play, which were "the effusions of an honest patriot heart expressed with energy and eloquence," he declared that the soliloquies were "seldom so conducted as not to wound probability" and that the dialogue in general, though "easy, sprightly, and often witty," needed "the pruning knife very much." The reviewer's own uncertain critical principles came out in a related remark about Manly: his long soliloquy on America in the second scene of act III creates an entirely unnatural situation, yet "the thoughts are so just, that I should be sorry they were left out entirely." Jessamy received criticism on the same grounds: he "is a closer imitation of his master than is natural, and his language in general is too good for a servant." Other than suggesting that the satire of Chesterfield was somewhat unjust and that Jonathan's part "sometimes degenerates into farce," the reviewer praised in general terms the great merits and "many beauties" of the play, which had received "the unceasing plaudits of the audience." [38]

Dramatist: The Contrast

Tyler gave the copyright for *The Contrast* to Wignell, who issued proposals for printing the play and eventually obtained a sufficient number of subscriptions so that the play could be published, in the spring of 1790, by Prichard & Hall of Philadelphia.[39] A review in the *Universal Asylum* several months later called the dialogue "sprightly, and correct," the servant plot "diverting," and the characters "well drawn," but wished that the play bore "less resemblance to the comedies of Charles II. reign, as there are some passages which border on indelicacy"; still, because it is "the first American attempt at this species of composition," it is "worthy of the public attention."[40] Isaiah Thomas' *Massachusetts Magazine* the same year printed parts of two scenes, act III, scene ii, and act V, scene i.[41] After several revivals in various cities in the 1790's, the play was not performed during most of the nineteenth century, but its occasional mention by critics and inclusion in anthologies suggest that its "novelty" (or historical importance) was deemed greater than its "merit." Dunlap, in his 1832 history, commented on it as "the commencement of the American drama as united with the American theatre," which, though it was "extremely deficient in plot, dialogue, or incident, . . . was relished by an audience gratified by the appearance of home manufacture." Various writers, like the editor Joseph Buckingham, mentioned *The Contrast* in the 1850's, and the Duyckincks included the Jonathan play-scene in their 1855 *Cyclopaedia*,[42] but it was not until the centennial of *The Contrast* that it was accorded much interest. In that year, 1887, the Dunlap Society, dedicated to the study of the early American theater, issued as its first publication an edition of *The Contrast*, with an introduction by Thomas J. McKee, who lamented "the neglect and inattention it has heretofore met with"; though "meager in plot and incident," it contained, he found, "considerable intrinsic merit" as an "acting play." Charles F. Richardson, in his literary history the following year, agreed that, however "crude and imperfect," the play possessed "adaptability for public presentation," and E. C. Stedman included the opening scene in his 1888 anthology.[43] Whether or not these reactions were responsible, the American Academy of Dramatic Art staged a revival of the play in 1894, but it received little other attention until the second decade of the twentieth century.

It was indicative of the fate of Tyler's reputation that when the Drama League of America produced the play (under Arthur Hopkins and Robert Edmond Jones), as one of its American Drama Matinees at the New York Republic Theatre on 22 and 23 January 1917, the author's name could appear on the program as "Royall Taylor." Nevertheless, the play was gaining recognition, having been performed five years before at the Brattleboro festival and given two other productions in 1917. Helen Tyler Brown, enthusiastically pursuing details of her ancestor's life, was responsible for some of this attention, and she wrote an introduction to the limited edition of the play which Houghton Mifflin published in 1920. James B. Wilbur contributed a preface describing a copy belonging to George Washington, whose name had led the list of subscribers to the original 1790 edition and whose copy was the basis for the 1920 edition. *The Contrast* had become a rare book, and the play was accorded the reverence due a key national document.[44]

This interest in the play, part of a general revaluation of our native literature in the 1910's and 1920's, was reinforced by a number of scholars who did not fail to mention the play in their literary histories or studies of the early drama.[45] In the decades which followed, *The Contrast* was given more than a dozen productions,[46] discussed in several scholarly articles and dissertations[47] as well as in popular magazines,[48] and anthologized eight times.[49] It is more widely known than most other literary works of the immediate post-Revolutionary years and is perhaps the most famous American play before the twentieth century. Attractions of "quaintness" and patriotism aside, the play, on the dual grounds of influence and merit, can be said to deserve its fame. If Tyler is usually remembered only as the author of *The Contrast*, it is no doubt largely for the reason implied in the prologue,[50] written "by a Young Gentleman of New-York":

> Yet *one*, whilst imitation bears the sway,
> Aspires to nobler heights, and points the way,
> Be rous'd, my friends! his bold example view;
> Let your own Bards be proud to copy *you*!

Tyler was to use American materials many more times, but the conjunction of circumstances and execution have given this "bold example" a special place. After nearly two centuries, one may find most appropriate the opening of that prologue, which has taken on additional meanings, unintended by the writer: "this night is shewn/A piece, which we may fairly call our own."

⁀❧ III ❧⁀

Dramatist: Later Plays

THE success of *The Contrast* encouraged Tyler to continue his playwriting, for his second effort appeared on the
John Street stage a month later, on 19 May 1787. Late April
and early May had seen productions of *The Beaux' Strategem*,
Romeo and Juliet, and *Macbeth*, and 19 May was to be a
benefit for Wignell. The first play of the evening was *The
Recruiting Officer* (performed only five days before for Mrs.
Harper's benefit night), and the second was announced as
"a COMIC OPERA in 2 Acts, (never performed) written
by the Author of the Contrast, (for this night only) called
May Day in Town, or NEW-YORK in an UPROAR." [1]
The music was "compiled from the most eminent Masters.
With an Overture and Accompanyments," and sheets of the
songs were to be sold on the evening of the performance.
One can only speculate on the plot and music of *May Day*,
for neither the play nor the song sheets are extant. It is impossible to know whether Tyler had sufficient musical knowledge to "compile" the score, and, if so, what kind of music
it was, since he shows little interest in music in his other
work; at least someone was having difficulty getting the music
put together, for the opera apparently had to be postponed
one day on this account. [2] The plot, perhaps in the vein of
The Contrast, probably arose from Tyler's own experiences
during his first May in New York, as he saw the city in the
"uproar" caused by the 1 May date for moving households.

The piece was less successful than *The Contrast*, since it was not repeated and did not elicit much comment in the newspapers, and one twentieth-century writer calls it a "trifle" and a "failure."[3] However, a contemporary witness, Congressman William J. Grayson, wrote to James Madison on 24 May admiring this play which "has plott and incident and is as good as several of the English farces"; but he admitted that "it has . . . not succeeded well" and suggested that the explanation was "the author's making his principal character a scold. Some of the New York ladies were alarmed for fear strangers should look upon Mrs. Sanders as the model of the gentle-women of this place."[4]

After these two plays, perfomed only a month apart in the spring of 1787, there is no record of further dramatic activity on Tyler's part for nearly a decade. His move to Vermont possibly was not conducive to writing for the stage, but the fact that his brother, John Steele Tyler, became manager of the Federal Street Theatre, Boston, in November 1795, combined with Dennie's prodding, may have provided adequate motivation for renewed efforts. Dennie wrote to Tyler in his usual style on 2 October 1795:

> I perceive by a recent Centinel, that your brother is appointed Manager of the Theater. This information cannot be premature, as the circumstance is corroberated [*sic*] in the Orrery. This revolution in the dramatic world cannot fail to shed select influence upon your plans. I propose residing here for some time. This information may induce you to descend from the mountains, to cooperate with your friend, and *now* to think seriously of writing for the stage; which under present auspices cannot fail to essentially promote your interest. Pray don't defer an instant *doing* on the present occasion. Your predecessor Gay and you have speculated enough in property: realise now fortune invits [*sic*]. The interest I have in your well being & the claims which genius has upon your contemporaries call loudly for that snug annuity, which I swear you can have, and which will give you a couch

for your gouty limbs, & Swift's daily pint, to dissipate the "curae edaces" of age. . . .

Whether you choose to have your opera sung or a future *new* comedy acted in great pomp, by his Majesty's servants, & praised by Gardner, heard by Morton, & puffed by me; this is the "mollia tempora." condescend for a day to vacate your indolent room, and entertain stock jobbing ideas. I wish you to receive that most honorable of pensions, which the dunces & knaves of a stupid mart have owed your talents since you first wove the web of fancy.[5]

Whether or not Dennie's persuasion was responsible, a play now attributed to Tyler appeared on the Boston stage five months later, on 6 May 1796. Entitled *The Farm House, or The Female Duellists*, it was announced as the afterpiece for *Every One Has His Fault*. Though no copy of the play survives, comparison of its cast with that of Kemble's 1789 *Farm House* (performed just a year earlier in New York and based in turn on the 1715 *Country Lasses*) suggests that it was an adaptation of Kemble. Tyler's brother had resigned as manager of the theater the month before, but Tyler's son reports, "The Dualists [*sic*] was performed and was especially popular." [6]

A year and a half later the Haymarket Theatre in Boston presented a play that can be assigned to Tyler with greater certainty. Dennie had written in the spring, "If I go to Boston this summer, which I am half resolved to do, I think I can lay a plan to start some Dramatic piece for you." [7] The *Independent Chronicle* duly announced, for 30 October 1797, as an afterpiece to follow *Wives as They Were*, "an original national DRAMA, in three acts, (never performed in any Theatre) entitled, The Georgia SPEC; *Or, Land in the Moon*. Written by R. TYLER, Esq. Author of the Contrast, &c." [8] The title suggests that Tyler was exploiting the current interest in land speculation in Yazoo County, Georgia, and that he was again utilizing native materials as the basis for satire.

Newspapers had been ridiculing the whole affair with such pieces as "an Elegy on the death of *Miss Georgia Purchase*"; [9] and the word "spec" was a common abbreviation for "speculation," particularly in connection with property, as in the advertisements for houses headed "A Spec!" [10] The names of the characters, as they appeared in the announced cast, offer a further glimpse into the nature of the play. In addition to "Old Spec" himself, there are Jasper Lunge, Charles Modish, Blunder Bubble, Slap Dash, and Billy Chatter, plus the ladies, Miss Bubble, Miss Prattle, and Miss Glib — and, finally, Old Bunker, identified as a Berkshire farmer. This is another instance of Yankee common sense contrasted with the ridiculous excesses of fashion. The *Columbian Centinel* commented, "It contains a rich diversity of national character and native humor scarcely to be found in any other drama of the language. Replete with incident, enlivened by wit and amply fraught with harmless mirth, the comedy is entitled to the applause of all without wounding the feelings of any." [11] The play moved to New York two months later, where it was performed at the John Street Theatre on 20 and 23 December under the title *A Good Spec: Land in the Moon, Or, The Yankee Turn'd Duellist*; it was given a third time in the New Theatre on 12 February 1798.[12]

One may suspect that Tyler had still further associations with the Boston theater: he did write an "Address" for the opening night of the 1795–96 season (under his brother's management), and as late as 1811 his brother was still asking him for prologues and inviting him to send "your Play which you mean to brush up." [13] It is a paradox (though not entirely unexpected) that the plays of Tyler which were performed have not survived (with the exception of *The Contrast*, which was printed), while those which in all probability were never staged have come down to us in manuscript. Until 1941 *The Contrast* was the only basis for a judgment of Tyler's skill in drama, although persons who had access to his son's memoir knew the titles of these other plays. In that year, however, the texts of four more Tyler plays, found among the Tyler Papers, were edited by A. W. Peach and G. F. Newbrough for the Princeton series of "America's Lost Plays." It may be that these plays do nothing to increase Tyler's stature, and it may be that they are so different in kind from *The Contrast* as to form almost a separate category of his work — but it is futile to wish that some of the produced plays had been saved instead, and in any case one is grateful for what meager material there is, material that does have its importance for an understanding of Tyler.

The Island of Barrataria

The first of the plays in the 1941 volume can be set apart from the other three but seems to fall in the same class with one final nonextant title ascribed to Tyler in that both are adaptations from foreign literature. Though nothing whatever is known about a play entitled *The Doctor in Spite of Himself*, which Tyler's son credits to his father, it appears to be an adapted version of the Molière play and can be dated approximately 1795 from a letter of Tyler's.[14] Similarly, the first of the four 1941 plays, *The Island of Barrataria* [sic], is based on the Barataria episode in *Don Quixote* (especially on chapters 45, 47, 51, and 53 of part II). While the Molière piece may have been little more than a revision of a translation, the Cervantes offers an opportunity for examining Tyler's dramatic technique, since in this case details from a prose work had to be selected and rearranged for dramatic effect. The Barataria sequence had previously been dramatized by Thomas D'Urfey, but if one is to accept Tyler's inscription on the title page of his manuscript, he wrote without a knowledge of previous efforts: "As the author is informed there is a farce in print — on the same subject — and perhaps with the Title first Proposed — the following is suggested as a substitute — Tantalization, Or The Governour of a Day." It has been suggested that the allusion is to Frederick Pilon's version of D'Urfey's *Barataria, or Sancho Panza Turned Governor*, performed at the John Street Theatre on 5 October 1789. Although there is no record that Tyler's play was ever performed, this reference, if correct, provides a *terminus a quo* for the play and suggests that it probably belongs to his second, or "Boston," period of play-writing — an inference supported by Tyler's further comment on his title page: "A Farce in Three Acts never before performed on any Stage [,] by a Bostonian." [15]

A comparison of *The Island of Barrataria* with the relevant chapters of *Don Quixote* reveals the skill which Tyler had acquired as a dramatic craftsman. If the finished play is not as important, nor even as interesting intrinsically, as *The Contrast*, it does show that Tyler knew how to put a play together, for in the course of its composition he had done three things: he had selected the most dramatic episodes from his source and omitted the others (compressing the time from seven days to one); he had added new incidents to create a romantic interest; and he had so arranged these elements as to form two interrelated plots, constituting a true intrigue as opposed to the episodic structure of the *Don Quixote* material. The basis of the intrigue (and Tyler's addition to the Barataria story) is, characteristically, a situation in which two lovers try to outwit an uncooperative father, his objections to the match founded on class consciousness and social pretensions.[16] Alvarez, a wealthy middle-class Baratarian, is determined that his daughter, Julietta, shall marry a nobleman, though she is in love with Carlos. Julietta, disguised, takes the initiative in arranging affairs, and the trick by which she attains her goal provides the main thread of "plot." It so happens that this family crisis occurs at the very time when

Sancho Panza takes over as governor of Barataria, and Tyler not only involves him in the plot but inserts portions of the traditional story into the framework thus provided. The result is that the two stories support each other, and what was an episodic adventure in the picaresque vein becomes a finished plot in the Aristotelian sense, with a beginning, middle, and end.[17]

The beginning shows the two strands before they become related. Of the four scenes in act I, the first and third concern the Alvarez story (Carlos talking with Alvarez, and Carlos and Julietta trying to outwit Alvarez through disguise), while the second and fourth introduce the Sancho Panza part (the Captain of the Guard announcing Sancho's arrival, and his entry itself). The future connection between the two, however, is disclosed at the end of the opening scene when Alvarez suggests the possibility of offering his daughter to the new governor, Sancho Panza (who is to arrive "this morning"), since Sancho is obviously of a noble family if he is to be governor; Carlos' protestations that Sancho is a "mere fool" and a "short thick fat squab boorish looking fellow" (p. 5) have no effect on the snobbery of Alvarez, who sees only that Sancho is a "grandee." The act also builds to a climax with the arrival of Sancho and the closing barrage of gunfire and shouts of the mob to welcome the governor. Tyler saw the theatrical value of pageantry and elaborated on the simple statement in Cervantes that Sancho entered amid pomp and the ringing of bells. He further perceived the usefulness of a comic motif and took a hint from the episode of Cervantes in which Sancho is not permitted to eat; Tyler leads up to that scene, in a degree that Cervantes does not, by emphasizing Sancho's appetite. The second thing Sancho says is, "And then let us go to dinner, for I am very hungry" (p. 10), and practically all his other remarks in the scene relate to food. He is a caricature, but one appropriate to the farcical world of Barataria, and the hunger provides a greater unifying thread than it does in Cervantes.

In act II the emphasis is on Sancho, but Tyler's device for interweaving the two plots makes him a very different figure from the one in *Don Quixote*. In the first scene Julietta, disguised as a page, slanders herself to watch Carlos' reactions and then asks her father (who does not recognize her) to recommend her as a page at the governor's palace. The two of them leave for the palace, which is the setting of the following scene. Although Sancho is still hoping for food (he has "all honour and no porridge"), the striking thing about the scene is his attitude toward his wife. Alvarez offers his daughter, and Sancho first replies that he is "noosed already" and that he "must not forget my good old spouse Terresa"; but when Alvarez mentions the money that will accompany Julietta, Sancho's attitude quickly changes, and he wishes "old Terresa was asleep in Paradise." He not only agrees to abandon Terresa and marry Julietta but accepts Alvarez's seal ring as pledge, though not without some pangs of conscience. He tells Alvarez, with a characteristic simile, to "speak softly that my conscience may not hear you, for it kicks like a mule colt," and he imagines Alvarez to be "a relation of that old gentleman who sometimes for his amusement sports a cloven foot" (p. 15). This Sancho is far removed from the one in Cervantes, who writes to Don Quixote asking him to forward letters from his wife Teresa because he longs for news of her and the children. Tyler's reason for the change appears to be a desire to make even more explicit the satire on rulers: when Sancho asks, "Would it not be wrong to make my spouse Terresa a castaway?," Alvarez assures him, "Wrong in private men, but in great men honourable. . . . a great man's conscience sleeps like himself in down" (p. 15). But the injection of this note weakens — not strengthens — the force of the satire. That the satire is more effective in the Cervantes chapters, or in Brackenridge when Teague O'Reagan is elected to an office for which he is not qualified, results not from the fact that Tyler is too direct, or overtly didactic, but from the more important fact that he has presented Sancho with an ethical dilemma foreign to the world of farce.

This is not to say that marital questions cannot be one of the main sources of farce, but that the heartlessness of Sancho's behavior in this scene, with the allusions to conscience and temptation by the devil, is not in accord with what we otherwise learn of Sancho, or even with the spirit of the entire play. The scene returns to farce at the end, when Sancho questions Carlos about Julietta (especially, "can she make a good dumpling?"), and Carlos replies with a ludicrously unpleasant picture of her — as he explains in an aside, "the fear of losing thee forces me to disparage thee" (p. 16). Julietta, still disguised as a page, is placed in the position of praising herself. Though the scene is not in Cervantes, the idea of describing Julietta as "a beauty if it were not that she is blind of one eye and squints with the other" and a good dancer "if she were not lame" probably comes from the similar (but much longer) description of a country girl in the Barataria section of *Don Quixote* (chapter 47). The whole scene is a crucial one for evaluating Tyler's effort because he is here carefully tying the threads of his plot together (foreshadowing the end with Alvarez's promise that whoever presents the seal ring shall have his daughter) and exploiting the comedy of Sancho's hunger — it fits admirably, that is, into the structure of the play. But in his zeal to comment more directly on the unscrupulousness of rulers, Tyler's method shifts to create the only serious blemish in the play: Sancho's lack of affection for his wife is not in itself objectionable; the problem lies in the approach to the matter. If Tyler is trying to make of Sancho a more complex character facing a serious moral and ethical decision, then he fails to pursue these implications through the rest of the play. The flaw is not in structure but in mood and characterization.

The final scene of act II is the longest in the play and presents the heart of the Barataria story — Sancho's decisions in his court of law. Though the first three cases which come up are from Cervantes, the ritual of the court is not; as a lawyer, Tyler was taking the opportunity to satirize the extravagances and jargon of his profession. After the crier calls the court to order, Don Ignatio Salkedor Ventris Fleta Bracton Comberback presents the first case and opens a roll, ten or fifteen feet long, listing the charges; when Sancho wants to know briefly what the man is accused of, Don Ignatio replies, "that would be against all precedent." In the second case Don Ignatio points out that the issue cannot be heard without a formal statement — "the Plaintiff," he says, "should have filed her declaration in haec verba":

Attach Joseph Nunnez of Algazanas in the Province of Andelusia, now resident in Barrataria yeoman, to answer unto Magdeline alias Martha alias Margery alias Dorcas alias Deborah alias Catharine alias Keturah Slammerkin alias Slubberkin alias Slipshins alias Slipshod of Avedo in the Province of Astrinas Spinster in a plea of Trespass on her case — For that the said Joseph at Astrog in Kamskatchka to wit in Barrataria and so forth et cetera and so forth — on the body of her the said Magdaline alias Martha alias Margery, alias Dorcas alias Deborah alias Catharine alias Keturah Slammerkin alias Slubberkin alias Slipshins alias Slipshod with staves clubs swords guns bayonets pistols crowbars Congreve Rockets boarding pikes steam boats masinos and Torpedoes and other deadly weapons — did make an assault and for that the said Joseph, aforesaid at Kamskatchka aforesaid to wit at Barrataria aforesaid — did aforesaid — then aforesaid and aforesaid there aforesaid — her aforesaid — the aforesaid said aforesaid Magdaline aforesaid alias Martha aforesaid alias Margery aforesaid — alias Dorcas aforesaid alias Deborah aforesaid alias Catharine aforesaid alias Keturah aforesaid Slammerkin aforesaid alias Slubberkin aforesaid alias Slipshins aforesaid — alias Slipshod aforesaid and for that also moreover nevertheless and likewise — and so proceed to set forth the Plaintiff's case. Clearness and precision, may it please your Excellency, are the glory of the Law. (pp. 18–19)

Thereupon Don Fabricio, a second lawyer, asserts that this suit should have been presented "by indictment — billa vera, my Lord," and goes on to declare that the only point on which lawyers agree is "that the law has been immutably settled for more than seven hundred years. But then how or in what manner or in which way, it is settled, we have been disputing about ever since." The pragmatic wisdom of Sancho's untutored judgment is of course illustrated in Cervantes and follows the immemorial pattern of native insight triumphing over elaborate dialectic; but Tyler's caricature of legal procedures and verbiage makes the incisiveness of Sancho's decisions stand out all the more.

The first case (which is one of the last in Cervantes' account, chapter 51) has to do with travelers on a bridge, each of whom is asked his reason for crossing. If he tells the truth, he may continue; if he lies, he is immediately hanged. The problem is that Lope de Stepaway said he was crossing the bridge for the purpose of being hanged; if he were executed, then, he would have told the truth and should have lived. Sancho answers quickly: "Let the prisoner go free for where the case is doubtful, the judge should always incline to mercy." When Don Ignatio reports that there is no precedent for such a decision, Sancho says, "Then put it in your books, that there may be one page at least an honest soul may love to read" (p. 17). The second case (from chapter 45 of *Don Quixote*, Sancho's second case there) concerns a woman who accuses a man of assaulting her, though the man claims he paid her what she had asked until she saw that he had more money. Sancho's solution is first to award the purse to the woman;

then, when the man tries to take it away from her, she defends it so energetically that Sancho can say, "if you had been as carefull to defend your Jewell as you have the purse, there are not many men in the old or new world who could have rob'd you" (p. 20). Though Tyler's Sancho does not castigate her as much as Cervantes', in both cases the man leaves with his money. The third issue (Sancho's first case in *Don Quixote*, chapter 45) turns on another trick: one peasant, casually handing his staff to a second, swears that he has paid the second peasant his debt; Sancho, after some thought, realizes that the money is concealed inside the staff.

These cases, while not related to the Alvarez plot, serve to reveal Sancho's character before he is faced with a case which does involve the love plot. After the two peasants leave, Julietta enters, disguised as an old woman, and tells Sancho a story about being abandoned by her husband, a story exactly parallel to Sancho's own projected behavior. "Such doings," says Julietta, "may do for emperors & governours & princes but won't do for Christian people" (p. 22). Sancho, who is aware of "a case as like this as two peas," advises her to tell her husband to "resist the devil," for "a good wife and children are the richest comforts a man can possess." Julietta asks for a token, as proof that she has talked to the governor, and Sancho gives her Alvarez's ring. Sancho's character has thus been righted, but dissatisfaction at his ambiguous role is not relieved. His inability to play the part of the unfeeling and corrupt monarch manifests itself in this decision as in the other three: all are consistently part of Tyler's satire on governmental hypocrisy, as brought into focus by naïveté and simplicity. But why did the Sancho who cuts through legal nonsense and refuses to submit to arguments about precedent ever attempt the role of the corrupt ruler or acquiesce to Alvarez's deal in the first place? If this episode is intended as a study of the good man who yields to temptation but sees his error in time, then the play is simply not up to the burden it must carry. Sancho goes through no agonized process of soul-searching, nor is there reason for him to in the world of the play; but one may feel that for a few moments he was in a different world.

The plot, in essence, is contained within those last two scenes of act II, for at the end of the act the ring has passed into Julietta's hands; there remains, in act III, only to make explicit the end of the affair. Of the two scenes in this act, the first is the culmination of the hunger theme. Sancho has not been permitted to eat since his arrival in Barataria, for the governor must traditionally appear at court before he dines. Now at last Sancho is confronted with a magnificent table of food, only to find (as in *Don Quixote*, chapter 47) that each dish he chooses is ruled out as unhealthful by the royal physician Don Pedro Physico Positivo Pulmonic Detergent; even the ale and wine are drunk by the official tasters. In the second scene, set in Sancho's private apartment, he is promised a special repast, but fresh matters of state interfere. First comes the announcement that the enemy is preparing to invade the island; then Julietta, disguised now as a gypsy, gives the ring to Carlos, who gives it in turn to Alvarez, who is forced by his earlier promise to award his daughter to Carlos; and, finally, the invading army arrives, Sancho is bound in armor so that he cannot move, he is trampled upon by soldiers, and at the end he is given credit for gaining the victory (based on chapter 53 of *Don Quixote*). Hypocritical praise is just as distasteful to him as the cant of the lawyers, and he can take no more of it. The play ends with Sancho, "in a sullen mood," delivering the moral to the audience: "I have for some time suspected I was the fool of the play. . . . Sancho is a simpleton I know, but as simple as I am, I have mother wit enough to find out in a brief day that I am unfit for office. But are there not some who govern it for years — bear abuse on abuse and have not wit enough to see that they are the Sancho's of the political play?" (p. 30).[18]

This final speech has no place in the play and may be regarded as a conventional eighteenth-century curtain speech to the audience. Otherwise, except for the wavering in the treatment of Sancho in act II, the play is successful enough to reassure one that Tyler's dramatic ability was not entirely exhausted in *The Contrast*. This play reveals a firmer (and less mechanical) grasp of dramatic structure and unity, and it demonstrates an insight into farcical situations and dialogue (which differ from those in drawing-room comedy). As in *The Contrast*, Tyler's underlying purpose is to deliver a sermon to the new republic, but, however overt, it is not quite so direct as in the earlier play. Even Sancho has been made into a kind of disguised Yankee, with his down-to-earth approach, his similes about peas and colts, and his expressions like "long locrum story" (p. 17), "how she kites it" (p. 23), and "Cork your peepers, good woman, and unstopple your mouth" (p. 18). Tyler's experimentation with words is again evident in colloquialisms, in characters' names, and in puns. Sancho constantly plays on words, particularly to bring the subject back to food — when Julietta is called "the toast of the town," it is inevitable that Sancho will say, "Very comfortable in a noggin of brisk ale" (p. 14).[19] One of his puns well illustrates the patriotic slant of the play: Don Ignatio's mention of a precedent causes Sancho to say, "President? — I never knew but one good President in my life & he is gone to glory" (p. 17).[20] The patriotism, as in *The Contrast* and *The Algerine Captive*, is critical and instructional; it is an attempted corrective of abuses in a system worth preserving. Only episodes from Cervantes' Barataria story which would contribute most directly to a satire of incompetence in high places are chosen (Sancho's "rounds" in chapter 49 are omitted), and a comparison of Cervantes' and Tyler's treatments of Sancho's exits from Barataria shows that Tyler's criticism is harsher and more biting. The unity he gives to Cervantes' incidents corresponds to the coherence of thought lying behind the play. Tyler knew the effectiveness of laughter and labeled his work a "farce" with no frivolous intent.

The Sacred Dramas

If *The Island of Barrataria* is not an unexpected successor to *The Contrast*, the other three plays, which are sacred dramas in blank verse, are so different that one student of Tyler has remarked that they "somehow hardly fit into the picture." [21] Yet the witty and satiric Tyler is not the whole man, as many of his poems show; and one should not be surprised to find a man who almost went into the ministry discovering a literary outlet in Biblical stories. These plays may have been intended as examples of the "coarse fabric" of the American "parnassian looms," which deserve patriotic support because they are "homespun," [22] but they are also the sincere products of a long familiarity with the Bible.

The shortest of the three, *The Judgement of Solomon*, may be taken as an illustration of the method used. This play, scarcely 750 lines, is made up of two approximately equal acts (the first of three scenes, the second of one), with a prologue and an epilogue. Its Biblical source, a short passage in I Kings (3:16–28), is the famous incident in which two women, each claiming a particular child as her own, appear before Solomon for settlement of the dispute. Solomon gives the command to have the child divided into two parts, one for each woman, and from the reactions of the women he determines which is the real mother — for one raises no objection to the division, while the other says she would rather lose custody of the child than see it slain. The latter is of course awarded the child, and the case is taken to represent one of the high points of Solomon's wisdom.

Out of this brief tale Tyler has constructed a well-rounded and dramatic work; he has exploited the conflict and suspense inherent in the story but not utilized in the Biblical version. The first act is of his own invention and serves, in three different episodes, to build up interest in the actual trial scene, which constitutes the second act. The opening scene is a conversation between two elders of Israel, Chalcol and Baanah. Chalcol, renowned for his wisdom, has been gone from Israel for many years in search of knowledge, and now, upon his return, he questions his old friend about the changes that have taken place. After all the strife that had occurred under Saul and David, Chalcol asks how it happens that now "peace and plenty crown this favour'd land" (p. 102); and the answer is that Solomon, "deemed of all mankind / The wisest," now rules. Although Chalcol, wise himself, is somewhat skeptical, Baanah explains that Solomon's wisdom is "from above, the special gift of God" (p. 103). Baanah points out Solomon's temple, and the scene ends as Chalcol amazedly tries to take in all these "genuine fruits of wisdom" (p. 104).

The second scene shifts to the house of the two women, Lernah and Maachah, and shows them quarreling. Whereas in the Biblical account the women are unnamed and undifferentiated, here they assume at least a small degree of personality; whereas in the Bible they simply appear before the King and explain the situation, here their conflict is dramatized, and we learn the dilemma through their quarrel. Lernah, the woman who speaks first and whose baby has supposedly died, is the one who speaks more gently, for the most part, and ultimately triumphs; Maachah, who is on the defensive from the start, is rather too sensitive about the question of whether the baby she is carrying is really hers, and her outbursts of anger suggest a guilty conscience. Tyler has provided in these women the rudiments at least of convincing characterizations. Lernah is determined to reclaim her child,

"if in Israel, in God's own land / Justice can yet be had"
(p. 106). "I'll fly straightway," she says, "to royal Solomon /
And at the footstool of his golden throne / Will cry for justice"; and Maachah follows her.

Like these two scenes, the third has its ultimate focus on
Solomon. This scene balances the first, with a conversation
between two men, one of whom (like Chalcol in the first)
remains to be convinced of Solomon's greatness. Liba, formerly a servant of Mephiboseth, extols Solomon, who has
awarded him half of Mephiboseth's property; Shimei, on
the other hand, considers Liba an apostate from the house
of Saul and curses Solomon and the race that took over Saul's
throne. So Liba suggests that they go to court, for that very
day a difficult case between two women is to come up, a
case in which the wisest men have declared that no justice
can be done. The symmetry of the first act is completed
when he names Chalcol, "This day return'd," as one of those
wise men. All three scenes have pointed toward Solomon
and have aroused curiosity (even in those who know the
story) about the scene in which Solomon will meet this test
of his wisdom.

The second act is set in Solomon's throne room and opens
with a herald's announcement that Belkis, the Queen of Sheba,
has arrived. Tyler is here joining, for dramatic effect, two
separate passages in I Kings, for the visit of the Queen of
Sheba (I Kings 10:1–13) is not connected in the Biblical
account with the decision in the case of the two women;
however, she does come to see if the reports of Solomon's
wisdom are true, and thus, in the play, she is another figure
like Chalcol and Shimei, doubting until she observes with her
own eyes. When the two women enter, Lernah first presents
her case, in words close to the King James version (this is the
very opening of the Biblical account) — for example, in the
King James the first woman explains that "there was no

stranger with us in the house, save we two in the house" (3:18); Lernah says, "There were with us no stranger in the house — / No one save us to see our infant babes" (p. 114). Then Maachah argues her side, and Solomon recapitulates the case, asks if there are witnesses, and turns to Baanah to determine whether there is a rule or precedent covering such a situation. The ritual symmetry of the play continues with the interpolated comments of Shimei (who believes that Solomon is baffled) and Liba (who still defends the King), balancing the brief discussion between Baanah and Chalcol just before the two women entered. When Solomon orders the child to be split, Shimei decries the barbarity of the decision, and Tyler continues to put off the climax by having Maachah speak before Lernah (in the Bible the true mother cries out first). There remains only for Solomon to award the child to Lernah and for Belkis, following closely the King James phrasing,[23] to deliver a glowing encomium to Solomon's wisdom.

It is understandable that Tyler should have been drawn to this subject, concerned with the administration of justice, and the Solomon case is only a serious presentation of the kind of legal puzzle that occurs in *The Island of Barrataria*. Furthermore, though overt preaching is kept out of the drama itself, the Prologue and Epilogue make clear the intended application. The Prologue centers on the question, "Has wisdom ceased her cry in modern times?" The answer is No, but modern man has turned to "earthly vanities," to "idols vain," and he may be helped by contemplating "How heavenly wisdom did in ancient days / Inspire the wisest of mankind." The Epilogue then points out that wisdom even greater than Solomon's is still bestowed "on all who rightly seek the Lord / And gain the honor of the Christian name." Finally, it is evident that Tyler knew these Biblical materials well, for all the names (except Belkis and Lernah) occur in the

Bible (chiefly in I Kings and I Samuel), and, if the incidents themselves are not authentic, the identities of most characters are.[24] The ease with which he sketches in political history in the third scene — the background of intrigue which led to Solomon's accession — is added testimony that Tyler had read his Old Testament more than casually.

To find that Tyler has skillfully employed various dramatic techniques to turn a short tale into a play is to find no more than one would expect, after *The Contrast* and *The Island of Barrataria*; more surprising, perhaps, is the quality of the verse. Tyler's blank verse reveals itself in this play to be a flexible, fluid instrument, capable of subtle effects and occasional power. He is in sufficient control of his medium that he is not afraid to run over certain lines, to vary the caesuras, or to cut some lines short (especially the last lines of speeches). The Miltonic patterns, with an attraction to place names, are illustrated in the seventh speech of the play, by Chalcol:

> In search of knowledge I have travel'd far
> Through Persia, Media and Chaldea's land,
> E'en to the peak of frozen Caucasus.
> Three years I sojourn'd on the banks of Nile;
> Thrice saw its mighty waters rush amain
> O'er Egypt's fertile plain; and three years more
> With wonder I in Babylon survey'd
> The huge remains of that stupendous pile
> Call'd Babel, raised by impious man.
> To mock Omnipotence I likewise climb'd
> The steep ascent of lofty Arrarat
> And hence have brought a piece of shittim wood
> Cut from the ribs of that same wondrous ark
> Which saved the righteous Noah from the flood
> Which delug'd the whole earth. (p. 101)

Alliteration and simile are not to any extent parts of Tyler's equipment,[25] but the short last line, as here, appeared so effective to him that it became a trademark of the longer speeches and emphatic short ones: "But Solomon is deemed of all mankind / The wisest" (p. 102); "To give just judgment in this wondrous case / So dark and intricate" (p. 109); "My Lord the King, I cannot bear to hear / Her lie so basely" (p. 114).

The strengths and weaknesses of Tyler's verse can be seen, at the beginning of act II, in the last lines of the prayer (modeled on the one in I Kings 3:6–9) which Solomon offers up before the trial:

> When I ascend the seat of judgment then,
> Hear thou in heaven, thy dwelling place,
> And me endue with wisdom to discern
> The good from evil, and still to award
> A righteous judgment to thy chosen race. (p. 110)

There is a faltering, as in the second and fourth lines, and occasionally an instance of overregularity, as in the first (with its filler word at the end); but there is also a sense of rhetorical effect, of how to construct and phrase a verse sentence for cumulative power, of combining movement and meaning. Tyler had learned to write by reading the masters, and, if his verse is derivative and filled with conventional expressions, it is not dull. He knew English poetry as well as he knew the Bible, and he practiced his lessons faithfully: his blank verse may not be always stimulating, but it is always competent. To say that much is to say a great deal, when one is speaking about a lawyer of the early republic, writing thirty years before Robert Montgomery Bird and sixty before George Henry Boker.

The other two plays, with a few distinguishing features of their own, manifest the same qualities of adaptation and prosody, and show invariably a flair for the selection and combination of inherently dramatic Biblical episodes. The Esther story is widely regarded as one of the best narratives in the Old Testament, though its brutality and secularism have raised questions about its appropriateness for inclusion in a sacred text. Tyler retells this story in 1150 lines, emphasizing (as the title indicates) the Hebrew celebration which grows out of it, in *The Origin of the Feast of Purim; Or, The Destinies of Haman and Mordecai.* This subtitle, contrasting the haughty Haman with the devout Mordecai, points to another aspect of the tale which Tyler stresses: the defeat of pride by righteousness, suggested by the epigraphs from Proverbs and Psalms [26] and by the concluding didactic lines: "pride and envy, baleful passions, / Altho' awhile they injure righteous men / Upon their base posessor oft recoil / And merge him in the ruin he design'd" (p. 60). A further subtitle suggests a certain amount of eclecticism: "A Sacred Drama in Three Acts Taken Principally from the Book of Esther." If Esther provides the material for the body of the play, the opening and closing choruses draw on the Psalms and some of the prophets. One may surmise that the opening lines of the male chorus were inspired by Jeremiah (see 4:8), but there is no question that the last speech of the female chorus in the opening section is a paraphrase (often repeating the King James wording) of Psalm 137 (pp. 34–35); then the prophet Haggai enters and, alternately with the male chorus, delivers what is in part a close paraphrase of passages in the book of Haggai; [27] and, after the action of the play, the choruses [28] speak again, this time with echoes of Psalms 98 and 100 (and perhaps 66, 81, and 95).

This combination of elements produces an anachronistic plot, since Haggai's attempts to arouse his people to return to Jerusalem and rebuild the Temple occurred about fifty years before the supposed deliverance of the Jews from Ahasuerus by Esther and Mordecai; but the result is greater dramatic effect and a more affirmative story, for Mordecai becomes the hero who not only saves the Jews but who, against his own personal wishes to go to Jerusalem with his friends,

stays behind to look after those of his people who remain.
The entire tale is given an added dimension, since the intrigue
is set against a background of renewed hope and purpose on
the part of the Jews. This expanded plot is in turn framed
by the choruses, so that it assumes the status of a metaphor.
The opening lyric section is a lamentation spoken antiphonally
by the men and women, who join nine times to pronounce
the refrain:

> Take up the burden of the woeful song:
> The Lord the God of Jacob hides his face;
> His promise to our Fathers is forgot. (pp. 33, 34, 35, 36, 37)

After the salvation of the Jews has been worked out, the
closing choral section is a hymn of praise, which repeats its
echo of the Psalms six times:

> O make a joyful noise unto the Lord
> Rejoice ye in the God of our Salvation,
> For the Lord hath remembered Jacob
> The Holy one hath redeemed Isra'l. (pp 60, 61, 62)

As in a formal elegy, uncontrolled grief is transformed to
serenity and happiness through a creative process which restores order; the activities of Esther and Mordecai against
Ahasuerus and Haman become symbolic of the ordering power
of righteousness and selflessness in a world that contains pride
and vicious conceit.

The intrigue itself follows closely the Biblical pattern,
though Esther is already queen when the play opens, and
we learn little here about her replacing Vashti (p. 39); it is
characteristic of Tyler not to allow us to see the main figure
at once, and Esther in fact does not appear until the next to
the last scene. Of the three scenes in act I, the first is Haggai's
appeal to the "pious remnant of this stubborn race"; the second, also not in the book of Esther, is a conversation between
Luzzi and Elam, two who are going back to Jerusalem fol-

lowing Haggai's advice; and the third, a domestic scene between Prince Haman and his wife Geresh,[29] reveals Haman's
anger over the failure of Mordecai to make obeisance to him.
While Tyler gives Haman's consultations with his wife (in
alternating scenes) in far greater detail than does the Bible,
we are not shown directly (as in Esther 3:8–15) Haman asking Ahasuerus to destroy all Jews. We learn about this only
when Mordecai tells Hatach, Esther's eunuch, in the short
second act; using Hatach as go-between, Mordecai persuades
Esther to approach the King and plead for the Jews (though
visiting the King unbidden can mean death). The other scene
of act II, again between Haman and his wife, reveals (following Esther 5:12) Esther's shrewdness in playing on
Haman's pride, for he is overjoyed that Esther has invited
him and the King to a special banquet.

Act III traces the downfall of Haman, following his false
elation. First Ahasuerus remembers that Mordecai once saved
his life and asks Haman to do Mordecai honor in the King's
name; Tyler sees the dramatic possibilities of the irony and
has Haman protest slightly (as he does not in Esther 6:11).
Then, after Haman and his wife talk over this unfortunate
reversal (scene ii) and after Esther has prayed (scene iii), the
banquet takes place in which Esther exposes Haman's treachery and Ahasuerus gives the order that Haman be hanged
on the gallows prepared for Mordecai. The play is built on
a kind of Sophoclean irony, for Haman thinks he is continually rising higher and still imagines the final banquet an
honor to him, even after the Mordecai celebration, in which
he had unwittingly arranged his own humiliation. Tyler concludes quickly with Ahasuerus' didactic speech and the
Chorus' joyful announcement of the Purim celebration, leaving out entirely the bloody descriptions of Jewish revenge
reported in the ninth chapter of Esther. This omission, as well
as his decision to elaborate certain scenes to dramatize Haman's

pride, underlines the fact that Tyler's interest is not in a tale of exciting (and cruel) adventure but in a poem of devout, yet active, faith.

The remaining play, *Joseph and His Brethren*, is the longest of the three (with about 1250 lines) and tells the familiar story from Genesis (chapters 37–50). With its long time span and wide-ranging scenes, the history of Joseph is the most intractable material Tyler attempted to dramatize. But the story does have highly dramatic moments, and Tyler wisely chose to concentrate on them. Act I recounts, in four scenes, the brothers' hatred of Joseph, their decision to cast him into a pit, their selling him to merchants, and their reporting to Jacob that he is dead. Tyler expands the Biblical account of Joseph's dreams (Genesis 37:3–10) in the opening scene so that there is some motivation for later action: Joseph's dreams may at first appear egotistical, but his soliloquy shows him to be self-sacrificing, and it is apparent that he is the victim of his brothers' jealousy and irritation, arising from his position as their father's favorite. Act II jumps to the second year of the famine; Tyler omits the account of Joseph and Potiphar's wife, and of Joseph's interpretations of the prisoners' and then of Pharaoh's dreams, resulting in his rise to power (Genesis 38–41). The seven years of plenty have passed and two of the famine, and Joseph's brothers now (in the first scene of act II) appear before him in Egypt asking for food. The second scene shows Jacob giving permission for Benjamin to go on the second trip, and in the following scene Joseph's steward welcomes the brothers to Egypt for a second time. This leaves the five scenes of act III [30] for the climactic action — Joseph's revelation of his identity (following the stolen cup trick) and Jacob's reaction to the news that Joseph is alive. The details of Jacob's later years in Egypt with Joseph (Genesis 46–50) are entirely omitted, and the play ends, much more dramatically than the Biblical account, with the effective scene in which Jacob and Leah are on the threshold of a new life. The last lines, taken almost without alteration from Genesis (45:28), are spoken by Jacob: "Joseph, my son, is yet alive / And I will go and see him ere I die!"

If the choice of scenes shows dramatic skill, the over-all form is less satisfying. Though there is no prologue, there is a Chorus of Israelitish Women which intrudes itself between the first two acts to explain that thirteen years are passing in this interval. The Chorus' twenty-eight-line speech, oddly enough, consists of an opening four-line quatrain (*abab*) in iambic pentameter, followed by twenty-four lines of iambic tetrameter, rhyming usually in couplets (except for the rhymes of lines 7 and 10, 13 and 21, 14 and 22). Why the first lines should be longer than the rest, why indeed the poem is in rhymed tetrameter at all, is not clear. These jingling lines, surrounded by blank verse, make the trite sentiments expressed all the more conspicuous. The Israelitish women tell us to turn to the Biblical account,

> Compar'd with which the feeble verse
> That our poor actors do rehearse
> On this our mean Scholastic Stage
> Seems dross beside the finest gold. (p. 78)

Surely Tyler did not shift to tetrameter simply in order to fit sound to sense, for the "feeble verse" of the rest of the play is above this; in any event the speech is a distracting and superfluous interlude. There is no similar break between acts II and III; then, after act III (which seems rather carelessly planned, with its two brief opening scenes), the Israelitish chorus pronounces a seventeen-line epilogue in blank verse, which is unusually didactic:

> . . . neglect not now, wisdom to win
> From these our scenes, and let our drama teach
> The lessons better taught in Holy Writ —
> That God for his own glory governs still

Human events, and turns the crimes of men
To the best good of all mankind. . . . (pp. 95–96)

Perhaps Tyler followed his model too closely in this effort. In his other two Biblical plays he combined episodes from different parts of the Bible or invented new scenes, so that, however closely he paraphrased at times, he was creating a new entity. In the Joseph play his task was only one of condensation, and he did not introduce new characters or scenes;[31] as a result, he perhaps felt that, instead of shaping something of his own, he was merely producing a weak substitute (as the chorus reiterates). He was not entirely in control of his material.

The point can be illustrated by the verse of the play. More than in the other two plays, Tyler resorts to inversions and periphrasis to fill out his lines (as "Ye well do know my wife to me two sons / Did bear," p. 90) and — a related matter — follows the King James wording more closely and more often.[32] The effect is not only dull, routine lines but a greater tendency toward moralistic pronouncements. Near the begining Joseph takes sixteen lines to explain that God works in mysterious ways (p. 67); he later indicates the meaning of the story when he asks God to turn seeming evil into future good (p. 73); and he points out at length that his earlier misfortune was part of God's plan to save Jacob's family (pp. 91–93). When, on the other hand, Tyler's instinct for drama leads him to elaborate on a hint in the Biblical story, the verse takes on life and the penetration of character is quite sharp.[33] For example, Joseph's relation to his brothers has a sound psychological basis: Levi recognizes a strain of pompousness in him and calls him "fond babbler" (p. 67), while Simeon's sarcasm (p. 69) reveals his own jealousy. Joseph's soliloquy (p. 69) shows him to be thoughtful and serious, and he emerges from the play a study in kindness combined with what others might take for pride. But the vigorous lines with which the play opens offer a promise that is not, except in isolated passages, fulfilled.

Tyler never expected that these plays would be performed, unless his reference to "this our mean Scholastic Stage" implies a school performance. They were the literary exercises of a man who gained great pleasure from such experimentation, and they were part of the same impulse that produced adaptations of Molière and Cervantes and projected "moral tales" for the instruction of youth. Both as exercises in adaptation and as materials for instruction, they provided the opportunity to write poetry and to construct dramatic situations. If phrases from the King James Bible account for the dignity of some of the verse, Tyler displays a facility of his own; if the Biblical stories provide a plot, Tyler demonstrates a sense of the dramatic. Tyler should not be measured entirely by these productions; but they are not negligible.

❧ IV ❧

Poet

AFTER the early plays, Tyler turned his attention to poetry. It is perhaps natural that a man with literary bent, for whom writing could be only a sideline, should find more occasion for producing verses than longer works. Tyler wrote with facility, however, and did manage to turn out some book-length efforts later; but during the middle 1790's his publications were almost exclusively in periodicals and in verse, and he continued to appear in the journals through the first decade of the nineteenth century. From the 108-line *Origin of Evil*, published separately in 1793, to the last poem for the *Polyanthos* in 1807, he wrote a considerable quantity of verse; nor did his efforts end in 1807 — he continued to write for his own amusement, if not for publication, and his later verse includes his longest poem, the 744-line *Chestnut Tree*, not published until 1931.

Although Tyler wrote verse sporadically during most of his life (at least after 1793), it is by no means clear exactly how much he wrote. Contributions to newspapers and magazines at this time were generally anonymous or pseudonymous, and, in the absence of a record kept by the author himself or by the editor, it is now virtually impossible to establish the complete canon of any particular writer's periodical work. Tyler's name appears on only a handful of poems; other poems may be identified as his through the comments of editors (either in their reminiscences or in marked copies of their publications); still others have been printed posthumously from his papers. Beyond that, there is little one can do, for stylistic tests, unsupported by external evidence, are hazardous, especially since Tyler wrote poetry in several styles, all of which were popular in the periodicals of the day. A further complication is the fact that a contributor might send in a poem, announcing in a prefatory note that it was the work of a poet he admired greatly, and his initial or pseudonym would be printed as the signature to the introductory note; this note would be enough to justify the periodical in labeling both it and the poem "original" (that is, not reprinted from another journal); finally, the poem might be by the contributor, despite his note, if he wanted to add an extra dimension to his protective mask.

With these difficulties, statements about Tyler's poetry must of necessity be approximate rather than precise, though a large enough number of poems can be identified to permit certain generalizations about the characteristics of his work.[1] Of the poems published during his lifetime, about fifty, totaling over 2900 lines, can be attributed to him with a great deal of certainty, and it is possible, with less assurance, to assign to him well over one hundred published poems (aside from that large category which could conceivably be his, or almost anyone else's). This count does not include the blank verse plays, the manuscript poems published since his death, or the fourteen passages used as epigraphs in *The Algerine Captive*. A survey of those fifty-odd poems that are undoubtedly Tyler's shows, beyond all question, that his favorite form was the four-beat iambic line. Fully two-thirds of his poems (amounting to half the total number of lines he published) are in tetrameter, either wholly or predominantly — sometimes arranged into couplets, sometimes into more intricate rhyme schemes with occasional short lines, but most frequently into quatrains rhyming *abab*. The fact that his longest poem (three times as long as any other) is in such tetrameter quatrains indicates his preference for the form. Of the remaining poems, the majority are in iambic pentameter couplets; a few are anapaestic; and those in the sonnet form or in blank verse (other than the plays) are negligible in number. Tyler did not reserve certain verse forms for particular kinds of work, for both serious and comic poems appear in the same metrical schemes; but in general his output does fall into three categories: satire, verse composed for specific occasions, and reflective or moralizing poems.

Publication

The story of the publication of Tyler's poetry begins with his meeting Joseph Dennie. Eleven years Tyler's junior, Dennie was to become one of the best-known essayists and editors of the young republic, but in the early 1790's he was in a position very similar to Tyler's — a graduate of Harvard, with legal training and an attraction to literature, who enjoyed the pleasures of the city but found himself in a small country town. Tyler knew who Dennie was as early as the spring of 1790, when he defended two of Dennie's classmates. In December of that year (a few months before Tyler settled in Vermont) Dennie moved to Charlestown, New Hampshire, to study law with Benjamin West,[2] and it is not surprising, given Tyler's traveling and Dennie's yearning for a literary life, that the two should have met and formed a lasting friendship. Nor was their distance from an urban center a disadvantage, because they discovered other young lawyers who would rather write verses than plead cases, and soon there were local outlets for their work that attracted national attention.

Dennie had published several numbers of his first series of Addisonian essays, "The Farrago," in the Windsor, Vermont, *Morning Ray* in 1792. By the middle of the next year Hanover, New Hampshire, had a four-page weekly paper which

Royall Tyler

was both Federalist in politics and literary in emphasis: *The Eagle, or Dartmouth Centinel,* started on 22 July 1793 by Josiah Dunham, Dartmouth graduate and Hanover printer.[3] Dennie's "Farrago" continued there, and by 1794 Tyler, more immersed in legal business than Dennie, was drawn into the circle of the paper's contributors. "A Christmas Hymn," which he had written for a celebration at Claremont, New Hampshire, the preceding year, appeared in the *Eagle* for 6 January 1794; it was followed, in July, by two serious poems signed "T." And at this time Dennie and Tyler conceived the idea of a collaboration.

It was the custom for newspaper contributors to adopt pseudonyms and to furnish series of essays or poems under that heading. Tyler and Dennie hit on the metaphor of a shop — their column would be a store which purveyed all varieties of prose and verse. They called it "From the Shop of Messrs. Colon & Spondee," and the first "advertisement" for their "wares" appeared in the *Eagle* of 28 July 1794:

Salutatory and Valedictory Orations, Syllogistic and Forensic Disputations and Dialogues among the living and the dead . . . Synaloephas, Elisions, and Ellipses of the newest *cut* — v's added and dove-tailed to their vowels, with a small assortment of the genuine Peloponesian Nasal Twangs — Classic Compliments adapted to all dignities, with superlatives in *o,* and gerunds in *di, gratis* . . . Anagrams, Acrostics, Anacreontics; Chronograms, Epigrams, Hudibrastics, & Panegyrics; Rebuses, Charades, Puns and Conundrums, by the *gross,* or *single dozen.* Sonnets, Elegies, Epithalamiums; Bucolics, Georgics, Pastorals; Epic Poems, Dedications, and Adulatory Prefaces, in *verse* and *prose.* . . . Serious Cautions against Whoredom, Drunkenness, &c. and other coarse Wrapping-Paper, *gratis,* to those who buy the smallest article. . . . *On hand a few Tierces of Attic Salt — Also, Cash, and the highest price, given for* RAW WIT, *for the use of the Manufactory, or taken in exchange for the above Articles.*

The metaphor was carried on in the column "To Correspondents" in the same issue: "Just arrived — a BALE OF GOODS from the SHOP *of Messrs. COLON & SPONDEE* — they shall be disposed of, on commission, as directed." The "Colon & Spondee" columns, thus begun, continued (often making elaborate use of the mercantile metaphor) in various journals for a decade. Consisting principally of satire and literary criticism, they quickly became famous for their wit, increased the circulation of the journals they appeared in, and inspired numerous imitators (such as "Messrs. Dactyl and Comma" or "Verbal and Trochee").[4] They represent one of the high points in early American journalism.

As Dennie later indicated, he was "Colon" and Tyler was "Spondee"; he wrote most of the prose and Tyler most of the poetry.[5] In the absence of evidence to the contrary, therefore, one can assume Tyler's authorship of "Colon & Spondee" poems;[6] in some cases they are signed with an "S." for "Spondee," and, indeed, "S." became established as Tyler's signature, even apart from the "Colon & Spondee" columns. By the end of 1794 six "Spondee" poems had been published in the *Eagle*, light verse with such titles as "Anacreontic to Flip," "The Rural Beauty," "The Widower," and "The Test of Conjugal Love." No further work of Tyler's appeared in the *Eagle*, and Dennie's contributions stopped in the spring of 1795, when he decided that he must get back to Boston and start a journal of his own.

At this time Tyler had about 500 lines of verse in print, but he was to increase that figure only a little during the next year. On 20 October 1794 Robert Treat Paine, a Harvard graduate somewhat younger than Dennie, started in Boston his strongly Federalist semi-weekly, the *Federal Orrery*.[7] Dennie published some satiric prose and theatrical criticism in it, and Tyler's main contributions were two theatrical poems, "Occasional Prologue, To the Mistakes of a Night; or, She Stoops to Conquer" (signed "R. Tyler, Esq.") on

29 December 1794 and, nearly a year later (9 November 1795), "An Occasional Address" on the opening of the new theater season (signed "By a Gentleman of Vermont"). By May of 1795 Dennie had arrived in Boston and was launching a small four-page weekly, the *Tablet*. It lasted only thirteen issues, from 19 May to 11 August 1795, and was principally an outlet for Dennie's "Farrago" essays. Some of the "Colon & Spondee" pieces were reprinted, but only one new identifiable Tyler poem appeared, "The Clown and Rose" (in the last issue, signed "S.").[8]

If 1795 was a slack year for Tyler's poetry, 1796 inaugurated the most spectacular period in his poetic career, his association with the *Newhampshire and Vermont Journal: or, the Farmer's Weekly Museum* of Walpole, New Hampshire. The *Farmer's Museum* (as it was later called) had begun on 11 April 1793 and, by 1796, had already reprinted some of Tyler's verse, but it was not until this time that he contributed original work to it. Walpole in these years, a town of 1400 inhabitants, was something of an intellectual center. For one thing, the printing shop of Thomas & Carlisle was turning out handsome volumes in addition to publishing the *Museum*. David Carlisle had been an apprentice of the great printer Isaiah Thomas, who gave him the financial backing in 1793 to set up a bookstore and printing shop in Walpole. Equally important, Walpole was the place frequented by a brilliant coterie of young Harvard lawyers and aspiring writers from the upper Connecticut Valley, who met between the court sessions and, according to Jeremiah Mason, "freely indulged in gambling, excessive drinking, and such like dissipation." Particularly after Major Asa Bullard took over the old Crafts Tavern (next door to Thomas & Carlisle), it became the rendezvous of this Literary Club, which included, besides Dennie and Tyler, Mason, Samuel Hunt, Roger Vose, Samuel West, and Thomas Green Fessenden ("Christopher

Caustic"). Dennie, leaving Boston after the failure of the *Tablet*, arrived in Walpole in the early fall of 1795 and became the leader of this group. He began contributing his "Lay Preacher" essays to the *Museum*, within a few weeks was directing the literary policy of the paper, and in April 1796 officially became editor. Though a number of important contributors to the *Museum* were not members of the Literary Club, much of the copy for the paper was produced next door, in between games of cards, jokes, drinks, and large meals. The spirit of the whole enterprise is suggested by one story about Dennie writing a "Lay Preacher" essay in sections during a game of whist; he finally had to ask Tyler to sit in for him, so that he could finish the last paragraph, which was already overdue at the printer's. In another version of the story Tyler completes the essay for him, with no discernible shift in Dennie's polished style.[9]

There is no question that, during Dennie's editorship (1796–1799), the *Farmer's Museum* reached a level rarely attained by a weekly literary and political sheet,[10] and its circulation was national. Its four large pages had a higher proportion of original contributions than most papers of the time, and its back page, "The Dessert," certainly printed more original poems and literary essays. The quality of the work, from the pens of John Curtis Chamberlain, David Everett ("Common Sense in Dishabille"), and Isaac Story ("Peter Quince"), as well as the Crafts Tavern group, was remarkably high for hastily written journalistic satire, and it often showed considerable learning and wit. The "Colon & Spondee" papers were one of the mainstays of the publication, and Tyler did his share in keeping Dennie supplied with material. At least, he published verse with more frequency than was usual with him, for twenty-five of his poems appeared in the "Shop of Messrs. Colon & Spondee" during the three years Dennie was editor — poems that represent Tyler's poetic range, from the literary satire of the "Address to Della Crusca" to the patriotism of the "Windsor Ode." A score of Tyler's poems were reprinted in the 1801 anthology *The Spirit of the Farmers' Museum*, and Dennie's annotations in the copy now owned by the Boston Public Library provide further assurance in attributing them to Tyler.

The next phase of Tyler's poetic career again follows one of Dennie's moves, for Tyler published no more in the *Museum* after Dennie left it in 1799. By summer of that year Dennie was ready to return to the city, but this time business took him to Philadelphia, where, after contributing to the *Gazette of the United States* for two years, he established in 1801 the *Port Folio*, a weekly of eight pages "in the manner of the Tatler," which became the leading American literary journal.[11] Although the *Port Folio* occupies an important place in the history of American magazines, it is of much less significance for Tyler's story, since he contributed little to it. Whether because Dennie was not able to prod him so much from the distance of Philadelphia or whether Tyler was too occupied with legal duties (these were his first years on the Vermont Supreme Court), he published only a few items in Dennie's journal, one of them the often-quoted "Love and Liberty" (signed "R. Tyler, Esq.") on 20 October 1804. Dennie, however, continued using the "Colon & Spondee" rubric, which now contained prose almost exclusively.

One of Dennie's principle themes in his column "To Readers and Correspondents" became a lament for the absence of Tyler. On 28 February 1801, in the second month of the *Port Folio's* existence, Dennie remarked, "The *poetry* of *Spondee*, was always fashionable, and in constant demand. Our credit will be affected, unless he attend with more diligence to the *business* of literature" (I, 69). Two weeks later he explained that poetry was Spondee's task, but "For some time, the poetical share of this work has been neglected"

(I, 87). On 17 October he sighed, "We hope soon to hear from our fellow-labourer, 'Spondee.' The Editor feels himself solitary indeed, without the cheering companion of his literary toils"; and he quoted, "One was our labour, one was our repose, / One social supper did our studies close" (I, 336). Throughout 1802 these pleas continued: on 10 July, "A valued friend, who has often assisted and cheered the Editor in his course, is affectionately addressed . . . , and the Editor hopes that in some pause of *judicial* care, his friend will forget for a moment the eloquence of the *forum*, and turn his 'bright fantastic eye' to every willing muse" (II, 215); a week later, "The Editor hopes soon to hear from his friend, and quondam companion, S. Our invocation to this much loved bard is frequent and fervent" (II, 223); and on 21 August, "S, we hope, will reflect on the following lines from the favorite Gifford. . . . 'Say, wilt thou from thy duties pause awhile, / To view my humble labours with a smile?' " (II, 263). But Tyler did not heed the call, and Dennie at last desisted.[12]

A more important magazine for Tyler, and the last major outlet for his verse, was the *Polyanthos*, a Boston monthly founded in late 1805 by Joseph T. Buckingham, who had been an apprentice to David Carlisle in Walpole in 1796 and who thus knew the old *Museum* crowd. It was a literary journal which gave special attention to biographical sketches of notable figures and to the theater. In his reminiscences, Buckingham reports, "Of the several writers, from whom I received aid, Judge Tyler of Vermont was the most liberal in his contributions. The series of numbers entitled 'Trash,' . . . and all poetical fugitives signed S. were supplied by him." Buckingham had written on 22 March 1806 asking for contributions, and Tyler sent one on 3 April, but with reservation: "I must, however, observe that the unvarying condition upon which you are permitted to publish it, must be your solemn promise, that I am not known as the author, either by private communication to your friends, or any public hints to patrons and subscribers." Later Tyler praised Buckingham for making the journal "lively" and criticized other Boston periodicals for being "very wise and very learned, and very dull: — dull, when they should have been witty." [13] Between April 1806 and July 1807 Tyler published thirteen poems in the *Polyanthos* (and a few prose pieces). These include three long poems in pentameter, two of them important theatrical criticisms and the third an elegy; a long tetrameter fable, "The Wolf and Wooden Beauty"; and some shorter lyrics and epigrams. They were Tyler's last important group of poems published during his lifetime, and they rank near the top of his output.

Tyler's poetry appeared in a few other journals, but generally just as occasional reprints — such as the "Convivial Song" in the Haverhill *Federal Gazette* (8 August 1799) or "Love and Liberty" in the *Columbian Centinel*, Benjamin Russell's Federalist paper in Boston (24 July 1805).[14] Among the poems still in manuscript at Tyler's death, a few were published in the 1920's and 1930's: "Lines on Brattleboro," "The Mantle of Washington," "On the Death of a Little Child," "Upon Seeing a Pair of Scales Suspended in a Justice's Office," [15] and *The Chestnut Tree*; others remained in manuscript until 1967, when the complete edition of Marius B. Péladeau appeared.[16] The publication record of Tyler's poetry emphasizes the fact that publication was not uppermost in Tyler's mind when he wrote; composing verses was an intriguing entertainment, a way to relax between court sessions. The verse had served its purpose before it reached the printed page.

Satiric and Humorous Poems
It is not surprising that the author of *The Contrast* should

find his best poetic outlet in light verse or in satires of current fashions. Many of his poems — and those for which he was most famous in his lifetime, aside from his patriotic poems — fall into the category of brisk, lighthearted (even flippant) jingles, lines dashed off rapidly by one who had a knack for rhyme and meter. But they are skillful in their way, they do not moralize, and they often catch the spirit of rural New England:

> Stingo! to thy bar-room skip,
> Make a foaming mug of Flip;
> Make it of our country's staple,
> Rum New-England, Sugar maple.[17]

Most of the light verse has to do with love and marriage and often celebrates sensual joys. "The Rural Beauty, A Village Ode" is characteristic in using irony to hide sentiment:

> Then I whisper wedlock joys;
> Future group of girls and boys;
> — Girls and boys, as fair, as SUE,
> Honest as their father too;
> — Now I feel her pulses beat —
> She burns me with her blushing cheek.

Although this "Ode" contains conventional phrases such as "fleecy sky," "dimpled cheek," and "eyes so blue," the lightness of tone and quickness of movement prevent it from becoming sentimental:

> Yes, I come, my tempting SUE,
> See she smiles to meet me too.
> Now my arms her waist entwine;
> Now her hand is lock'd in mine.[18]

Another poem about "Sue" illustrates the kind of twist that frequently forms the basis of the humor; when a bachelor rejects Sue as a possible wife because she is too young, a neighbor says he must "speak to *clear her reputation*": "She's old enough to be your lady, / For *two years past, she had a baby!*" [19] This ending also shows that Tyler was not particular about his rhymes.

The epigram was a useful form to a man with Tyler's turn of mind and limited time for writing, and he produced several on the marriage theme. One of the best points out that, of the husbands who are "grumble tonians," each probably "chose his *dearest* by the *eye*":

> Ye fools, if you were buying houses,
> You'd be more cautious than in spouses;
> Not one of you would glance the windows,
> And buy with out once entering indoors,
> Nor yet about the doors be dodging,
> But try the house with one night's lodging.
> The house so tippy outside door,
> Might prove within a cursed bore;
> I think, says Tim, that's all I'll say,
> Wives might be chose in SOME SUCH WAY. [20]

The colloquialisms, the feminine rhymes, the risqué metaphor or amusing comparison, all occur in other epigrams. Puns are common, as when Sue, "at a female tea-drinking," asks the girls what business they would like their husbands to be in and declares her own preference for a cooper (that is, T. A. Cooper, the English actor in Boston at the time); this epigram rhymes "pass on" with "parson," "witty" with "pretty," and "tomorrow" with "follow." [21] Another "Epigrammatick Sketch" (which, with forty lines, goes beyond the bounds of an epigram) ridicules the ladies' pursuit of fashion; Tom Tweezer, a devoted husband, is running home with a present for his wife so that he will get it in her hands before it is out of style:

> Stop me not, I must not falter,
> I must hasten to my true one,
> The fashion else I fear will alter,
> And my Duck will want a new one. [22]

Satire of the artificiality in feminine fashions was a favorite eighteenth-century subject on both sides of the Atlantic, and Tyler in these poems is simply carrying on in the tradition of *The Contrast*. Echoing *The Rivals*, "To Miss Flirtilla Languish" enumerates the current cosmetics (paste for the neck, rouge for the cheeks, wigs, and so on) and ends with the beau's wish that Flirtilla would "press *me* to what *once* was her breast." [23] Despite the anapaestic movement, there is a seriousness here not present in the similar poem about Tom Tweezer.

Another set of fashions — those in literature — had been touched on in *The Contrast* and became one of Tyler's main subjects for satiric verse and parody. He chose, as his object for repeated attacks between 1797 and 1799, the work of the Della Cruscan poetasters, who had enjoyed great popularity in England and were being reprinted and imitated in America. Their verse, most of it a parody of itself, was characterized by extreme sentimentality and elaborate, high-flown diction. The group was originally composed of a few Englishmen who gathered in 1784 in the Florence salon of Mrs. Hester Lynch Piozzi.[24] They amused themselves by writing flattering verses to each other, and, as these became known in England, other would-be poets felt the urge to express themselves in similar fashion. Robert Merry, one of the original group, signed his work "Della Crusca" because he was a member of the Florentine Accademia della Crusca, and the name came to be applied to the entire coterie and then to all the writers of newspaper effusions in this vein. Tyler's main targets, besides "Della Crusca" himself, were two of the later followers, Mrs. Hannah Cowley ("Anna Matilda") and Mrs. Charlotte Smith. The attack had already begun in England, led by William Gifford (whom Dennie continually quoted when addressing Tyler in print), and Gifford's second onslaught, the *Maeviad* (1795), had appeared two years before Tyler's first Della Cruscan parody; Dennie and Tyler were the most energetic and influential of the attackers in America. The whole movement represents one of the excesses of romanticism and was an inevitable concomitant to the growing emphasis on personal feelings; it was not, however, solely to blame for all the affected expression in America (like that which Timothy Dwight called the "Boston style" of oratory). In ridiculing these tendencies Tyler was attacking not romanticism but an insidious sentimentalism which had far deeper roots than the Della Cruscan writers.

The *Farmer's Weekly Museum* on 4 April 1797 printed Tyler's first effort along this line, "An Ode to a Pipe of Tobacco, Addressed by Della Yankee, to Anna Jemima," in seventy tetrameter lines, with its obvious parody of Della Cruscan pseudonyms and circumlocution. He vows his eternal faithfulness to his pipe, which becomes his "extatick tube," his "sweet, assuaging tube," and his "lenient solace of dank care." [25] A month later he wrote a more skillful satire, in sixty-six lines of pentameter couplets, entitled "Address to Della Crusca, Humbly Attempted in the Sublime Style of That Fashionable Author." The main part of the poem describes the triumph of Della Crusca in America, with epithets assigned to each Indian tribe:

> Gods how sublime shall Della Crusca rage,
> When ALL NIAGARA CATARACTS THY PAGE.
> What arts? What arms? Unknown to thee belong?
> What ruddy scalps shall deck thy sanguin'd song?
> What fumy calmuts scent the ambient air,
> What love lorn Warhoops, CAPITALS declare.
> Cerulean tomahawks shall grace each line,
> And BLUE EY'D WAMPUM glisten through thy rhyme.

At the end he exclaims, "Proclaim thy sounding page, from shore to shore, / And swear that sense in verse, shall be no more." [26] Four months later, in his "Sonnet to the Indian Muckawiss," Tyler (signing himself "Sensibility") gave an example of an American subject treated in Della Cruscan fashion and parodied the work of Charlotte Smith. The sonnet (Shakespearean in form) is replete with such phrases as "tuneful art," "lorn numbers," "dusky plain," "Child of the sober eve," and "sad delight"; it is followed by a note explaining its particular beauties to the ladies.[27]

In 1799 Tyler wrote two more Della Cruscan sonnets that illustrate his parody at its height. In one he explains that he is going to take a rhyme from the *New England Primer* — "The Cat doth play, / And after slay" — and amplify it in the manner of Charlotte Smith:

Sonnet to an Old Mouser
Child of lubricious art! of sanguine sport!
Of PANGFUL MIRTH! sweet ermin'd sprite!
Who lov'st with silent, VELVET STEP to court
The bashful bosom of the night.

Whose elfin eyes can pierce night's sable gloom,
And witch her FAIRY PREY with guile,
Who sports fell frolic o'er the grisly tomb,
And gracest death with dimpling smile!

DAUGHTER OF IREFUL MIRTH, sportive in rage,
Whose joy should shine in sculptur'd bas relief,
Like Patience, in rapt Shakespear's deathless page,
Smiling in marble at wan grief:

Oh, come and teach me all thy barb'rous joy,
To sport with sorrow first and then destroy.[28]

The other sonnet has a prefatory advertisement in which Messrs. Colon & Spondee

inform their kind customers that they brighten the dullest compositions in prose and verse by the apt and judicious insertion of capital letters, italics, asterisks, brackets, apostrophes, carets, hyphens, idiopathics, ichnographics, ellipses, and synalephies, notes manual, digital, and astral, with notes of the interrogation, obnubulation, and admiration, by the gross or dozen.

N.B. They have some capitals of an uncommon large size, for the use of the female muse.

The ensuing "Sonnet to the Turtle Dove" illustrates most of these devices in its opening lines:

SWEET CHILD OF WOE!! who pour'st THY LOVE LORN LAYS
ON THE DULL EAR! of PENSIVE night,
Who with THY sighs protract'st the pitying gale,
WHICH seeks with GOS'MER WING the INFANT LIGHT.[29]

If the Della Cruscan extravagances formed the most repeated subject for Tyler's verse satire, he wrote individual poems ridiculing other literary excesses. In "The Exile," Messrs. Colon & Spondee set up a "Caledonian Loom" and parody Burns and other writers in Scottish dialect; the theme of the poem occurs in lines 7–8: "While Bessy wha is far awa, / Is faithfu' unto me." A glossary is provided and a significant introductory note, which comments ironically on the lack of American nationalism in both literature and business: "we hope to be na farer behint the Europeans, than is common wi' the youthful manufactures of America." [30] Excessive use of alliteration is parodied in "An Alliterative Address" (illustrating also Tyler's love of playing with words), in which each line repeats the same initial sound (it opens, "The sweetest Seraph's softest smile").[31] The "Poetical Paraphrase of our General's Journal" is a skillful if exaggerated mock epic, in heroic couplets, satirizing the *Memoirs* (1798) of Major General William Heath. The General is depicted as rising to announce to his children, in the most elaborate terms ("Shoots of my glory, scions of my name, / Twigs of my hope . . ."), the publication of his reminiscences.[32]

Poet

Satire of pedantry is a recurring motif in Tyler's work, and the "Irregular Supplicatory Address to the American Academies of Arts and Sciences" tries (in 112 lines) to deflate the "learned wights, who all the heights / Of science still are soaring, / The comet's tail, or tail of mites / Sagaciously exploring." He explains why he would like to be elected to the Academy and then lists his qualifications — he has several items which should be investigated, such as "a full grown Pumpkin . . . No bigger than a pullets egg." That Tyler could utilize devastating metaphors is evident in the poem: the botanists, he says, "Lasciviously delight to act, / As pandars to the flowers." [33] Finally, one may notice "The Sun and the Bats," a political satire of 120 lines in which the sun is the principle of Federalism, sending good things downward to all, while the bats (Anti-Federalists) are active in the absence of the sun and resent such centralization of power as the sun has.[34] The satire is competent but, with the sun's speech at the end, tends too much toward the overtly didactic — a fault which Tyler usually avoids in his satiric verse.

Occasional Poems

One important category in the Tyler canon consists of poems which he wrote for particular occasions. His talents were well suited to such versifying, for he could produce, at short notice, a smooth and graceful lyric; if it was not particularly striking or profound, it expressed the usual sentiments conveniently and served as a focal point for a celebration, which was all that was expected of it. His first poem in the *Eagle*, "A Christmas Hymn," had been sung at the Claremont services on Christmas 1793. Though in part a conventional hymn praising "the joyous day, / On which our Lord was born," it proceeds to show how the Lord is responsible for the freedom of the United States:

Royall Tyler

> He crown'd fair freedom's cause;
> He made our nation great;
> The Leader of our wars
> He raised to rule our States.
> Your voices raise!
> To HIM who brings
> To earth proud kings,
> Be deathless praise.[35]

There are ten such stanzas in the poem, the first four lines of three beats each, rhyming alternately, and the last four of two beats, rhyming *cddc*; the fifth line is the same in every stanza, so that the final word in each case rhymes with "raise." In the satiric poems Tyler did not experiment very widely with verse forms, but the occasional poems show that he could, if necessary, manipulate a variety of stanza patterns with ease. "A Christmas Hymn" was evidently popular, for it was reprinted in broadside many years later, after Tyler had become Chief Justice, with his name on it. In the few cases where Tyler allowed his name to appear on a poem, it was always an occasional poem. Perhaps he felt that, if the authorship were known at the time of the celebration, there was no need to hide it later; but, more important, such poems were serving a socially approved purpose, and a gentleman's name could be openly attached to them.

If the "Christmas Hymn" expresses patriotic sentiments,[36] the poems for Independence Day do so even more. The "Ode Composed for the Fourth of July," which appeared in the *Newhampshire and Vermont Journal* on 19 July 1796, is probably Tyler's most famous poem; certainly it is the one most often reprinted. It is a jolly and fast-moving piece, which sounds like the calling of a square dance:

> Squeak the fife, and beat the drum,
> INDEPENDENCE DAY has come!!
> Let the roasting pig be bled.
> Quick twist off the cockerel's head,

> Quickly rub the pewter platter,
> Heap the nutcakes fried in batter.
>
> . . . .
>
> Sal, put on your ruffel skirt,
> Jotham, get your *boughten* shirt,
> To day we dance to riddle diddle.
> — Here comes Sambo with his fiddle;
> Sambo, take a dram of whiskey,
> And play up Yankee Doodle frisky.

So it goes for fifty-five lines, building up enthusiasm for the celebration, giving a good picture of late eighteenth-century rural customs, and, at the same time, working in a few references to current social problems:

> Sambo, play and dance with quality;
> This is the day of blest Equality.
> Father and *Mother* are but men,
> And Sambo — is a Citizen,
>
> . . . .
>
> Come, one more swig to southern Demos
> Who represent our brother negroes.[37]

Another of Tyler's best-known poems, "Love and Liberty," is similar:

> In bri'ry dell, or thicket brown,
>   On mountain high, in lowly vale,
> Or where the thistle sheds its down,
>   And sweet-fern scents the passing gale;
>   There hop the birds from bush to tree,
>   Love fills their throats,
>   Love swells their notes,
>   Their song is Love and Liberty.[38]

The varied rhythm and well-manipulated sounds make the three stanzas of this poem one of Tyler's most graceful lyrics.

For the Independence Day celebration in Windsor, Vermont, in 1799, Tyler wrote two poems, a serious one, the "Windsor Ode," for the main ceremony, and a lighter "Convivial Song" for the evening festivities; both were published under his own name in the *Farmer's Weekly Museum*.[39] The "Windsor Ode" consists of six ten-line stanzas, mostly tetrameter, with a four-line refrain at the end of each stanza. It begins by praising "Columbia's natal day," then refers to the country's enemies, first the "haughty Britons" and now the "faithless" and "bloody" French, then surveys American heroes and forces, and ends with praise of Adams and Washington. Despite occasional clichés ("blushing east," "warlike swords"), the poem has an honesty and strength, suggested by the refrain (which varies slightly from stanza to stanza):

> Shout, shout Columbia's praise,
> Wide through the world her glory raise,
> Our Independence bravely gain'd,
> Shall full as bravely be maintain'd.

"The Convivial Song," in eight eight-line stanzas of a rather complex metrical and rhyme pattern, is composed of a series of toasts. The first is a general one:

> Come, fill each brimming glass, boys,
> Red or white has equal joys,
> Come, fill each brimming glass, boys,
> And toast your country's glory;
> Does any here to fear incline,
> And o'er Columbia's danger whine,
> Why let him quaff this gen'rous wine,
> He'll tell another story.

There follow toasts to Washington, to the gallant tar, to the native land, to Vermont, and finally to Adams, who with "temp'rate head . . . sits sublime, / And for our good is thinking."

Besides these enthusiastic lyrics which he produced for patriotic celebrations, Tyler wrote verse for theatrical occasions. Just as the prologue to *The Contrast* emphasized that it was a native play, so Tyler's prologues follow the theme of literary nationalism. In his "Occasional Prologue" to *She Stoops to Conquer*, he devotes the entire thirty-eight lines to showing that, despite "Proud *Europe*, and still prouder *Britain*," the liberal arts "have stemmed the atlantic wave":

> Let candor then, imprint this thought alone,
> *The painting, acting, music, are our own.*

He prophesies that a "future *Avon* shall meandering glide" through the Green Mountains and that England, "humbled" and "awed by our success, / In arts and arms, our triumph shall confess." [40] The following year (1795), Tyler wrote "An Occasional Address" for the opening of the Boston Theatre's new season, the first under his brother's management. Again in pentameter couplets (though considerably longer, 118 lines), it takes up where the other left off, even using some of the same lines about England's yielding to American success. After an opening passage praising the culture of America ("*That* land, where genius soars sublimest heights; / Where *Trumbull* painted, and where *Trumbull* writes"), he addresses, in turn, the boxes, the pit, and the upper gallery. The artificiality of the coquettes in the boxes contrasts with the natural laughter from the gallery ("the warm impulse of the glowing heart"); as for the critics in the pit, Tyler speaks to them of a native literature and suggests their duty in fostering it:

> For *me*, sustained by *you* — the task be mine,
> Where native genius droops in shades to find,
> The tender buds from wintery vales to bring,
> To where your bounty sheds perpetual spring.

When this occurs, the "*Charles* shall rival British *Avon's* pride," and there shall be "Columbian *Shakespeares*" and "Yankee *Garricks*." [41]

If these two poems are companion pieces of the 1790's, two later poems, occasioned by the theatrical season of 1805–

1806, are in effect one work. The "Epilogue to the Theatrical Season: Or, A Review of the Thespian Corps" appeared in the *Polyanthos* for April 1806, followed two months later by "An Epistle to My Muse: Or, A Postscript to the Epilogue to the Theatrical Season." [42] Together they total 402 lines of heroic couplets and constitute one of Tyler's major poetic efforts, his only extended attempt at satiric portraits in the grand eighteenth-century manner. After invoking the Muse and her sister Candour, he presents ten vignette portraits of members of the Boston company during the past season, deciding that each is unfit for the laurel, until he comes to T. A. Cooper, who is "beyond all praise." Behind his criticism of most of the actors is a concept of realism: he can always recognize one actor, in whatever role, because of his yellow shoes; another moves like a "clock work man"; and a plump actress ("Great ton of beauty") plays roles not compatible with her physique ("thine is the comick mien / To strike broad humour from the saddest scene"). Since "men of sense" are offended when "virtuous speeches flow from lips impure," those actors are best who play good roles not only on stage but off, so that their acting is natural ("The Voice of Nature is thy mother tongue"). The populace is easily pleased and has little discernment in such matters, but an actress of Mrs. Powell's quality will never overstep "nature's modest aims" to become the "screaming favourite of a tasteless age":

> What though thy scenick pencil oft portrays
> Fine strokes of nature lost to common gaze?
> The purblind many can't read nature's line,
> Unless in lamp-black capitals it shine.
> What though less frequent shouts thy worth reward,
> And the house slumbers when it should applaud?
> Be thine the approving smile of all the chaste,
> Thine the proud plaudit of the man of taste.

Similarly, William Twaits, who played comic roles, is praised for doing what Tyler himself was trying to do: "With squint-eyed satire a bad age reclaim, / And vice and folly laugh to open shame."

This was the harshest attack Tyler had indulged in, and the editor Buckingham, in a prefatory note, admitted that he found some of the portraits "rather too severely handled." In his second installment, the "postscript" to the "epilogue," Tyler capitalized on the stir the earlier part had created. He addresses his Muse, describing how "the Green Room quakes with wild uproar," everyone discussing who was praised, damned, or omitted in the "Epilogue." Beginning with line 60, he announces that he will survey the actors again, this time more gently, although they are all eager for fame and would "rather be lampoon'd than be neglected." But instead of naming individuals, he simply enumerates certain faults common among actors: there is the tragic actor whose grimace is comic (lines 79–92), the actress whose effective anguished pause is caused by her forgetting the line (93–106), the man who exemplifies all the mistakes mentioned in Hamlet's advice to the players (107–132), and actresses who are either overly timid or overly aggressive (133–148). This poem, like the other, is imitative of the tradition of Churchill's *Rosciad* and Lloyd's *The Actor*, but its high spirits, comic rhymes, and witty criticisms make it more than a literary exercise. All the occasional poems are sprightly and, either directly or indirectly, patriotic in intention without being mawkish. To use Tyler's own criterion, it is the naturalness and sincerity of these poems which make them an attractive group.

Reflective Poems

Tyler was at his best in light or satiric verse; when he attempted serious reflective or philosophical poems, he committed most of the faults he ridiculed in others.[43] Although a few redeeming features can be found in some of them (particularly the two long ones), the most that can be said for the rest is that they are mediocre — competent enough for newspaper verse (when compared with others in the same papers), but in no way distinguished. Tyler needed the mask of humor or satire to present serious ideas effectively; his straightforward attempts partook too much of the sentimental cliché, of what was, after all, the accepted mode of popular utterance.

The point is illustrated by some of his didactic verse, which he often called "fables." "The Sensitive Plant," in 120 tetrameter lines, tells of all the qualities (from Venus, Minerva, Cupid, and so on) that contributed to Anna's character, in rhymes that are frequently inexact: "Some seek Arabia's balmy sweets, / To give the fragrance of her breath; / Some dive for pearls old ocean's deeps, / To form the whiteness of her teeth." At length Minerva says that she will root the sensitive plant "deep in Anna's breast," for it removes all "unchaste desires";

> And know, each maid, this plant is yours;
>   Each bashful virgin feels its aid;
> For sage Minerva's gift secures,
>   The beauties of each virtuous maid.
>
> This plant, the heart, the garden yield;
>   Though men have different names assigned;
> Called Sensitive, when in the field,
>   And Modesty when in the mind.[44]

The same theme recurs in "The Clown and Rose": Laura is like a rose because she has sweet looks combined with thorny anger to protect her virtue; she will be kind only if approached with an offer of wedlock, just as the rose allows soft breezes to touch its petals but will prick the hand that tries to break off a blossom. The rose speaks at the end and explains the comparison in detail:

To guard the beauties, nature gave,
　She all my thousand thorns prepar'd,
And LAURA's lovelier charms to save,
　Gave Thorny Virtue for a guard.[45]

Similarly, in "The Wolf and Wooden Beauty: An Old Fable New Vamped," a wolf makes advances to a beautiful carved figure and is confounded to discover that she is not real. Though this part is recounted in a jocular fashion, the explanation of the moral — that beauty is the least important quality in a good wife — is entirely serious: "*But she* who fills with nobler pride, / That female throne the fire side" is a "help-meet on life's weary way" who nurtures the children "by her fostering hand," and so on.[46] Another treatment of this idea (occasioned by Proverbs 31:10) is "The Properties of a Good Wife," 102 solemn lines spoken by Israel's King:

Through all his prosp'rous, joyous days,
Her virtues shall command his praise,
　And, though to blame inclin'd,
No action of her blameless life,
Shall stain her conduct as a wife,
　To vex her husband's mind.[47]

Tyler never tired of writing on this subject, but one should turn to his epigrams on marriage rather than to these verses for his best statement of it.

In blank verse, which Tyler always used for serious purposes, he shows himself to be a competent versifier, but, more than anything else, he reveals his familiarity with the tradition of English poetry, for his lines are highly derivative. The seventy-four lines of blank verse labeled "Author's Manuscript Poems" which serve as epigraphs to twelve chapters in *The Algerine Captive* are only fragments, varying from two to nineteen lines in length, but they show his aims in blank verse. The chapter which records a dream of the hero's mother carries an eight-line passage:

Nor yet alone by day the unerring hand
Of Providence, unseen directs man's path;
But, in the boding vision of the night,
By antic shapes, in gay fantastic dream,
Gives dubious prospect of the coming good;
Or, with fell precipice, or deep swoln flood,
Dank dungeon, or vain flight from savage foe,
The labouring slumberer warns of future ill.[48]

The varied caesura, the occasional run-over line and alliteration, the elaborate syntax and inversions, and the formal diction all reflect established practice from the time of Milton on; the lines are an exercise in versification more than a piece of poetry. For the other passages the same may be said, with such phrases as "The beaming dignities of man eclipsed," "the dear pledges of their mutual love," "hellish rage," "firm foundations of a Saviour's love," and "the young sighings of a contrite heart." [49] Tyler published in the April 1806 *Polyanthos* a passage of twenty-six lines, which he entitled "Extract from 'The Divine,' A Poem in Six Books." It is an exposition of all the virtues of the Reverend Joseph Buckminster, founder of the Boston Athenaeum, and furnishes in its ending an example of sustained parallelism and inversion:

From the rich pages of the inspired pen,
Which mock all human rhetorick to scorn,
The classick christian breathes the chaste discourse;
With temperate zeal the wandering sinner warns;
Sustains the pious with the promis'd grace;
Confirms the doubting; wakens the secure;
With mild consoling voice the wretched cheers;
And, with purest elegance of speech,
Gives new attraction to the gospel truth.[50]

When the man who so often argued for native literature expresses himself in this fashion, the result must seem ironic. In another of the epigraphs he says, "Still let the faithful pen unerring point / The polar truth" (II, 97); but one cannot help seeing a disparity between the sentiment and the style. That Tyler was familiar enough with the Miltonic tradition to turn in an able performance is a fact for the cultural history of America; that he wrote such lines with greater seriousness than his rhyming genre pictures of New England life is a fact of his own limitations as an artist.

Of the two remaining long poems, one, a 108-line unsigned work entitled *The Origin of Evil: An Elegy*, was published separately as an eight-page pamphlet in 1793 (with no publisher or place indicated on the title page). The main evidence for attributing the poem to Tyler seems to be that the unique copy in the American Antiquarian Society has "By Royal Tyler" written on the title page in a contemporary hand thought to be that of Isaiah Thomas. If it is Tyler's, it precedes his earliest published poem in the *Eagle* and is unlike his other poems in content; but if he could write blank verse plays on Biblical subjects, it is not unlikely that he should have tried his hand at versifying the Adam and Eve story in tetrameter quatrains. Indeed, the poem is semi-dramatic in form, concentrating on one episode presented largely in terms of conversation between the two characters — a method which perhaps owes something to one of the works quoted in the epigraphs, Sébastien Châteillon's *Dialogorum sacrorum* (1543). The "Proem" of three stanzas, with its jingling rhythm, hardly seems an appropriate introduction to the cosmic tragedy to follow:

> Ranting topers, midnight rovers,
> Cease to roar your fleshly lays;
>
> . . . .
> Let each lovely *Miss* and *Madam*,
> Quit the dear joys of carnal sense,
> Weep the *fall* of *Eve* and *Adam*,
> From their first state of Innocence.

The poem deals with the moment when Eve sees the forbidden fruit and questions the justice of the divine command. It is noteworthy only in one respect: the emphasis throughout is sensual, and Eve, foreseeing the consequences of her action, nevertheless cannot restrain herself from the allurements of sensual pleasure:

> "Threaten'd death will soon o'ertake me,
>   If this forbidden tree I pluck,
> But life itself will soon forsake me,
>   Unless its cordial juice I suck."

Detailed sensuous descriptions recur frequently:

> Her bosom, heaving for caresses,
>   Seem'd blushing berries cast on snow.
> . . . .
> As *Eve* cast her arms so slender,
>   His brawny chest to fondly stroke;
> . . . .
> As her arm Eve held him hard in,
>   And toy'd him with her roving hand,
> In the middle of Love's Garden,
>   She saw the Tree of Knowledge stand.

This dramatic juxtaposition suggests a real insight which is unfortunately obscured by the structure and meter of the context in which it is set.

The other poem, Tyler's longest production in verse and the one on which he was working despite his illness near the end of his life, was not made public until 1931. In that year Walter J. Coates (who had already printed in the *Driftwind* a few unpublished Tyler poems which Helen Tyler Brown had given him) brought out, at his Driftwind Press of North Montpelier, in a limited edition of 250 copies, *The Chestnut Tree: or, A Sketch of Brattleborough at the Close of the Twentieth Century, Being an Address to a Horse Chestnut Presented to the Author by the Rev. A. L. Baury*. It consists of 186 of Tyler's usual tetrameter quatrains and takes as its starting point the planting of a chestnut tree, which will still be living long after the present generation has died. The first eighteen stanzas (lines 1–72) [51] introduce the poem by suggesting that "the sorceress Fancy" can lift the veil of the future, reveal the "vista of two hundred years," and depict what will take place under the tree during that time.

The procession of future scenes then begins. People of all kinds (students, businessmen, lovers) rest in the shade of the tree (lines 73–144); the "village Hoyden" climbs the tree (145–156); and a group wanders along laughing at the eighteenth-century fashions in a copy of *The Ladies' Diary* (157–176). Next (177–204) come the sick and diseased ("dropsy's bloated bulk," "gout with crutch and flannel armed," "corroding cancer"), accompanied by two arguing physicians, like those Tyler satirized in *The Algerine Captive*: "I had well hoped this wordy war / Would cease before that distant day." Lawyers, too, are still "wrangling at the noisy bar" (205–224), and there are derelicts thinking of the tree for suicide (225–236). A Quaker couple appears, "firm in noiseless faith" and "stiff in moral rectitude" but acknowledging the power of love (237–272); then the drunkard "with burning breath," a "wilful, lingering suicide" (273–296); and then (297–340) "boisterous youngsters" in "rude athletic play," along with grown men fishing ("solace for a vacant mind") and hunting (the "cruel sportsman" shoots a bird which "bleeds his little life away"). "Manufactory's fetid halls" are responsible for the condition of the "haggard mottled crew" which comes next (341–376), a contrast to the happy group climbing the nearby mountain (377–432). Thirteen stanzas then describe the "female Pauper," a lonely old woman ill-treated by those she had befriended earlier in life (433–484), followed by an extended picture of a lonely man, a "stale bachelor of 42," and a description of the joys of wedlock which he is missing (485–600) — a familiar Tyler theme. The remaining stanzas place side by side the pedant gazing at "a worm-eaten, smoke-dried page" (601–628) and the "studious young divine" learning the "charms of pulpit eloquence" under the old tree (629–652), then a "pensive party" visiting the graveyard (653–692) and youthful lovers sighing vows of "eternal love and truth" (693–708).

After this long succession of visions, Tyler concludes, rather irrelevantly, that his own situation is not unlike that of the chestnut seed, a symbol of immortality:

> Misshapen seed! I too like thee
> Shall in our parent earth be cast,
> And with new life shall quickened be
> When the grave's wintry season's past.   (729–732)

The poem as a whole, though it contains many of Tyler's favorite themes, is a disappointing production — perhaps it contains too many themes, for the final effect lacks unity. Several descriptions are obviously given adjacent positions for contrast, and the idea of imagining a tree in the future provides a loose framework; but many of the individual portraits have no connection with the tree, and the ending, stressing a Christian afterlife, has not been prepared for in the social criticism dominant in the bulk of the work. Individual phrases, and even whole stanzas, are effective, such as the satire of the scholar or the description of the bachelor; and occasionally there is a sensitive picture of early nineteenth-century New England life (the mountain-climbing episode, for example). But the tetrameter becomes tiresome, some of the portraits are one-sided and sentimental (like that of the "female Pauper"), and the whole is permeated with stock phrases: "the ravages of time," "quaff the dulcet tide," "sicklied age," "the surge of ocean," "changing like the inconstant moon." There is no firm conception shaping the entire work, and the result has greater value as a social document than as a poem.

Tyler cannot hold rank as a poet, but he himself realized as much. It is enough that in eighteenth-century America he had the background and the inclination to amuse himself by writing verse and at times to put in a public word on behalf of the arts. He personally was unwilling to work harder at poetry, but he knew some of the places to look for shallowness in others. With some justice he has been called "an earlier and coarse Wendell Holmes." [52] At the end of *The Chestnut Tree*, his self-estimate is more than a literary convention:

> When ardent youth crowned life's gay scene
>   I could bright fancy's dreams create,
> And from a stubborn flinty theme,
>   The flickering sparks could scintillate.
>
> My ebbing mind and troubled head
>   Both bid me cease the poet's strains;
> Invention's gone, and fancy fled,
>   And naught but chiming rhyme remains.   (713–720)

It may be unkind to point out that the "chiming rhyme" was there all along, but one must admit that so was the "flinty theme" with its sparks.

❧ V ❧

Novelist

O N 17 August 1797, Joseph Nancrede, the Boston publisher and bookseller, inserted an advertisement in the *Independent Chronicle* that concluded with a special note: "*The Algerine Captive*, which has, for a few weeks since excited so much curiosity, and which on perusal, has been pronounced by a *few men of taste, The Rabelais* of America, is hourly expected at the above Store." [1] This book, in two well-printed volumes, purporting on the title page to be a factual account of Algerian slavery by Dr. Updike Underhill, had been published at Walpole early in August by David Carlisle, in an edition of 1000 copies. [2] That it was actually the work of Royall Tyler (who knew no more about Algerian slavery than what he had read in newspapers and books) seems to have been recognized from the beginning, for, after Nancrede did obtain copies late in September, he changed his advertisement: "These two volumes, attributed with some foundation, to *Royal Tyler*, Esq. have been pronounced by Gentlemen of taste, to be fully equal to Mr. Tyler's reputation. They are offered to the American Public, as a specimen of indigenous Wit." [3] Joseph Dennie, who was continually prodding Tyler to write and had suggested the idea for the book, echoed these advertisements in a letter from Boston late that August:

Your novel has been examined by the few and approved. It is however extremely difficult for the Bostonians to supply themselves with a book that slumbers in a stall at Walpole, supposed, by the latest and most accurate advertisements, to be situated 400 miles north of their meridian. . . . People are pretty well convinced that you are capable of writing well on any subject, and, for your encouragement, I can assure you, that a taste for letters begins gradually to obtain here.[4]

The Federalist journalist William Coleman, for a time the law partner of Aaron Burr, wrote in a similar vein a month later:

When I have heard you mentioned here, with much tribute of applause, for your literary talents, as I have often; and when I see your publication of the "Algerine" announced with great eclat, as it has repeatedly been in different papers, and "the public curiosity is said to be alive to read it;" I feel proud that I was once so intimately acquainted with the man and the Author.[5]

The book continued to be advertised during the next few months, and it was still listed among the "Fresh Supply of Books," as "an original and entertaining work," in the Walpole paper the following summer.[6]

Interest in the work was, in fact, more prolonged than this, and its contemporary appeal no doubt resulted largely from the widespread public curiosity about the Barbary pirates. Years later, Tyler himself commented on this topicality in a preface he wrote for a proposed new edition of the book:

In the year 1797, when the sufferings of our unfortunate seamen, carried into slavery at Algiers, was the common topic of conversation, and excited the most lively interest throughout the United States, the Author . . . embodied such information as could then be obtained as to the manners, customs, habits and history of those Corsairs in a little work, entitled The Algerine Captive.[7]

Trouble with the Barbary States was one of the most difficult problems faced by the new government. The vessels of a young country, no longer under the protection of England, were a natural target for the privateers; at the same time the situation helped to unify the American states in a single cause, for meeting the challenge was a matter of national pride. Several American seamen had been captured in 1784 and 1785, after the Treaty of Paris, but it was in the fall of 1793 that America suffered most, with eleven ships and 109 men taken in less than two months. At one time in the early 1790's there were 1200 Christian slaves in Algiers, exposed to cruelty and plagues; in 1794 smallpox alone took the lives of 4 American captives. Through the efforts of Joseph Donaldson and Joel Barlow, peace (of sorts) was made in July 1795; the 85 remaining Americans were ransomed, set sail on 13 July 1796, and after further attacks of disease reached home in February 1797, six months before Tyler's book appeared.[8]

The American public was interested in any scrap of information or myth about the Barbary States, and the newspapers were happy to comply.[9] Books also appeared, so many eventually that one may legitimately think of the Algerine captivity narrative as a distinct species of adventure story. Tyler was not the first to use these materials as the basis for a literary and patriotic work: Peter Markoe wrote in 1787 *The Algerine Spy in Pennsylvania; or, Letters Written by a Native of Algiers on the Affairs of the United States of America* (with the early letters set in Gibraltar); Susannah Rowson's first play, *Slaves in Algiers; or, A Struggle for Freedom*, was performed and published late in 1794; and in 1797, besides Tyler's book, a poem in two cantos (695 lines of pentameter couplets) called *The American in Algiers; or, The Patriot of Seventy Six in Capitivity* (which also attacked Negro slavery in America) was published.[10] Tyler's information about Algiers could have been derived from any number of sources. In the same year as his own book James Wilson Stevens' *An Historical and Geographical Account of*

Algiers appeared, as well as the American edition of Donald Campbell's *Journey over Land to India* (which included shipwreck and imprisonment); in 1794 Mathew Carey had published *A Short Account of Algiers*; in 1795 James Leach, *A New and Easy Plan to Redeem the American Captives in Algiers*; and in 1796 Emanuel de Aranda, *The History of Algiers*. In addition, there were many European books on the subject, some of which were probably available to Tyler — works like J. Morgan's *Voyage of the Mathurin Fathers to Algiers and Tunis, for the Redemption of Captives* (1735); Thomas Shaw's *Travels and Observations* (1738); *A Compleat History of the Pyratical States of Barbary* (1750); *The Female Captive* (1769); Alexander Jardine's *Letters from Barbary* (1788); Abbé Poiret's *Travels through Barbary* (1791), and others.[11] Whatever his sources, Tyler epitomized a large amount of material successfully enough that his account became the basis for at least one later work (Thomas Nicholson's *Affecting Narrative*, 1818) [12] and was not completely lost amid the increasing flurry of reminiscences that appeared after the prisoners' return.

Reception

The Algerine Captive is not, as all this might suggest, a work of history. It is a fictional account of Updike Underhill's adventures, the first volume entirely devoted to Updike's American experiences and the second to the Algerian. One of the first commentaries of any substance on the book, a letter to the editor of the *Farmer's Weekly Museum* on 24 April 1798, did call the work a novel but attributed it to "Peter Pencil," another of the paper's regular contributors. Before criticizing some minor faults of the book, the correspondent began with a statement to which exception cannot be taken even today:

An American novel has lately been presented to the public,

from your press, under the title of the Algerine Captive. The subject of this work is well chosen, the publication well timed, and the execution does great credit to the talents and erudition of the writer. In delineating the national character, and in describing the local peculiarities, in manners, customs, and language, of the people of New England, there is no preceding work, either from Europe or America, which can claim the smallest pretence to rivalship.

The faults mentioned are really only two: that "a geographical errour has been committed, in working the voyage of his hero from Gibralter to Algiers; from which the Rover is made to sail a distance of five or six hundred miles in a single night," and that the stress on New England uprightness is a little hypocritical and may be offensive to inhabitants of the South (such as the Southern minister satirized in chapter 24):

In the sympathetic watering of the preceding voyage to Africa, an errour is thought to be committed, by people at the southward, by the use of an ingredient seldom to be met with in those parts, called *yankee conscience*. It has been a subject of common observation, that the industrious people of the northern states, who have so eminently distinguished themselves in this humane traffic, whenever they proceed for the coast of Africa, make a point of leaving this old, and somewhat unfashionable staple of their country at home, to be resumed again at their return, as the decorum of religion or morality should render expedient. . . . I am apprehensive, that the smart of the lash will be felt too severely, by the clergyman of V———a, and that the sympathetic interest of his parishioners may diminish the demand for such valuable wares.

The letter was as much an occasion to comment on the "Colon & Spondee" and the "Peter Pencil" columns as on *The Algerine Captive*, and there was no discussion of the literary quality of the book. But the work was to come in for more, rather than less, comment as the years passed. In early 1802, four and a half years after the book's publication, Dennie quoted in his *Port Folio* a statement from the *Farmer's Museum* (which incidentally takes Tyler's authorship as a matter of fact) to the effect that, while some books receive unjustified praise and some are unaccountably forgotten, others "are only neglected for a while, till their deserts call them from an unjust oblivion. Amongst the latter, may be classed the Algerine Captive, written by R. Tyler, Esq. a work of much humour and merit, and for which we are happy to see a late and increasing demand." Dennie added his own praise, as Tyler's friend:

From our partiality for Mr. Tyler, and our conviction of the ingenuity of his mind, we are much delighted with the above information. A second edition of his work, enlarged to two volumes octavo, and published in the style of "Mordaunt," by Dr. Moore, is greatly wanted, and would afford the author an opportunity to extend his chapters, which are now too brief, and fill a fine outline, with very captivating colours.[13]

The last point is well taken, for the two volumes, totaling only about 65,000 words, are made up of sixty-nine chapters, some of which are no longer than a good-sized paragraph.

But if Tyler was not immediately given the opportunity for an expanded edition, a new edition did appear within a few months after Dennie's remarks. In April 1802 a two-volume edition, printed by S. Hamilton and published by G. and J. Robinson, appeared in London, and as a result *The Algerine Captive* is usually called the first American novel to be reprinted in England. That distinction properly belongs to Charles Brockden Brown's *Ormond*, published in England in 1800,[14] but Tyler's book was one of the earliest, for very few pre-1820 American novels were reprinted there.[15] Although Tyler was later to remark regretfully that this was the period of Sydney Smith's "Who reads an American book?,"[16] he at least had little cause for complaint about the way his work was presented. Robinson's two volumes were handsomely printed, and the text was not expurgated, not even the patriotic preface or such references to England as "that haughty exasperated power" (though it did embody nearly 250 alterations of wording — usually for the better — and many hundreds more of punctuation).[17] Unfortunately this edition did not have a large circulation because Hamilton's warehouses and printing office burned down while the edition was stored there, destroying nearly all copies. To remedy the loss, the Robinsons decided to issue the work serially in the *Lady's Magazine*, which they published, and it appeared there in 1804, divided into thirteen installments and adorned with several engraved plates (illustrating such scenes as "A Medical Consultation" or "Updike Underhill seized by the Algerines").[18] A note to the initial installment announced, "The narrative is almost entirely founded on facts; and it is the first genuine American production of the kind that has been published in this country." The text (including the preface) followed the 1802 edition (with a few more changes in punctuation), except for one episode near the beginning, which must have been thought too daring to include in an *Entertaining Companion for the Fair Sex* (as the subtitle of the magazine reads), though it is actually one of Tyler's most amusing sketches. The narrator, telling of his ancestor John Underhill, reports that the venerable man was once charged with adultery because, at a public lecture in Boston, he gazed "stedfastly, and perhaps inordinately," upon Mistress Miriam Wilbore,

who it seems was, at that very time, herself in the breach of the spirit of an existing law, which forbad women to appear in public with uncovered arms and necks, by appearing at the same lecture with a pair of wanton open worked gloves, slit at the thumbs and fingers, for the conveniency of taking snuff; though she was not charged with the latter crime of using tobacco.[19]

At the trial Master Cotton "quoted Gregory Nazianzen upon

good works" and Master Peters averred that "these opennings [in the gloves] were Satan's port holes of firy temptatione." Thus the Robinsons thought best to omit the last three paragraphs of chapter 1 and all of chapter 2, so that their serial version contains sixty-eight chapters, all suitable for ladies.

The London *Monthly Review* devoted eight pages to *The Algerine Captive* in its September 1803 issue, but most of the space was given over to extracts from the book or to plot summary, with the only critical comments coming in the last two paragraphs. The writer predictably finds the book wanting when compared with British or European works — the "management of the story" is below *Robinson Crusoe*, the "exquisite humour" of *Gulliver's Travels* is absent, and the "delicate and refined irony" of the *Lettres Persanes* is not to be found here; nevertheless, the reader is "carried along by a train of probable and touching events," presented with "natural and lively painting" of "the folly or wickedness of human kind." The laudable sentiments in the book — the exposure of the evils of captivity and of the African slave trade, the "able and warm" defense of religious freedom, and the disapproval of certain aspects of European policy — according to the British critic, "may be allowed to atone for partial failures in the execution of [Tyler's] plan." Of the three faults he singled out, one is natural to come from the British viewpoint (that "the moral picture of London is darkened with shading not its own"), and the other two have become almost standard comments (that "the contents of the first volume are more diversified and more amusing than those of the second" and that, in Updike's debate with the Mohammedan priest, "the author too feebly defends that religion which he professes to revere").[20] Dennie's *Port Folio* also commented on the English edition with its usual loyalty: in June 1803 it announced that an "elegant" edition had appeared and asserted that American works received better treatment in England than at home; in April 1804 it commented on the "soothing *triumph* to the ingenious author to learn that his book is perused in the country of his *ancestors*," even though somewhat neglected in his native land.[21]

If the book then passed out of public attention for a time, it did enjoy a more prolonged life than the average publication, for it was still being discussed in 1810 and was reissued in 1816. The Boston *Monthly Anthology*, in one of its "Retrospective Reviews" for 1810, lamented, "This little work is very undeservedly hastening to oblivion. It contains an admirable picture of the manners of the interiour of New England." The book was also to be praised for the instruction that it gave, especially in the matter of children's education, where conceit is too often mistaken for genius. But again there are three flaws, two of them familiar by now. First, Updike's journeys as a doctor form "the most amusing part," and the second volume is "much inferiour," being "a collection of common-place remarks upon the Barbary powers, and a relation of common incidents, accompanied with many trite reflections." Second, the religious debate puts Christianity in too weak a position; and, finally, the "perpetual invective against classical learning" is to be deplored.[22] Though Tyler later expressed wonder that the book could be criticized for infidelity, he must have been pleased with the recurrent interest in the work. There was at least enough demand for it that Peter B. Gleason of Hartford set up a new compact one-volume edition in 1816 (rather carelessly proofread).[23] And Tyler himself, who was working on a revision and expansion of the work in the last years of his life, must have sensed its importance, even if he did not realize that he had failed by only a few degrees to produce something as significant in the history of American fiction as *The Contrast* had been in American drama.

The Preface

For a book that purports to tell about a captivity in Algeria, the preface makes some unexpected points about America and American works. This preface is one of the important early manifestoes of American literary independence.[24] The use of native materials and the creation of a distinctive literature, perennial concerns of American writers, had special relevance in the years when the country was becoming politically independent as well, and Tyler's pronouncement is of a piece with those of the Connecticut wits and other gentleman-writers of the young republic. His preface introduces a strain of Americanism — praise of freedom and the glories of America — that recurs continually in the book, like the poets' conventional survey of the country's golden future. He calls for realism at a time when only one or two earlier novels (such as *Modern Chivalry*) could be said to treat the American scene with fidelity, although approximately twenty-five books that qualify in some way as fiction had already been published in the United States. A glance at the titles of other novels of 1797 (Hannah Foster's *Coquette*, Mrs. Patterson's *The Unfortunate Lovers*, Samuel Relf's *Infidelity*, and James Butler's *Fortune's Foot-ball*) shows that sentimentality reigned supreme, even among works which sometimes claimed to be based on fact.[25]

But Tyler's preface is interesting also because it is made an integral part of the book. That is, since the title page announces the work to be an autobiographical narrative by Updike Underhill, Tyler must step into his persona even in the preface and express his views both about fiction in general and American works in particular from the point of view of a contemporary educated New England writer of nonfiction. The nine pages of the preface are divided into three paragraphs which mark the three stages in his argument. Underhill begins, having just returned from his seven years' captivity, by noting how many more books are being read purely for amusement by "all ranks" of New Englanders (whereas formerly such books had been available only in seaports), and he proudly points to American education as the cause of this rapidly increasing "taste for amusing literature" — for in no other country "are there so many people, in proportion to its numbers, who can read and write." Tyler's taste in literature, as well as Underhill's character, is reflected in his description of the reading material previously available to rural communities: "certain funeral discourses, the last words and dying speeches of Bryan Shaheen, and Levi Ames, and some dreary somebody's Day of Doom, formed the most diverting part of the farmer's library." What replaced these works was not always better, because the "social libraries" and "country booksellers" had "filled the whole land with modern Travels, and Novels, almost as incredible" — an oblique comment, if the critics had seen it, on the form of the book itself, for, under these circumstances, the best approach to truth might be a fictitious travelogue. Underhill's description of this shift in taste to frivolous works demonstrates Tyler's allusive style and light touch and is consistent with the Underhill we follow through the book; he explains that all

forsook the sober sermons and Practical Pieties of their fathers, for the gay stories and splendid impieties of the Traveller and the Novelist. The worthy farmer no longer fatigued himself with Bunyan's Pilgrim up the "hill of difficulty" or through the "slough of despond;" but quaffed wine with Brydone in the hermitage of Vesuvius, or sported with Bruce on the fairy land of Abysinia.

If the hired man and the maid no longer wept over sad ballads, they "amused themselves into so agreeable a terrour, with the haunted houses and hobgobblins of Mrs. Ratcliffe, that they were both afraid to sleep alone."

Given this state of affairs, Underhill goes on to point out what is to be "deplored" in it and what can be done to rectify it, observing parenthetically what the function of novels is. The first objection is that these books often "are not of our own manufacture," a fault to be remedied simply by producing "our own books of amusement." The second problem, inseparable from the first, is more serious — since novels present a "picture of the times" and since most of them are British, "the New England reader is insensibly taught to admire the levity, and often the vices of the parent country. While the fancy is enchanted, the heart is corrupted." The argument, then, is not quite the usual appeal for a native literature on patriotic grounds, for here the morality of novels and their practical effects are most important, though these questions do involve patriotism of a more subtle sort:

If the English novel does not inculcate vice, it at least impresses on the young mind [American, presumably] an erroneous idea of the world, in which she is to live. It paints the manners, customs, and habits of a strange country; excites a fondness for false splendour; and renders the homespun habits of her own country disgusting.

The implication is that American customs (as in *The Contrast*) are pure, unaffected, and simple — and therefore more desirable; that novels do have a lasting effect on the behavior of their readers; that novelists reflect the manners and customs around them; and that, as a result, the best novels for Americans to read are novels written by Americans depicting American manners.

Underhill then follows the tradition of pretending that he would not have been so presumptuous as to write his own story if the idea had not been suggested to him by "a friend."

This anonymous friend had told him that an account of his own life would "at least display a portrait of New England manners, hitherto unattempted." This remark brings us, however circuitously, to a rationale for the first volume of the work, for it does portray American (not only New England) manners; yet Underhill's reasoning is still a bit shadowy, since his discussion of the faults of British fiction for American readers leads one to expect him to announce a proper work of American fiction, not an autobiography. The second volume, a large part of which describes the customs of the Algerines, is even more puzzling and is explained only by the statement that "the manners of that ferocious race" are "so little known in our country" — and would therefore at least be "interesting." One can only conclude that it is more dangerous for Americans to read about the customs of the British (for whom a touch of loyalty might yet remain in many minds) than those of the Algerines (for whom there could be no sentimental attachment and about whose evils it would be beneficial for Americans to be informed). Underhill's closing satirical touch is to point out that his work will be just as exciting as fiction to all readers except one like the lady described by Addison, who threw her Plutarch (which she had been enjoying as a novel) aside "with disgust, because a man of letters had inadvertently told her, the work was founded on FACT."

It is characteristic of Tyler, as a Federalist lawyer and amateur man of letters, to write a novel pseudonymously, in the guise of a truthful autobiography, with both a patriotic and a social purpose in mind. The two purposes show through the dedication (dated 20 June 1797) to David Humphreys, a Connecticut wit and a minister to Spain. Underhill (who signs the dedication) first makes a distinction between European dedications (in which "the author oftener looks to the plenitude of the pockets, than the brains of his patron") and those of America (which involve no pecuniary gain and are determined by the "acknowledged merit" of the individual chosen). With exact parallelism (Underhill is "a lover of the Muses" and "a biographer of private life," and Humphreys is "a Poet" and "the Biographer of a Hero" — Israel Putnam), he explains the appropriateness of his dedication in a book about "those miseries of slavery, from which your public energies have principally conduced to liberate hundreds of our fellow citizens." Humphreys' efforts toward a treaty with the Algerines helped correct a social evil and so, Underhill implies, can a book informing the public fully about the situation.

The First Volume

If patriotic and social purposes are present throughout the novel, they operate in different ways in the two volumes. In the second volume the exposure of the evil of Algerine captivity offers the opportunity for occasional remarks on the glories of America; in the first volume the satire of certain American customs is only gentle criticism by one who hopes to make an excellent country even better. The patriotism remains; the social criticism changes. The first volume is light, satirical, and picaresque; the second is humanitarian and informative. Among American works, the first is reminiscent of Brackenridge's *Modern Chivalry*, the second of an Indian captivity narrative. The divergence between the two volumes is too great to be accommodated even in the tradition of the wandering rogue; the two volumes must be considered separately, for they constitute essentially two books.

The first volume, if it is reminiscent of *Modern Chivalry* in its picaresque framework and its satire of American customs, is not so consistent in approach nor methodical in coverage. *Modern Chivalry*, whose method may not be apparent immediately, eventually presents a thorough investigation of the practice of democracy; *The Algerine Captive* touches here and there sporadically on many social follies — perhaps in almost every case related to democracy but not explicitly so. Tyler, as *The Island of Barrataria* shows, knew his Cervantes as well as Brackenridge, and he makes allusions which reveal his familiarity with Smollett. But the unity of a picaresque novel requires more than the presence of a hero, and the individual incidents (about election procedures, for example) in *Modern Chivalry* add up to a coherent whole in a way those in *The Algerine Captive* do not.

The underlying organization of the first volume is a chronological account of the life of Updike Underhill to the time when, at the age of twenty-six, he is taken captive by the Algerines. Inspired in part by stories of the captivity of his great-uncle Thomas, Tyler traced his hero's ancestry back to the famous Captain John Underhill, author of *Newes from America* (1638). After three chapters on the Captain's gallant exploits (following the account in Jeremy Belknap's *History of New-Hampshire*), and some brief comment on his eldest son, Benoni (a fabrication of Tyler's), from whom Updike is supposedly descended, we come (on page 49) to a description of the hero's birth on 16 July 1762.[26] This event is accompanied by the proper omens, for his mother dreams that Updike is captured by an Indian "playing at foot ball" with his head, signifying that he would "one day suffer among savages." His childhood (chapters 5–6) is represented by a few paragraphs on his attendance at a private school and his ensuing study of Greek and Latin (which he greatly enjoys), and soon (chapter 7) he takes a position as country schoolmaster (which he thoroughly dislikes and from which he is released by a fire that destroys the schoolhouse). By this time his father has decided that he should be in a profession (chapter 8), so Updike commences his study of medicine with a celebrated doctor (chapters 9–15), a process interrupted occasionally by his encounters with polite society (chapters 11–14). His studies completed in June of 1785, at the age of twenty-two, he visits Boston and Harvard (chapters 16–17) for medical supplies and sets out, "full Speed, to seek Practice, Fame, and Fortune, as a Country Practitioner." When he becomes dissatisfied with his first place of residence (chapters 19–21), he decides to move to the South, where he had heard "that the inhabitants were immensely opulent" and "paid high fees with profusion" (chapter 22). Though his journey begins well, with a visit to Benjamin Franklin in Philadelphia (chapter 23), his experiences in the South (chapters 24–25), needless to say, are not as he had anticipated, and he soon accepts an offer to sail as surgeon on a ship bound for England. One chapter (26) is devoted to his impression of London and three (27–29) to Thomas Paine, whom he meets before he sets sail again on 18 July 1788 in the ship *Sympathy*, bound for the coast of Africa to pick up Negro slaves. As physician, it is Updike's duty to inspect the slaves, and, when an epidemic breaks out, he recommends that they be taken ashore to get well (chapters 30–31). While camping there with five slaves who are still recuperating, he is abandoned by his ship and, on 14 November 1788, is captured by the Algerine *Rover*, which eleven days later "hove in sight of the city of Algiers" (chapter 32). It is here, at the beginning of Updike's Algerine captivity, that the first volume ends.

This course of events has been arranged to serve an obvious purpose. Tyler wants to satirize or comment on certain customs and practices, and he plans Updike's life so that they are included. When Updike first tries teaching school and then becomes a doctor, Tyler has the opportunity to say something about two professions; when Updike's ancestry is described, Tyler can comment on the American past and particularly on the Puritans; when Updike goes to the South, Tyler can point out the hypocrisy of aristocratic life and can criticize one part of America for not being American; when the hero finds his way to England, Tyler can make comparisons with the splendors of his native country. The portraits of Franklin and Paine are patriotic and political; the chapter on Harvard is a plea for greater Americanism; and the description of conditions on the slave ship is humanitarian protest. The volume is a kind of anthology of targets for the satirist and scenes of inspiration for the patriot. Tyler seems to have assembled his opinions on almost all subjects in which he was strongly interested and has strung them together on a biographical thread; the result, if not quite inconsistent, is certainly less than unified.

But to say that restraint, shaping, and subordinating would have produced a more coherent whole is not to say that there is no power in individual scenes, for some of the sketches are among the most skillful and amusing in early American literature. Updike's love of Greek, for instance, which could almost be called a motif of the volume, forms the basis of several episodes and serves a double purpose: his recitations at inappropriate moments are part of the general ridiculing of pedantry, and the common people's ignorance of Greek is taken, at the same time, as a mark of their general lack of culture. Both the pedantry and the social gap are evident when Updike, as the country schoolmaster, begins talking to a group of men in a tavern about Achilles' horse (chapter 7) or when, at a women's quilting party, he brings up the subject of Andromache at her loom, and then he speaks of Penelope:

This was received with a stupid stare, until I mentioned the long time the queen of Ulysses was weaving; when a smart young woman observed, that she supposed Miss Penelope's yarn was rotted in whitening, that made her so long: and then told a tedious story of a piece of cotton and linen she had herself woven, under the same circumstances. She had no sooner finished, than, to enforce my observations, I recited above forty lines of Greek, from the Odessey, and then began a dissertation on the *caesura*. (I, 73)

This humor of exaggeration and incongruity is nearly always successful — as when Updike leaves the party:

> I was about retiring, fatigued and disgusted, when it was hinted to me, that I might wait on Miss Mima home; but as I could recollect no word in the Greek, which would construe into *bundling*, or any of Homer's heroes, who *got the bag*, I declined. In the Latin, it is true, that Aeneas and Dido, in the cave, seem something like a precedent. (I, 74)

Earlier (chapter 6), on his father's farm, he "gave Greek names to all our farming tools; and cheered the cattle with hexameter verse":

> After I had worked on the farm some months, having killed a fat heifer of my father's, upon which the family depended for their winter's beef, covered it with green boughs, and laid it in the shade to putrify, in order to raise a swarm of bees, after the manner of Virgil; which process, notwithstanding I followed closely the directions in the georgics, some how or other, failed, my father consented to my mother's request, that I should renew my career of learning. (I, 65–66)

The comedy of book learning which does not work out in practical life recurs in the volume, as does the device of the anticlimactic twist.

Other branches of learning come in for mild thrusts as well. When Updike, as a child at school (chapter 5), is asked to read from Dilworth's spelling book, he recites as loud as he can "without regard to emphasis or stops." The teacher considers Updike his "best scholar," and the minister, "who prided himself on the strength of his own lungs," is so pleased by the volume of Updike's recitation that he recommends college for him (I, 53–54). If this incident reflects on the quality of both the teaching profession and the ministry, Updike's own career as a teacher is a commentary at once on the lack of excellence in the country schools and the related lack of interest in education on the part of the people. Updike is not a good teacher, but one feels that he had the ability, if he had not been defeated by the community. To be sure, he is not so dedicated as to rise to the challenge, but he at least has considered the matter seriously: "As I had been once unmercifully whipt, for detecting my master in a false concord, I resolved to be mild in my government, to avoid all manual correction, and doubted not by these means to secure the love and respect of my pupils" (I, 68). In one sentence Tyler has suggested the hypocrisy (or incompetence) of the schoolmasters, the need for more humane treatment of children, and the ironic contrast between a teacher's idealistic intentions and actual experience. The "love and respect" of the pupils never come, and, equally expected, the parents take the children's side. Thus, when Updike is forced to strike a student who will not relinquish the master's chair by the fire, the father of the student soon appears with threats — "the only instance," Updike remarks sarcastically, "of the overwhelming gratitude of parents I received." The public appreciation of education is further reflected in the low salary (tendered in produce each fall) which causes Updike to go into debt. Altogether it is not a very pretty picture of colonial education, and the good humor of the telling (with the exception of Updike's one sarcastic comment) is more effective than an angry protest, though one may wonder occasionally, here and elsewhere, if the comedy is not sometimes indulged in for its own sake and its ostensible purpose lost sight of. In any case, the split between the educated minority and the Philistine majority is just as evident here, if not treated so militantly, as it is in *Main Street* or other works of the 1920's. Doubts about the utility of education are present even in Updike's own family. Although the book does not show us Updike's development enough to be considered a *Bildungsroman*, it does contain an element often present in such works, including recent ones — a mother who is "a little spare woman," interested in the arts and education, and a father who is practical and worldly, "a large bony man" (I, 55).

The minister who appreciates strength of lung more than vitality of thought is a characteristic Tyler clergyman, though religion in *The Algerine Captive* is not simply a subject for ridicule. It is true, however, that references to public worship are usually made with irony and the hypocrisy of divines is repeatedly emphasized. Even Updike's account of his illustrious ancestor alludes to the time "when the zeal of our worthy forefathers burned the hottest against heretics" (I, 32) and includes the glove episode. When Updike's father seeks a professional opinion on the value of Greek (chapter 6), he learns from a Boston clergyman that it is now useless, for there are fashions in divinity as in everything else:

When our forefathers founded the college, at Cambridge, critical knowledge in the mazes and subtleties of school divinity was all the mode. He that could give a new turn to an old text, or detect a mistranslation in the version, was more admired than the man, who invented printing, discovered the magnetic powers. (I, 61)

What appears at first to be a didactic episode (chapter 14) on the importance of Bible-reading — an incident which "contains a lesson, valuable to the reader, if he has penetration enough to discover it, and candour enough to apply it to himself" — ends by connecting religion with monetary gain, for, when Updike belatedly turns to the Bible his mother had given him, a guinea falls out: "[I] resolved that, in gratitude, I would read a chapter in the bible, every remaining day of my life. This resolution I then persevered in, a whole fortnight" (I, 120). The deflating of sentiment present here represents the tone of the first volume, and it is not until the second that the comments on religion, at least, take on a different character.

Another minister in volume I (chapter 24) is criticized

for his behavior, in an episode which also contrasts the solid worth of New England with the frivolous hypocrisy of the South. In a state "south of Philadelphia," the parson arrives at church cursing and beating his slave, only to deliver an "animated" sermon on sinning with one's tongue. When the short service is over and the congregation has "prayed fervently," everyone rushes outside to the horse race, where the parson "descanted, in the language of the turf, upon the points of the two rival horses, and the sleeve of his cassoc was heavy laden, with the principal bets." Updike, the true Yankee, expresses his disapproval in his best dead-pan manner:

The whole of this extraordinary scene was novel to me. Besides, a certain staple of New England I had with me, called conscience, made my situation, in even the passive part I bore in it, so awkward and uneasy, that I could not refrain from observing to my friend my surprise at the parson's conduct, in chastising his servant immediately before divine service. My friend was so happily influenced by the habits of these liberal, enlightened people, that he could not even comprehend the tendency of my remark. He supposed it levelled at the impropriety, not of the minister, but the man; not at the act, but the severity of the chastisement. (I, 162–163)

The reader is then directed to "interlard those quotations" with oaths, so that the scene will be both more natural and less "tasteless and vapid" to the Southerner.

Tyler's satire of social customs is again effectively expressed through Updike's naïveté, in the episode in which he becomes involved in a duel (chapter 12). Updike had presented an ode, full of classical epithets, to a young lady, one of whose suitors took the description "ox-eyed" as an insult rather than a compliment. In a letter revealing all his lack of education but showing his knowledge of the code of honor, the suitor demands an explanation for "Them there very extraordinary pare of varses." Fooled by the polite tone, the innocent Up-

dike believes it to be a request to discuss the ode, "to be indulged with an explanation of some of its peculiar beauties":

I began to recollect illustrations and parodies, from some favourite passages in the Iliad. But, what we were to do, in wasting a few
charges of powder, was utterly inexplicable. At one time, indeed,
I thought it an invitation to shoot partridges, and bethought myself of scouring a long barrelled gun, which had descended as an
heir loom in our family. . . . Then again, I reflected, that the
lower end of a wharf, in a populous town, was not the most probable place, to spring a covey of partridges. But what puzzled me
most, was his punctual attention to hours, and even seconds.
(I, 104–105)

A fellow student explains the code and advises Updike to
accept. The challenger, "a raw lad, from the country," is
surprised, and the town officials step in to settle the matter
peacefully — Updike escorted "by the high sheriff, two depu-
ties, three constables, and eleven stout assistants . . . guarded
by a platoon of the militia, with a colonel at their head." The
exaggeration, the piling up of detail, the pose of innocence,
the matter-of-fact tone, all contribute to skillful satire of
social pretentiousness. After this occurrence, Updike says, "I
verily believe that, if I had spouted a whole Iliad, in the ball
room, no one would have ventured to interrupt me: for I had
proved myself a MAN OF HONOUR."

The most extended satire in the book, however, is not of
ministers, teachers, or men about town, but of physicians.
Medical jargon is a favorite target (the ninth chapter describes
"A Philosophical Detail of the Operation of Couching for
the Gutta Serena"), as are the deceptions of quacks. In one
town where Updike settles (chapter 19), he encounters a
learned doctor (who follows the books, measures out medicine carefully, and is opposed to fresh air), a cheap doctor
(who is "careless, daring, and often successful"), a safe doctor ("if he did no good, he never did any harm"), and a musi-

cal doctor (that is, "entertaining or facetious"). He also comes across a quack (barely distinguishable from the four preceding) who has captured the faith of the public by making elaborate spiels in his own version of Latin. When Updike meets him (chapter 20), the quack has just "prescribed a gill of burnt brandy, with a pepper pod in it, to keep up the patient's spirits, under the operation, and [takes] another himself, to keep his hand steady" (I, 138). The two work out a successful partnership: Updike provides the knowledge, the quack the clientele; needless to say, the patients attribute all success to the quack. Soon after, when a jockey falls off a horse, the poor man is subjected to a professional consultation by this entire group of practitioners. The learned doctor is not able to venture an opinion since he "had unfortunately left at home his Pringle on contusions," but the safe doctor does not hesitate to propose "brown paper, dipped in rum and cobwebs, to staunch the blood." It is the quack's opinion that the jockey will recover since his soul has not been damaged, a jockey's soul being in his left heel. Finally (chapter 21) one doctor pours "a dose of urine and molasses down the patient's throat: who soon so happily recovered as to pursue his vocation, swop horses three times, play twenty rubbers of all fours, and get dead drunk again before sunset" (I, 150).

As with the double-edged satire of schoolmasters, the criticism here, though good-natured, is by no means limited to the pedantry or incompetence of the physicians themselves, for the gullible public that will support quacks is equally to blame. Updike has a difficult time finding a practice, where the quacks have already gained their patients' confidence, and he discovers (chapter 18) that doctors often command no more respect than schoolmasters:

In the neighbouring town, they did not want [need] a physician, as an experienced itinerant doctor visited the place, every March, when the people had most leisure to be sick and take physic. He practiced with great success, especially in slow consumptions, charged very low, and took his pay in any thing and every thing. Besides, he carried a mould with him, to run pewter spoons, and was equally good at mending a kettle and a constitution. (I, 130–131)

The picture of the medical profession which Tyler presents is just as discouraging as that of the teaching profession. The few good doctors are unrecognized, unrewarded, and driven to odd jobs on the side; the doctors that prevail are ignorant, unscrupulous, and mercenary, playing on an equally ignorant and hypochondriac public. That a serious purpose underlies Tyler's satire becomes evident in several straightforward passages, like the description of a blind man in the process of emerging from a successful operation (chapter 9), the anecdotes of the "celebrated Doctor Moyes" (chapter 10), or Updike's praise of his own teacher, who "possessed all the essence, without the parade of learning" (chapter 15). This combination of the overtly serious with the satiric — and with irony that verges on self-indulgent humor — is characteristic of the kind of mixture found throughout *The Algerine Captive*. But the solemn statement or direct comment is often isolated in a separate chapter and rarely intrudes to break the tone of a satiric sketch; Tyler's gift for comedy, gentle ridicule, and telling social criticism is nowhere better displayed than in these portraits of physicians.

The Second Volume

If the first volume is made up of groups of chapters relating to certain objects of satire, the second must be thought of in terms of topical headings, such as history, religion, law, public ceremonies, language, finance, and so on — for volume II is, more than anything else, a direct and unadorned account, supposedly factual, of the Algerines, their history, their customs, and their country. The text of this volume is longer by some forty pages than that of the first, but it is likely to seem even longer to most readers. Its subject matter is remote from general interest, unenlivened by satire or whimsy except in a few brilliant passages, and plot is almost nonexistent. The first volume, a digression from the story of Algerine captivity which has little plot other than the successive escapades of the hero, is important historically in its use of native materials and is still entertaining today. In the second volume, Tyler is not able adequately to integrate details of an unfamiliar setting with whatever action is taking place in it, and the resulting passages of description are more irritating than diverting.

Most of the intrigue is concentrated in two chapters near the end, chapters 30 and 36.[27] Earlier references to what Updike is doing are rarely inserted for themselves; they are employed to put him into situations where other aspects of Algerine life can be expounded. In this respect the picaresque plan of volume I is continued, with the course of the hero's life predetermined by the subjects for discussion; the difference is in the tone of those discussions, which is factual and expository, not satirical and anecdotal. The volume begins with a description of the palace of the Dey of Algiers, Vizier Hassen Bashaw, before whom Updike and the other captives are brought. Since Updike cannot promise ransom, he is exhibited in the slave market, where he is purchased by Abdel Melic, who then takes him to his mansion (chapters 2–4). Updike's attempt to help a fellow slave who is being whipped is an occasion for comment on the freedom of America (and causes Updike to be assigned to the stone quarry); his conversation with an Englishman who has espoused Mohammedanism provides the opportunity for religious commentary (chapter 5), followed by a comparison with Christianity in his debate with the mullah (chapters 6–7). Upon returning to the quarry after the debate, he feels more familiar with the language, so we are given a chapter on "The Language of the Algerines" (chapter 8). Although there is a hint of plot in chapter 9, when Updike makes plans to escape, these plans are thwarted by the occurrence of a public celebration, which is duly described in the following chapter.

The trend of the account may be said to take a slight turn with chapter 11, because there we return to the subject of medicine. Chapters 11 through 14 describe Updike's collapse from exhaustion and depression, his stay in the infirmary, his purchase by the head of the hospital (due to his former medical experience), his new duties, his trips for medical supplies (an occasion for comment on Algerine medicine), and his visit to a sick lady. But these four chapters together lack one page of being as long as the next chapter, the longest in the book, a "Sketch of the History of the Algerines," which begins a long expository section that is the center, if not the heart, of the volume. We have a description of the city of Algiers (chapter 16), an account of its government (17), revenue (18), and military forces (19), and a discussion of Algerine dress (20), marriages, and funerals (21); then follows a "Life of the Prophet Mahomet" (22) and two chapters on various sects and religious practices (23–24); an analysis (25) of the sources of Algerine power (why Europeans have not been able to suppress the Algerines) is succeeded by an example of an Algerine lawsuit (26) and an Algerine sermon (27). It is not until chapter 28 that we are given any assurance that Updike has not forgotten his story:

I have thus given some succinct notices of the history, government, religion, habits, and manners of this ferocious race. I have interspersed reflections, which, I hope, will be received by the learned with candour; and shall now resume the thread of my more appropriate narrative. (II, 178)

Despite this promise, we still have to hear about the position of the Jews in Algiers — an account which, surprisingly, leads us directly into the largely narrative framework of the last nine chapters, for Updike, with his greater freedom as a medical slave, wanders into the Jewish section and makes the acquaintance of Adonah Ben Benjamin, who promises to help him escape.

The only true plot (in the sense of an intrigue in which the order of events makes a difference) occurs in these last chapters, although even there four chapters (31–34) are given over to a description of a pilgrimage to Medina and Mecca. In the space of one chapter (30), Updike makes arrangements with the Jew for his escape, having turned over all his savings, only to call at the Jew's house on the appointed day to find him dead of apoplexy and the Jew's son unwilling to acknowledge any of the money as Updike's. This chapter, if it does nothing to redeem Tyler's sense of narrative proportion, does demonstrate his feeling for melodramatic turns of events. The hero's hopes are built up, and then are destroyed, just before the final happy outcome. Updike is more discouraged than ever until, after he cures the Jew's son of a fever, the son is so grateful that he confesses his perfidy, repays Updike's money, and lends him enough more to make up the ransom (chapters 35–36). Even here Tyler attempts to create suspense by having the son not make the payment at the appointed time, but a day later; and the abrupt vicissitudes continue when Updike, on the ship making his escape, is seized and taken captive by a man from Tunis. After an agonizing forty-eight hours, enlivened by a storm, a Portuguese ship comes alongside and frees Updike and the other slaves. It is then a simple matter for Updike to get to Portugal, to arrange passage to England, and to return to the United States (chapter 37). He lands at Chesapeake Bay on 3 May 1795, after an absence of seven years, buys a horse, and rides to a happy reunion with his parents.

In spite of the large amount of expository material, volume II does approach a unity of tone and does make a connection with volume I through its comments on two subjects — religion and American freedom. While one of Tyler's purposes was undoubtedly to alert his fellow countrymen to the evils of the Algerian depredations, another was certainly to inspire patriotism and, to a slighter degree, love of Christianity. The principal motif of the entire work is the glorious freedom of America. In volume I certain American habits may be satirized, in the interests of improvement, but patriotism is always a solemn subject. Even in that anecdote criticizing the religious zeal of early New Englanders, Updike does not fail to mention their "love of liberty, which under God enabled us to obtain our own glorious freedom" (I, 44). When Updike visits Harvard he is indignant that the museum has so few American objects (chapter 17); and he loses no opportunity to make invidious references to England — thus the English took over the land which rightly belonged to John Underhill (chapter 3), and the common man in England, as Updike observes on his visit to London, was "rotting in dungeons, languishing wretched lives in foetid jails, and boasting of the GLORIOUS FREEDOM OF ENGLISHMEN" (chapter 26). Social and economic criticism of the English is intended as indirect praise of America: their "little smoky fire of coals was rendered cheerless by excise, and their daily draught of beer embittered by taxes." Americans, especially New Englanders, also have a greater feeling for justice than other nationalities. So, on the slave ship *Sympathy*, Captain Russell fears that Updike is "moved by some *yankee nonsense about humanity*" (I, 201) and, in the South, Updike is uneasy because of that "staple of New England . . . called conscience" (I, 162). The visits to Benjamin Franklin and Thomas Paine, inserted partly to increase the verisimilitude of the work, serve a patriotic purpose as well. Franklin is praised (chapter 23) for his democratic rise from a lowly position by his own efforts (and for the inevitable qualities of frugality and wisdom, illustrated with anecdotes); Paine, on the other hand, a "spare man, rather under size," whose "bodily presence was both mean and contemptible" (I, 176), is a "missionary of vice" and a "modern vandal" who has "vilified a great prophet, the saviour of the Gentiles," and has "railed at Washington, a saviour of his country" (I, 183–184). Updike delights in telling a story (chapter 28) in which Paine is defeated in a clash of wit by Peter Pindar, Paine's point of view being that the United States would be better off if it were still a colony, without a Washington as the great leader.[28] Finally, at the end of volume I, when Updike is in the dungeon of the Algerine ship, he exclaims, "Grant me . . . once more to taste the freedom of my native country, and every moment of my life shall be dedicated to preaching against this detestable commerce" (I, 213). The humanitarianism and didacticism of the work, then, are a function of its patriotism, for the existence of slavery anywhere in the world is an affront to a free American. As Updike says of his role on the slave ship, "I thought of my native land and blushed" (I, 190).

This relation between freedom and patriotism is particularly clear in volume II. As early as the second chapter, Updike declares that any American citizen who, "in the warmth of . . . patriotism," condemns him for lack of spirit in submitting to Algerine slavery should have been there to "avail himself of a noble opportunity of suffering gloriously for his country" (II, 25). In the fourth chapter he continues in the same vein:

Judge you, my gallant, freeborn fellow citizens, you, who rejoice daily in our federal strength and independence, what were my sensations. . . . Let those of our fellow citizens, who set at nought the rich blessings of our federal union, go like me to a land of slavery, and they will then learn how to appreciate the value of our free government. (II, 35, 39)

At the public spectacle, one look at a tortured slave is "enough to appal a New England heart" (II, 76). Updike's homesickness for New England is revealed in his many allusions to native foods, customs, or language and in his eagerness to see another American: "the idea of embracing a fellow citizen, a brother christian, perhaps some one, who came from the same state, or had been in the same town, or seen my dear parents" (II, 187). But his own feelings are less important than the lesson he hopes to impart:

A slave myself, I have learned to appreciate the blessings of freedom. May my countrymen ever preserve and transmit to their posterity that liberty, which they have bled to obtain; and always bear it deeply engraven upon their memories, that, when men are once reduced to slavery, they can never resolve, much more achieve, any thing, that is manly, virtuous, or great. (II, 79)

It is this sentiment which Tyler gives the final position of emphasis in his closing chapter. Updike, who has been restored to the "rights and protection" of "the freest country in the universe," intends to support the "excellent government" which he "learnt to adore, in schools of despotism" and thus to be a "worthy FEDERAL citizen":

My ardent wish is, that my fellow citizens may profit by my misfortunes. If they peruse these pages with attention they will perceive the necessity of uniting our federal strength to enforce a due respect among other nations. Let us, one and all, endeavour to sustain the general government. Let no foreign emissaries inflame us against one nation, by raking into the ashes of long extinguished enmity or delude us into the extravagant schemes of another, by recurring to fancied gratitude. Our first object is union among ourselves. For to no nation besides the United States can that antient saying be more emphatically applied; BY UNITING WE STAND, BY DIVIDING WE FALL. (II, 241)

The shift from indirect to direct statement, which begins in the closing chapters of volume I, reaches its culmination here. Tyler seems to have been aware of the changed tone, for he has Updike comment that the doctors in the Algerine infirmary are "more ignorant than those of my own country, who had amused me in the gayer days of life" (II, 81). What was a subject for humor and satire in volume I has become matter for sober reflection and didactic exhortation.

The serious directness of volume II is also evident in the treatment of religion. To be sure, the satire of religious pedantry and of hypocritical ministers is balanced, even in volume I, by more direct assertions of faith, as when the physician who restores sight has a pleasure surpassed only, "with reverence be it spoken, by the satisfaction of our benevolent Saviour, when, by his miraculous power, he opened the eyes of the actually blind, made the dumb to sing, and the lame and impotent leap for joy" (I, 93). Of his role as doctor on the slave ship, Updike observes:

I have deplored my conduct with tears of anguish; and, I pray a merciful God, the common parent of the great family of the universe, who hath made of one flesh and one blood all nations of the earth, that the miseries, the insults, and cruel woundings, I afterwards received, when a slave myself, may expiate for the inhumanity, I was necessitated to exercise, towards these MY BRETHREN OF THE HUMAN RACE. (I, 193–194)

However much such references to God are discounted as conventional expressions, the subject of slavery and captivity, as opposed to freedom, has religious, as well as patriotic and political, implications. It is also evident, by the end of the first volume, that the discussion of religion will not be so one-sided as that of patriotism, for Updike remarks of the Algerines on shipboard, "the regularity and frequency of their devotion was astonishing to me, who had been taught to consider this people as the most blasphemous infidels" (I, 214).

Novelist

The religious element in the second volume takes the form either of a dramatic clash between Christianity and Mohammedanism or of an exposition of practices and customs in Mohammedanism — the first more likely to occur in the opening and closing sections of the volume, the second in the middle expository section. Chapters 5, 6, and 7 offer the best example of the dramatic conflict. In chapter 5 Updike encounters an Englishman who has adopted Mohammedanism, and he clarifies the connection between liberty and religion:

> I looked at him with astonishment. I had ever viewed the character of an apostate as odious and detestable. I turned from him with abhorrence, and for once embraced my burthen with pleasure. Indeed I pity you, said he. I sorrow for your distresses, and pity your prejudices. I pity you too, replied I, the tears standing in my eyes. My body is in slavery, but my mind is free. Your body is at liberty, but your soul is in the most abject slavery, in the gall of bitterness and bond of iniquity. (II, 43)

But Updike does consent to give a hearing to the Mohammedan priest, so that, as the Englishman says, his decision will be based on reason, having a knowledge of both systems. Updike is taken to the luxurious palace of the priests, or mullahs, in chapter 6 and is treated very courteously for eleven days. His reactions well illustrate the mixture of tone in volume II, for he is still capable of wry commentary, but within a few paragraphs he is verging on the sentimental:

> I have often observed that, in all countries, except New England, those, whose profession it is to decry the luxuries and vanities of this world, some how or other, contrive to possess the greatest portion of them. (II, 47)

> Though I viewed his [the mullah's] conduct as insidious, yet he no sooner retired than, overcome by his suavity of manners, for the first time I trembled for my faith, and burst into tears. (II, 51–52)

When Updike is in this frame of mind the mullah comes to

debate the relative merits of the two faiths. Chapter 7 summarizes in dialogue form their five days' discussion — it is this chapter which was criticized in contemporary discussions of the book. The *Monthly Anthology* objected to the fact that the mullah came out much better in the argument than Updike.[29] While the total context makes it impossible to believe that Tyler is attacking Christianity here, one must admit that the course of the debate does not lead very logically to Updike's final reaction: "disgusted with his fables, abashed by his assurance, and almost confounded by his sophistry, I resumed my slave's attire, and sought safety in my former servitude" (II, 65). In long and eloquent speeches, the mullah attempts to prove that the Koran is of divine origin and that Mohammedanism has multiplied more than Christianity, has greater miracles, was not promulgated by force, and does not have a sensual paradise; by comparison Updike's replies seem weak. Tyler's rationale, however, lies in the statement of the Englishman two chapters earlier: if his readers are brought to see that a good case can be made out for other religions, they will approach their own more thoughtfully, with more knowledge and with less bias. But whether Updike has set a better example of the thoughtful approach to religion or of Yankee stubbornness is debatable.

Tyler has created in Updike, for those of his readers able to see it, a subtle characterization of the typical New Englander with his prejudice and narrowness. In the expository chapters, when Updike is supposedly reporting facts, his preconceptions are obvious. He may praise a Mohammedan sermon (chapter 27) and say that it "was received . . . with a reverence, better becoming christians than infidels" (II, 172), but his very use of the term "infidels," and his conception of the relative worth of the behavior of the two, negates the seeming praise. Or, at the beginning of the three chapters on Algerine religion (chapters 22–24), Updike's assertion that he will "endeavour to steer the middle course of impartiality" is belied in the same paragraph by his reference to Mohammed as a "fortunate impostor." Mohammed's rise is depicted as the result of a calculated plan to gratify his ambition:

Mankind are apt to impute the most profound abilities to founders of religious systems, and other fortunate adventurers, when perhaps they owe their success more to a fortunate coincidence of circumstances, and their only merit is the sagacity to avail themselves of that tide in the affairs of men, which leads to wealth and honour. . . . The system of Mahomet is said to have been calculated to attach all these. To gratify the Arian and the Jew, he maintained the unity of God; and, to please the Pagans, he adopted many of their external rites, as fastings, washings, &c. . . . The stories of Mahomet's having retired to a cave with a monk and a Jew to compile his book; and falling into fits of the epilepsy, persuading his disciples that these fits were trances in order to propagate his system more effectually, so often related by geography compilers, like the tales of Pope Joan and the nag's head consecration of the English bishops, are fit only to amuse the vulgar. (II, 144–146)

The pose of impartiality is strengthened by mentioning certain points that one proceeds to deny, for the sake of getting those points on record, and by appearing to treat allegedly parallel situations in one's own religion in the same light.

This passage illustrates another aspect of Tyler's persona — Updike's Yankee common sense. Throughout the chapters on Algerine religion, it is the natural, rather than the miraculous or romantic, explanation that appeals to him. There were stories, he says, of Mohammed's being poisoned by a monk, but, "when we consider his advanced age and public energies, we need not recur to any but natural means for the cause of his death" (II, 149). Later, in the narrative chapters on the pilgrimage to Mecca (chapters 31–35), Updike constantly denies the supernatural explanations favored by the leader of the group, only to make this observation in the same breath:

We passed near the north arm of the red sea, and then pursued our journey south, until we struck the same arm again, near the place where the learned Wortley Montague has concluded the Israelites, under the conduct of Moses, effected their passage. The breadth of the sea here is great, and the waters deep and turbulent. The infidel may sneer, if he chooses; but, for my own part, I am convinced beyond a doubt, that, if the Israelites passed in this place, it must have been by the miraculous interposition of a divine power. I could not refrain from reflecting upon the infatuated temerity, which impelled the Egyptian king to follow them. Well does the Latin poet exclaim; *Quem Deus vult perdere, prius dementat.* (II, 210–211)

Either the satire has turned upon Updike himself, or he is directing his sarcasm toward Christian as well as Mohammedan miracles. But if the latter is the case, it is difficult to reconcile Updike's purple eloquence at other times, as when he describes a dream:

That Beneficent Being, who brightens the slumbers of the wretched with rays of bliss, can alone express my raptures, when, in the visions of that night, I stepped lightly over a father's threshold; was surrounded by congratulating friends and faithful domestics; was pressed by the embraces of a father; and with holy joy felt a mother's tears moisten my cheek. (II, 72)

It is true that Updike does approach the sarcasm of volume I in most of his description of the pilgrimage — he ridicules the practice of visiting the holy shrines by proxy, the ceremonial connected with the shrines, and the economic motive of the pilgrims. These cynical observations, however, are consistent with his tendency to seek the rational or practical explanation and do not (in conjunction with the sentimental statements of faith) constitute evidence of such impartiality that Christianity could also be ridiculed.

It is more reasonable to see Tyler here casting a few rationalistic doubts about religious extravagances through the less broad-minded attitudes of Updike. Volume II, while perhaps not so intrinsically interesting to an American, does have a form and consistency of its own, for it shows a New Englander trying to report foreign customs accurately and exhibiting his own prejudices in the process. The flaw in *The Algerine Captive* may best be expressed in terms of a satiric shift. In volume I, Updike, though naïve at times, is aware of the stupidities and hypocrisies around him and consciously satirizes them; in volume II, he is still willing to satirize certain things occasionally, but in the main he is explaining unfamiliar customs and in so doing displays his own hypocrisies and becomes the chief satiric object. If it was Tyler's plan, as it presumably was, to expose certain follies in the American scene through the eyes of a shrewd New Englander, and then to reveal the provinciality of the New Englander himself by placing him on a larger stage, it would have been to his advantage to consider the difficulties inherent in changing the stance of the narrator. This is not to say that we are witnessing a different Updike in the two volumes; rather, in volume I, Updike was in with us on a joke from which he seems to be excluded in volume II.[30] The question has to do, not with the plausibility or justice of Updike's portrait as a New Englander, but with the artistic method of producing that portrait. *The Algerine Captive*, quite simply, fails to achieve a unity of tone that would hold both volumes together.

Language

The book is most successful in individual satiric sketches, rather than in the fusion of the whole, and that success is partly accounted for by the skillful handling of language. Irony is the principal device, both verbal and dramatic — sometimes through direct statements of Updike's which are obviously the opposite of what he means, at other times through the contrast between his expectations and actuality. Updike is at one moment the naïve observer, overly impressed with strange customs, and at another the objective historian, whose own bias is clear. Professions of objectivity occur from the beginning. In the second chapter Updike says that he hesitates to present anything which will reflect on his ancestors, but he has "the impartiality of a historian" (I, 43); two chapters later he observes, "I only relate facts, and leave the reader to his own comments" (I, 51). The supposed factual quality of the book is also supported by the frequent recording of detail, as when Thomas Paine appears before Updike "dressed in a snuff coloured coat, olive velvet vest, drab breeches, coarse hose. His shoe buckles of the size of half a dollar" (I, 176).

Another source of irony is the title and the epigraph to each chapter — usually incongruous with the contents. Thus, the chapter describing Updike's unpleasant experience as a schoolmaster is headed with a quotation from Thomson's *Seasons* beginning, "Delightful talk! to rear the tender thought" (volume I, chapter 7); the account of the Harvard museum begins with two lines from Mrs. Barbauld, "A hornet's sting, / And all the wonders of an insect's wing" (volume I, chapter 17); the absurd consultation among the different types of doctors starts with Pope's "For man's relief the healing art was given" (volume I, chapter 21); four lines from Cowper on beauty form the epigraph for the dismal picture of London (volume I, chapter 26); a Biblical verse, "The heaven of heavens cannot contain thee," is placed at the head of the description of Mecca (volume II, chapter 34); and a quotation from Blair's *Grave* adorns "The Infirmary" (volume II, chapter 12). One of the best examples of this technique occurs in chapter 16 of volume I: the epigraph, from *Tristram Shandy*, is "The lady Baussiere rode on," and the title is "Doctor Underhill visiteth Boston, and maketh no Remarks." As one might expect, most of these humorous headings occur in the first volume and, when they are found in the second, come in the less straightforward chapters near the beginning and end. Similarly revealing, there are six quotations from Pope in volume I and only one in volume II, while Shakespeare is called on more in volume II (six times, as compared with three in volume I), and Tyler resorts to verses which he himself has composed (in a serious vein) more frequently in the second volume (nine times; four in volume I).

This interest in playing with language (as well as the familiarity with English poetry) is not unexpected from the author of the "Colon & Spondee" poems and manifests itself not only in the discussion of the Algerines' lingua franca or in the ungrammatical challenge to a duel but in the balancing of sentences and the ability to produce fluent prose on several stylistic levels. There are the oversentimental excesses (laden with adjectives) of some of the references to God and family — these to be placed next to the straightforward, generally unadorned style of the expository chapters, contrasted in turn with the elaborate prose poem which Tyler allows himself as an example of a Mohammedan sermon.[31] On the omniscience of deity, the Mohammedan priest presents Tyler's best metaphorical and balanced style: "Michael, whose wings are full of eyes, is blind before him, the dark night is unto him as the rays of the morning; for he noticeth the creeping of the small pismire in the dark night, upon the black stone, and apprehendeth the motion of an atom in the open air" (II, 174). For a concentrated example of the stylistic devices that make up Tyler's satiric skill, the best choice would be one of the final chapters of volume II, here quoted entire:

Chapter 32
The Author is blessed with the Sight and Touch of a most holy Mahometan Saint
Procul! O procul! este profani. — Virgil
When we were within one day's journey of Medina, we halted for a longer time than usual; occasioned, as I found, by the arrival

of a most holy saint. As I had never seen a saint, being bred, in a land, where even the relics of these holy men are not preserved, for I believe all New England cannot produce so much as a saint's rotten tooth or toe nail, I was solicitous to see and converse with this blessed personage. I soon discovered him, in the midst of about fifty pilgrims, some of whom were devoutly touching their foreheads with the hem of his garment, while others, still more devout, prostrated themselves on the ground, and kissed the prints of his footsteps in the sand. Though I was assured, that he was filled with divine love, and conferred felicity on all, who touched him; yet, to outward appearance, he was the most disgusting, contemptible object, I had ever seen. Figure to yourselves, my readers, a little decrepit, old man, made shorter by stooping, with a countenance, which exhibited a vacant stare, his head bald, his finger and toe nails as long as hawks' claws, his attire squalid, his face, neck, arms, and legs begrimed with dirt and swarming with vermin, and you will have some faint idea of this Mussulman saint. As I was too reasonable to expect that holiness existed in a man's exteriour, I waited to hear him speak; anticipating, from his lips, the profoundest wisdom, delivered in the honied accents of the saints in bliss. At length he spake; and his speech betrayed him, a mere idiot. While this astonished me, it raised the respect of his admirers, who estimated his sanctity in an inverse ratio to the weakness of his intellects. If they could have ascertained, that he was born an idiot, I verily believe, they would have adored him; for the Mahometans are taught by their alcoran, that the souls of saints are often lodged in the bodies of idiots; and these pious souls, being so intent on the joys of paradise, is the true reason, that the actions of their bodies are so little suited to the manners of this world. This saint however did not aspire to the sanctity of a genuine idiot; though, I fancy, his modesty injured his preferment, for he certainly had very fair pretensions. It was resolved, that the holy man should go with us; and, to my great mortification and disgust, he was mounted behind me on the same camel; my Mahometan friends probably conceiving, that he would so far communicate his sanctity by contact, as that it might affect my conversion to their faith. Whatever were their motives, in the embraces of this nauseous being, with the people prostrating themselves in reverence on each side, I made my entry into the city of Medina.

Here one finds the matter-of-fact pose, the specificity of detail, the exaggeration, the incongruity, and the solemnity of logic misapplied that give satire its richest double meanings. Occasional flaws in syntax (as in the first and ninth sentences) do not obscure the control in diction and structure of the whole movement, ending with an appealing flourish in the final periodic sentence.

A passage of this sort indicates both the strengths and the weaknesses of *The Algerine Captive*. The merits of the book are found in such individual sketches, which rarely fail to be amusing and effective, but the work seems less impressive when viewed as an artistic entity. Tyler's very skill in the restricted form of journalistic squibs was perhaps his undoing in the longer form. At any rate, *The Algerine Captive* can hardly be called a novel, except in the sense that it is a narrative recounting fictitious incidents. The whole intent of the work, from its preface to its final patriotic paragraph, is nonartistic. Tyler, a true Federalist and devout Christian, is writing to impress upon his readers the advantages of their new government and the greater importance of inner faith than of ritual. He does find a metaphorical approach useful at times, but the mixture it creates is at the heart of the dissatisfaction which a modern reader must feel about the structure of the book. Updike is Tyler's mask, but without the dimensions of a real character (he is never described physically); he is the mouthpiece for certain ideas, but the way in which that mouthpiece operates in volume II (with the exception of a few passages like the one just quoted) is different from its mode of operation in volume I. The factual material about the Algerines in volume II is not in itself inappropriate, since it becomes the vehicle for Tyler's indirect exposure of provinciality; but neither is it the basis for a coherent metaphorical structure, like the cetological information in *Moby-Dick*. It would be foolish to search for a symbolic reading of

The Algerine Captive, with Updike, "lost . . . and now found" as he says at the end, charting the course to spiritual rebirth after a trial of faith and a dark night of the soul. The subjects of freedom and slavery — political, spiritual, and physical — do unite the material of the book; but the embracing context of direct exhortation prevents a final dramatic unity. While the value of the book as a historical and literary document is not disputed, there is no reason to be patronizing about its artistic qualities either. Its quaintness is of slight importance compared to the firmness of mind inherent in it, the realism of its approach, and the undeniable skill of which it gives evidence if not fulfillment.

❧ VI ❧

Essayist

IF Tyler had completed all the works he planned, the proportion of nonfiction prose in his output would be considerably larger than it is, for most of his projected writings fall into this category. In addition, Tyler of necessity did a great deal of writing in the course of his profession, and his legal reports and transcripts of jury charges add to the bulk of his prose writings, though they can hardly be classed as literary essays. His speeches, like the Washington oration in 1800, are only extensions of his role as lawyer and public servant, as are his contributions to official documents of the University of Vermont, the "Laws and Regulations," for example, which he and William C. Bradley drew up on 28 July 1811.[1] Further, certain ideas which he mentioned to publishers grew out of his professional interests; he wrote to Isaac Riley in 1810 to suggest the publication of an "American Law Dictionary," which he had been compiling for some time.[2] Other ideas, not directly related to law, reveal his love of learning and of factual information; he approached Joseph Nancrede in 1800 with a proposal for a "Cosmography," which, he said, he had thought about for such a long time that it was almost written.[3]

One unfinished prose work, which missed completion by only a slim margin, was entitled "The Touchstone, or a Humble Modest Inquiry into the Nature of Religious Intolerance." In 1817 the well-known printer Simeon Ide, of

Brattleboro, began setting this tract in type before Tyler had finished writing it. When, by 26 January 1818, Tyler had not yet furnished the complete copy, Ide drew up a formal agreement, which Tyler signed, whereby Tyler agreed to provide copy for a seventy-two-page work by 4 March, or else pay Ide twelve dollars to cover the cost of the paper already used. It seems likely that Tyler never completed the work, for no copy of the book can be located, and the only copy which has ever been noted in print was an incomplete one of thirty-six pages. What Tyler had to say about religious intolerance in 1817, then, must remain conjectural.[4]

That Tyler esteemed these serious works more highly than his lighter and more "literary" productions is suggested in one of his letters to Nancrede about some children's tales he had written: the only reason for publishing the tales, he says, is to make his name better known before the "Cosmography" appears. These "Moral Tales for American Youth" were a series of stories intended to amuse and instruct at the same time; according to Tyler, nothing of the kind had been produced in America, though many such books had been imported from England. The work contained a story about Dr. Franklin and his mother, "A Philosophical Experiment"; a Green Mountain tale entitled "Home"; a story about a "tub woman," adapted from a British magazine; a parable illustrating the folly of believing gossip and of embroidering the truth — and so on.[5] Dennie wrote enthusiastically in 1797, "Vose has read your 'Moral Romances;' and, he assures me, it rendered a gloomy and snowy Fast day pleasant, He declares it more uniformly pure than Updike, and, in elegance, greatly its superior. For myself, I have always assured you of the sure and certain hope of popularity & profit."[6]

With such encouragement Tyler envisioned a large sale for the book and even planned further volumes to take advantage of the same market, "a little library," as he called it. The second volume would contain dialogues reminiscent of Berquin and character studies like those of La Bruyère and Theophrastus; the third would be a "Comic Grammar," in which the rules were to be illustrated not only by entertaining quotations from authors of the past but by amusing stories of Tyler's own invention which would bring the meaning home to a child. In describing the idea to Nancrede, Tyler explains that he once had to teach grammar to a young lady reluctant to study:

I accordingly wrote a grammar in *usum puellae*, and being forwarded in twelve letters, folded as billet doux, she condescended to read. . . . A lover at the feet of his mistress, gave a passionate example of interjection; a lady crowned her favored lover's virtuous wishes in the passive voice, and dismissed an unsucessful admirer in the imperative mood. Thus every rule of syntax was associated with some pleasing anecdote, brilliant quotation, or quaint observation, which familiarized the stubborn rule to a mind open only to the amusing and pleasing.[7]

Tyler perhaps anticipated modern educational ideas; certainly his plans for books took a practical and utilitarian direction.

On the question of publishing the "Moral Tales," Tyler had some difficulties with Nancrede. In a fascinating series of letters,[8] which reveal the kind of bargaining that took place between author and publisher in 1800, Nancrede argued that he expected a work twice as long and that he could not pay $200 for one hundred pages which cost the author "eight days' amusement." He claimed on 7 March, however, that the work had gone to press, but it is unlikely that the negotiations were ever straightened out sufficiently for the printing to be completed; at least, no copy of the book is known to exist today. Tyler sent three more stories in an attempt to lengthen the work, but he emphasized that he was not primarily a writer. "You certainly misconceived me," he had written on 14 February, "if you concluded that I was anyways anxious to have the work published. . . . So far from this, it is with [a] great degree of reluctance I have consented to its publication." The most significant part of the letter may stand as a remarkable summary of Tyler's entire position as a writer:

I have a profession, and my abilities in the exercise of it in this wooden world are esteemed above mediocrity. This profession affords me the comforts and conveniences of life, for myself and family; and I have learned that great secret of felicity to find enjoyment at home. From certain disgusts perhaps uncharitably admitted, I had renounced the ambition of authorship. Your charming plausibility drew me from my retreat and made me willing — not anxious — to write again for the press. I rely upon your uprightness; and am ready to believe that what you offer is all that you can afford to give for this little work: but if writing for the public is attended with no more profit, I had rather file legal process in my attorney's office, and endeavor to explain unintelligible law to Green Mountain jurors; and when the *cacoethes scribendi* assails me, I will write sonnets to rustic loves, and tales for children; and look for my reward in the exhilarating smiles of partial friends round my own fireside.

Tyler had stated the case eloquently, not only for himself, but for many others as well. Literature, in the United States of 1800, was not a profession, and one wrote, when the urge came, between the rounds of business.

Periodical Essays

In a day when newspapers and magazines were filled with Addisonian essays, it is inevitable that Tyler, as a member of an informal club of writers and a facile versifier, should have tried his hand at light essays. The problem of determining just which ones he wrote, however, is even more difficult than in the case of the newspaper verse. Since prose was generally Dennie's province in the "Colon & Spondee" partnership,[9] the attribution to Tyler of particular essays under this heading requires especially strong evidence. In point of fact, Tyler probably wrote a sizable number of these essays, just as Dennie contributed poems from time to time (signed "C." in the early columns). But the graceful, polished style and the ubiquitous allusions to English literature do not serve to distinguish between the prose of the two men, and it is probable that some essays result from a collaboration of both, given the conditions of composition in Crafts Tavern and the pressures of the printer's deadlines. The safest course, therefore, is to take the few pieces linked to Tyler by contemporary evidence and allow them to serve as examples of his work in the informal periodical essay.

Tyler's prose contributions to the *Farmer's Museum* ranged from short notes — largely puns, anecdotes, and quotations — to brief paragraphs and essays for the "Colon & Spondee" column, according to the annotations which Joseph Dennie made in a copy of *The Spirit of the Farmers' Museum* (1801).[10] Most of his topics are predictable: quack doctors, the law, the Bible, fashions, language. He wrote "Colon & Spondee" essays with such headings as "Fine Comb Points," "Between You and I," "State of Literature in England and America, at Different Periods," and "Oilnut, or Butternut." [11] On one occasion he satirized the handbooks which oversimplify complex material by announcing a similar work for children, to be called "The Pap of Science; or, Goody B——'s Nursery Gift"; its contents, with nursery rhymes under such divisions as "Geographical Lullabies," "Cypher Candy," "Biographical Bon Bon," and "Political Sugar Plumb," recall Tyler's plans for a comic grammar.[12] Of the twenty-six "Colon & Spondee" essays in the *Spirit*, Dennie credits Tyler with fifteen, and, if the selection is at all representative, he may have written even more of the prose than is usually thought. But the sample is large enough to show that these pieces, sufficiently entertaining for space-fillers in a newspaper, do not represent Tyler's satire at its height.

Although most of Tyler's essays seem to have been literary in content, the Hall files of the *Port Folio* attribute one political satire to him.[13] Entitled "Logic," [14] it begins by announcing that "those profound logicians, Colon and Spondee," deny the effectiveness of majority rule in carrying out the will of the people. The position is not an unlikely one for a Federalist, but the ensuing argument shows that Tyler's wit transcended party lines. He "proves" in four ways that the minority should always prevail: from reason (fools make up the bulk of mankind); from experience (witness the blunders of British ministers); from expediency (the masses of men could then stay out of public affairs and tend to their own business); and from religion (only the few are to be saved, the majority damned). The essay, like others of this class, involves a triple satiric mask: the writer is seemingly serious; he constructs his argument to reveal that he is after all being playful; but there is point to the playfulness, and he does mean part of what he says.

Tyler's other prose contributions to the *Port Folio*,[15] according to the Hall files, are three essays in early 1802 in the "Colon & Spondee" series called "An Author's Evenings." [16] This series was designed (partly as a filler) to accommodate random remarks on literary figures of the past, usually accompanied with copious quotations from their works. It had begun, under the "Colon & Spondee" rubric, in the *Farmer's Weekly Museum* in 1799, and Dennie continued it for several years in the *Port Folio*. Like the "Colon & Spondee" label, it inspired imitations and parodies, such as "An Author's Moonlight Nights, from the Garret of Messrs. Lunatic and Lumbago." [17] Tyler begins his column for 21 January 1802 in the spirit of the title: "To night, after my return from the theatre, into which I sometimes saunter, to smooth the wrinkles of my brow, to surrender myself to the illusions of imagination, and derive fresh spirits for my lucubrations, I could not help reflecting. . . ." And he launches into a discussion of the "new pantomime of *Obi*," which leads into reflections on the power of magic over men's minds, references to a related magazine article, quotations from Jonson's *Masque of Queens* and from *Macbeth*, and a comparison of sorcerers' charms in different cultures.

This literary wandering is repeated on 27 February when he first quotes an "exquisite" poem from a British magazine, then quotes British critics on the subject of Sir William Jones, and finally gives a prose translation by W. Ouseley of an ode of Hafiz. He pays attention to diction and parallelism in prose no less than in poetry: Jones, he says, had the good fortune "to resist the sleep of sloth and withstand the blandishments of pleasure." Tyler also comments in this essay that he is "too laboriously engaged in *reading* poetry to have any leisure to combine a couplet." In the third of these essays (on 15 May), he is prompted, by taking up a volume of Chesterfield, to consider the usefulness of proverbs and to lament their current lack of fashion. He points out many parallels between ideas in Chesterfield and old adages and ends with a final thrust at Chesterfield: "Much more might be added, but the printer's boy calls, and I much fear, by tracing the sentiments of this polite writer to so unfashionable a source, I may destroy that relish for his works, which gives the true zest to most of his readers." As in *The Contrast*, Chesterfield represents the extreme of vicious artificiality, Tyler's perennial subject of attack, whether it occurs in the Della Cruscans or in the courtroom.

One other series of essays, under the title of "Trash," Tyler contributed to Buckingham's *Polyanthos* in 1806 and 1807.[18] In his opening column, he explains the title of this "department" as inspired by a friend who bound miscellaneous sermons and pamphlets together and labeled the spine "Trash":

Those who are too wise, grave, and learned to be *amused*, when they see my *title*, may pass my humble lucubrations — they can regale themselves on the *ripened* fruits of science; but there are many, who may wish to cheer the gloom of a stormy evening, or relieve the tedium of busy life, with what may relax without tainting the mind; and such may have a relish for TRASH.

The amusement which he offers is not without a satiric bite. After commenting on the habit of giving scriptural names to babies and after quoting an English and Latin poem signed "B.," he turns to current stage pronunciation. His own "Yankee utterance," he claims, has been "wonderfully corrected in various important particulars" during his attendance at the theater, and he composes a poem in which he attempts through spelling to "delineate the elegant tones of our more polished players." The ensuing thirty-six lines, "Love Varses to the Bucheous Daffodel," have a glossary "for the benefit of the *unlearned* reader," explaining such words as *ajore* ("adore") and *churn* ("turn").

The other "Trash" columns proceed in the same rambling way. The second is a poem, "The Town Eclogue," but the third and fourth are again essays. They illustrate Tyler's familiarity with English literature, for in the third he draws on Chaucer, Drayton, and Shakespeare as he attempts to construct realistic and unsentimental portraits of Jane Shore and Edward IV; in the fourth he surveys famous riddles of the past and quotes Wyatt's "Riddle of a Gyft by a Ladie." There is very little explicit literary criticism here, but occasionally Tyler does express a judgment, as when he comments that "Drayton seldom rises above mediocrity as a poet, and these epistles [to Jane Shore] are not among the most excellent of his labours." The most revealing passage occurs in the fourth "Trash" essay, in which Tyler recalls that Dr. Johnson found certain lines without rhyme in Dryden's Cecilia ode:

Now this is the case with all of us when we set down to criticise. We are forced to discover some defects in order to evidence that we have some penetration. But yet, great as the Doctor is, I, who am an enthusiastick admirer of the Ode, would no more thank him for his discovery, than I would the officious person who should approach me at dinner, and point out something disgusting in my favourite dish. At the literary feast, I wish to cater for myself, and an austere, captious critick is as disagreeable to me as the Physician in Don Quixotte was to Sancho Pancha, when he criticised away the best viands from the table of that governour in the island of Barataria.

Using the dining metaphor (with its allusion to the subject of his *Barrataria* play), Tyler sets forth "the acknowledged triumph of publick taste over the fastidiosity of referred criticism."

This attitude — as well as all the other elements of Tyler's newspaper essays: the random associations, the literary allusions, the graceful but detached manner — is suggestive of the gentleman who dabbles in literature, the littérateur rather than the writer. But Tyler's love of literature was real, his acquaintance with it extensive, and his concern for its standards sincere; the gentlemanly approach did not preclude satiric attacks on patent absurdities like the Della Cruscans, and the "publick taste" that would triumph was to be an informed one. For Tyler, like Dennie and other serious writers of newspaper prose, the Addisonian manner lent dignity to a calling that was not highly regarded in a new country; they could not avoid being artificial in that sense, but the basic integrity of their efforts, at the same time, was laying the foundations for an authentic native tradition.

The Yankey in London

The Yankey in London, a small volume of 180 pages printed in New York by Isaac Riley, appeared in early October 1809. Like *The Algerine Captive,* the book was issued not only anonymously but under a mask — in this case concealing Tyler even from his publisher. Throughout the spring and summer of 1809 Tyler was in correspondence with Riley about the first volume of the Vermont *Reports*, and he casually mentioned another work which he could procure; in June he sent it:

Captain Holbrook will communicate the work I mentioned some time since. He is instructed and empowered to agree with you on the terms of publication. The copy sent will, I am sensible, make but a small book; but, from the preface, you will learn it may be enlarged. The present object of those concerned is merely to feel the public pulse, by the publication of a small edition. If the thing takes, it can be extended to any size: and even the present edition, if you should so agree with Captain Holbrook, can be enlarged by a few more letters; say, ten or fifteen more pages of the manuscript. The remainder of the letters are not in Vermont, but can be commanded. To give it currency among the class of readers who will most probably purchase, the edition must be elegantly edited. If you cannot agree upon terms, I have every reliance on your word, that any concern I may have in ushering this little work into public notice, through the medium of some other press, will be scrupulously concealed.[19]

Riley pushed the work through the press ahead of the *Reports* and wrote optimistically to Tyler on 7 October:

By the mail I send you one copy of "The Yankee in London" hastily put up. Some, more handsomely bound, I shall forward soon. . . . I have to ask you to aid me in procuring the future Letters to make a more enlarged edition. I did not print but few of this, merely to get it into notice. I believe the work will have a good sale: it is however but this week before the public.[20]

The following spring, when Tyler had further ideas to suggest to Riley, he included in his letter a comment on the book: "I am exceedingly pleased with the elegant impression of the Yankee, but can say nothing as to another edition until the beginning of July, when I will write you on the subject."[21]

The secret seems to have been kept better than with Tyler's other writings, for even a Brattleboro friend, William Wells, was completely fooled, thinking that the book was an authentic account of a visit to England.[22] Tyler's wife, however, in her reminiscences, openly asserted her husband's authorship.[23]

The mask, intricate enough in Tyler's dealings with Riley, was preserved throughout the book, which becomes a kind of parody of the Tocqueville tradition of travel writing. Giving no hints, the title page merely reads, "By an American Youth." A preface, signed "The Friends of the Writer," purports to explain that the author is "a native of Boston, in Massachusetts, known to his fellow-townsmen as a young man of modest merit, and only known to a few particular friends as a gentleman of an active and inquisitive mind, and of quaint, and ofttimes original remark." He has supposedly written a series of letters from London which these "friends" have persuaded him to consent to have published, "upon the express condition of expunging such passages as might lead to a discovery of the author." The "friends" give the impression that, out of a large number of letters, the present ones have been selected so as not to offend the English; but they hope that "the approbation of the public will give confidence to our friend to publish the remainder of his letters" under his own name, and they label the collection "Volume I" (causing librarians, ever since, to stamp the card "No more published").

The pretense is even more elaborately carried out by choosing random numbers to identify the letters, suggesting that many have been left out in the intervals. Consisting of thirteen letters, the book begins with "Letter III" and ends with "Letter XLV." All but one are addressed to a friend named Frank (see pp. 27, 28, 48, 64, 150), usually referred to as "My excellent Friend," and the remaining one, on fashions in clothing, is directed to his sister. There are allusions to an Amelia (pp. 98, 99, 132), who is presumably his sweetheart, and memories of his home at Brookline (pp. 85–86). He is established as a character, whose personality reveals itself in the course of the letters as intelligent, patriotic, and somewhat naïve — not unlike Updike Underhill, though the author of these letters rarely seems to be the object of Tyler's satire, as Updike sometimes was. A final element of the mask is the appearance of editorial ellipses: proper names are given with asterisks, and, at the end of Letter XLII, there appears a note in brackets (signed "The Editors"), to the effect that "it was deemed expedient to omit" the remainder of this letter, since it "contained certain pointed observations" on English political figures (p. 143).

The epistolary device permits Tyler to write individual essays on a wide range of subjects and yet achieve unity and dramatic interest through the cumulative reactions of his letter writer. The book is sometimes classified as a novel since there is a main character visiting London and writing to a friend about it; but there is no further plot, and the emphasis of the work — a direct, not a metaphorical, exposition of ideas — is such that the more meaningful label is "essay." A quick glance at the sequence of chapters suggests the diversity of materials. Letter III discusses traits of the English character and literary fashions, followed by two (V and VIII) on the Houses of Parliament and one (XI) on English biographical writing. This leads, in Letter XIX, to the subject of books and etymology; Letter XX returns to the House of Commons, with remarks on the merits of seriousness. The next two letters deal with fashions — in clothing (XXIII) and in language (XXX) — and the following two with deception (literary forgery in XXXIII and quacks in XLII). Finally there are further strictures on the English character (XLIII), on travelers (XLIV), and on the English language (XLV).

The unity of the book comes not only through the constant presence of the letter writer but through his interest in two dominant concerns. In the vein of *The Contrast* and *The Algerine Captive*, every subject discussed in *The Yankey in London* contributes directly or by implication to two propositions: first, that America is a glorious place, with a proud heritage and a promising future; second, that hypocrisy and artifice irrationally govern the lives of many supposedly rational beings. The satirist's exposure of man's folly is again joined with the patriot's desire to improve his country. English habits and institutions are compared unfavorably with those of Americans; and the existence of quacks, of slang, and of rapidly shifting fashions is testimony to the sway of artificiality over naturalness. Letter VIII could perhaps furnish the motto: "let us, my friend, endeavour to guard against the delusions of forms, and look to the essence of that national liberty for which our fathers successfully fought" (p. 45).

Rarely does the application to the United States have to be inferred. When a London bookseller discovers that the author can quote the classics, he is prompted to observe that "the country of Franklin, Adams, and Jefferson, must produce scientific men. Sir, you were born in a new world; every thing there evinces the vigour of youth; Europe, sir, I fear, is in her dotage. — You have withstood our arms, and, I fear, will soon rival us in the arts and sciences" (p. 72). The patriotism is broad enough to encompass England as part of the American heritage; yet current practices in the British government make one ashamed: "I felt the dignity of my nature violated. I felt more — I remembered I was of English descent, and I blushed for the land of my ancestors" (pp. 27–28). This patriotism, however, should not be blind; it is natural, the author says, to be patriotic, but there are proper limits, and English vanity goes beyond them in assuming that people in all other countries must be wretched. He takes his illustration from the weather: the English are proud of their climate (which, to an American, "presents, every day, an apology for suicide"), but a bright, sunny American day "is one of those few common blessings which the Bostonians have sensibility to relish" (pp. 157–158). To argue that the superiority of America extends even to its atmospheric conditions may suggest that the letter writer has a touch of the national vanity he is condemning; but he is generally frank in acknowledging America's faults and here implies that Americans often do not have the perception to recognize their strengths.

As one might expect, the British government is one of his prime examples to show, by contrast, the superiority of the United States. Letter V, describing his visit to the House of Commons, provides one of the best instances of the naïve approach. "I justly expected," he says, "to find the talents, the learning, the wisdom and political science of a wise nation collected in one brilliant focus" (p. 18), but he is disappointed. When he overhears one member say, in reference to a horse race, "Creeper against Sweeper, feather weight," he reacts with a characteristic comic device: "I was so simple that, at first, I thought the learned Creeper might have written a commentary on Smith's wealth of nations, and that the erudite Sweeper had illustrated Dr. Price's essay on finance, by the negative quantities of algebra. *Feather weight*, I naturally concluded, alluded to the balance of power in Europe" (p. 20). His uncertainty "whether to laugh or weep" is repeated when he gets to the House of Lords (Letter VIII), where he also manifests a certain objectivity about American institutions. Although the idea of a hereditary legislature contains "something essentially ludicrous to the mind of a republican" (p. 35), a hereditary court (the Lords were judging a case at the time) "might provoke the risibility of even

Littleton himself": "This baronial bench seemed to me even more absurd than the court of errors in the state of Connecticut, where the council of that state, composed generally of plain farmers, correct the judgments of their supreme court, composed of men of the first legal talents" (pp. 35–36). This is a natural point of view for Tyler the lawyer, but he has his letter writer recommend such a common-sense court for England, where an exaggerated respect for precedents and forms is destroying the spirit of the common law, the Britons' "richest legacy, to their posterity" (p. 45). When his correspondent objects that he has been too harsh, he replies (Letter XX) that the frivolity and facetiousness found in the House of Commons are never among the qualities of great men; decorum and gravity are the essential marks of greatness, and for proof he has only to point to the dignified group of men who produced the American Declaration of Independence (p. 81).

If the British government deserves criticism, so do the British national traits, but again not without some penetrating comments on the American character. The author remarks, in his opening letter (III), on British "national reserve and hauteur," shyness, and class consciousness (pp. 4–6), but proceeds as usual to make the comparison with America explicit:

> The difference between the English and their American descendants, in this particular, is — the Englishman is shy and suspicious, grows more suspicious, and is surly. The New-England man is suspicious and inquisitive, grows more suspicious, and is familiar and troublesome. When once the Englishman's suspicions are dissipated (no matter how) he is unbounded in his confidence; while the Yankey shews very little distrust, is never silent or surly to the stranger, but his suspicions never leave him. (p. 6)

Vanity, however, is the most prominent trait applicable to all classes in England (Letter XLIII), and government is "the

gas which inflates the full-blown bladder of English vanity"
— a government, based on "commercial aggrandizement,"
with laws too complex to guide behavior and with a criminal
code so harsh that it "violates the moral sense of justice"
(p. 154). Despite these weaknesses, the English expect all
other countries to see the superior merits of their form of
government and imagine that other countries cannot win
battles without their support. One Englishman, proud of
Britain's "dense and sombre" fogs, was made ill by Boston's
clear weather and had to shut himself in a room with a damp
coal fire (p. 160). This vanity is also seen in such phrases as
"English courage," but Tyler's writer finds "English bull
dogs" the most apt illustration. The trait, he says, leads to
prejudice against foreigners and the association of certain
habits with particular nations.

The generalizing in this letter has been doing that very
thing — classifying a nationality; but the letter writer explains
that he would not be above the level of the English traveler
if he had intended all his comments seriously. This awkward
conclusion to Letter XLIII raises more problems than it
solves, for the contradiction, obviously, is still there. Either
Tyler is engaging in subtle irony at the expense of his letter
writer; or he is identifying himself with the letter writer at
the cost of the logic and forcefulness of his argument. Here
is the same confusion in the use of a persona that came up in
The Algerine Captive. But part of the irony directed at Updike was based on his behavior in various episodes, as he reported it; in the present instance one has only the comments,
not the behavior, to look at, for the letter writer tells us not
what he has done but only what he thinks. Since his opinions
at most times are straightforward expressions of Tyler's own,
there is no reason, in the context of the book, for not accept-
ing at face value these closing remarks in Letter XLIII. The
letter writer says that he has made friends among the English

and that England does have things to be proud of. Tyler no doubt imagined that a show of broadmindedness would strengthen his other criticisms; but, having created a mask, he at least opened the possibility for a moment that he was also exposing American narrowmindedness.

The subject of national traits leads to the third major topic of the book — fashions — when we are told that one of the Englishman's desires is not only national glory but individual glory. He attempts to achieve personal distinction by adopting eccentricities, which eventually are imitated by others. One man "cut off the skirts of his coat, close to his waistband, and set the fashion you now have in Boston, called the spencer," while another *"eat a live cat"* (p. 9). The principal discussion of fashion, in Letter XXIII, emphasizes its changeability and unnaturalness. The writer predicts that, if he should attempt to describe the current styles, the information would be obsolete by the time the letter arrived; but such changes are essential since many people's incomes depend on them. Fashions pass down from the upper classes to the lower, and then to the United States; when a manufacturer wants to revive something, he persuades the royal family to wear it and it becomes common. This entire diatribe is part of a larger concern with artificiality, and chief among the criticisms of fashion is that it seems unrelated to beauty and to climate. Tyler's gift for comic elaboration helps him to explain the appearance of a modish, but excessively thin, shawl by comparing it to wet drapery in statuary, at the same time pointing out the dearth of statuary in America:

Next washing-day, if you will quit your piano-forte and follow Betty into the clothes'-yard, and direct her to cover one of the old red posts with muslin dripping from the wash-tub, you will have a distinct idea of wet drapery, and, if you have the eye of a connoisseur, will certainly notice that, although the post is completely enveloped, yet, none of the beauties of its fine form are lost. (p. 92)

Fashion is the "conqueror of decorum, modesty, beauty, and health," and the letter writer tells his sister that she could come to London dressed as an Indian and "set the fashion at court." He has had some suits sent to her, along with "a turban or cap which, as it is very gaudy, very odd, and extremely homely, I conclude must be very fashionable" (p. 99). As a parting thought, he cautions her, when wearing the new clothes, not to expose herself to the evening air, "especially after dancing."

There are fashions in all things, not merely clothing, and in every case they result from a thoughtless preference for the artificial over the natural. Quacks of all kinds (Letter XLII) flourish by appealing to man's irrationality, and in England "the belief in panaceas is a national weakness" (p. 133). For example, there are mechanical quacks who insist, "with grave effrontery," that their arms and legs are superior to natural ones and are so eloquent that they "had almost persuaded me to submit to amputation" (p. 139). One manufacturer of glass eyes asserts that "they excel the natural in displaying the finer and nobler emotions of the soul" (p. 136), and cites the testimonial of a man who met his wife through the attraction to such eyes:

[He was] peculiarly impressed with the fascinating glances of her brilliant eyes: upon after acquaintance, although he was not insensible to the expression and good sense which beamed from her right eye, yet, the mild serenity of the left gave such happy presage of that suavity of temper which promised a plenteous harvest of conjugal peace. (pp. 137–138)

Tyler is unrelenting in his ridicule of affectation, whether it is Dimple worshiping Chesterfield, the Bishop of Cloyne drinking tar-water, or a West Indian praising his cork leg. There are even culinary quacks, and a cookbook by John Perkins, linking alphabetically foods and diseases ("Apple-pye and Asthma," "Pickles and Piles," "Ragouts and Rheumatism"),

Tyler's letter writer wittily imagines to be "an ethical work, exhibiting the dreadful consequences of a life devoted to intemperance" (p. 142). But the evils of affectation are not overlooked when they occur in an American, and the brief Letter XLIV exposes the folly of a young Bostonian in London, dressed in the latest fashions, spending a great deal of money, and visiting all the tourist attractions ("he went to see a man who eat himself, but found this was a joke," p. 169). This young man is important enough, as an illustration of the superficiality of most travelers, that he is referred to again (spending his money) in the final lines of the book, a postscript to the last letter.

A fourth main topic of the volume — language and literature — perhaps bulks largest and is by no means unrelated to the question of fashion. There are literary quacks (forgers and perpetrators of hoaxes); there are slang phrases adopted by everyone as the proper things to say; there are styles of writing, decidedly not natural, which make their authors popular. Enough is said on these subjects here, even if we did not have the satire in *The Contrast*, *The Algerine Captive*, and the newspaper poetry, that we should still know where Tyler stands on literary questions. His position emerges obliquely from the cynical discussion of literary "larceny" in Letter XXXIII. After relating the stories of Chatterton, Ireland, and Ossian, he asks why, if they had such genius of imitation, they are not honored. These men, he says, were more modest than Michaelangelo, since he revealed his imitation of classic work; but literature is a trade in England, and the English do not want to admit that their great writers can be equaled. Furthermore, "as most of their modern books are made up by plagiarisms from old works, the English book-makers are admirably qualified to detect literary fraud" (p. 126). After this double irony, he turns, still with tongue in cheek, to "our happy land," where Americans "prize books, as the principles of our excellent republican government teach us to value men, not for their origin but their intrinsic merit" (p. 132).

Tyler's interest in writing manifests itself throughout his work in a concern with language, and his keen observation of linguistic habits appears again and again in *The Yankey in London*.[24] He tries to record dialect (p. 39) and observes several differences in diction between England and New England (pp. 104–109); he remarks on phrases like "certain people" (p. 7), "smoked the quiz" (p. 141), and "Yankey" — a corruption of "Yorkshire," as pronounced by the Indians (p. 75) — in letters that are otherwise not on linguistic subjects. But two letters in particular, XXX and XLV, show that Tyler gave a good deal of serious thought to language. At first glance they seem to contradict one another. The first attacks current slang phrases as "*scoria* floating on the English language" (p. 101) and deplores the fact that "there are a number of words now familiar, not merely in transient converse, but even in English fine writing, which are of vulgar origin and illegitimate descent, which disgust an admirer of the writers of their Augustan age, and degrade their finest modern compositions by a grotesque air of pert vivacity" (p. 103). Among such words, the most objectionable is "clever," "not derived from those pure and rich sources which have given all that is valuable in the English language." To set against this prescriptive attitude are the sentiments of Letter XLV:

Indeed, the perfectibility of language is as ridiculous as the perfectibility of man. Language, as pertaining to man, partakes of the laws of our nature: it is ever changing; it has the incoherency and simplicity of youth, the vigour of manhood, and the decline and decrepitude of old age. This has been its fate in all ages: it has begun in barbarism; had its age of elegance and refinement, and became nerveless and weak. (p. 175)

Here are the rudiments of a scientific approach to language, not disentangled from prescriptive considerations. Though modern linguists would not agree with Tyler that his own period represented a "decline" in language, they could join him in pointing out the futility of national academies and in saying, "New discoveries will call for new terms to express novel ideas" (p. 177). Tyler is aware of the way in which language changes (even if his discussion is occasionally confused), and his earlier strictures on slang are more concerned with the slavish and unthinking repetition of fashionable phrases than with an attempt to keep language "pure" — directed more at warning writers to avoid clichés than constructing a theory of language.

His comments on language are part of his argument against artificiality and are related to matters of literary taste. One of the marks of the deplorable taste of the English, according to the letter writer, is the kind of biography they currently produce (Letter XI). He believes that lives of great men should be instructive and inspiring; he admires Dr. Burnet's account of the Earl of Rochester because every sentence is a "homily" (p. 53). Recent biographies, however, follow their subjects in their most trivial daily activities, reveal their infirmities, and are "not only disreputable to the subjects of them but injurious to the cause of virtue" (p. 56). One might guess that "the lives of most of the eminent men in England were written by their valets, or rather by their grooms or scullions" (p. 54); it is as if West, instead of painting William III mounted on his horse, had chosen to show him in his water closet with a bellyache: "Oh, it is vile! it is descending from the dignity of the biographer, to expose the infirmities of the wise for the gratification of the idle; to patch the venerable garb of wisdom with the motley of Harlequin, and hold it forth as a laughing stock for folly" (p. 58). Dr. Johnson, the writer continues, set the fashion for such "gossiping biography" and has now been paid back with three of the same kind written about him, the one with the largest amount of irrelevant material being Boswell's. The *Gentleman's Magazine* also furnishes an illustration of the trivial when it publishes the life of a man who "was remarkable for having never used but one pen during this period [of forty years], which was made of a gray goose-quill" (p. 62). This moralistic theory of biography therefore condemns the memoirs of prostitutes and suggests that prosecution of the printers of "these apologies for pollution" makes more sense than the imprisonment of those who publish pamphlets against the ministry, since their crime, "in the next administration, may be considered a virtue" (p. 66).

Such a remark shows that, however much Tyler approved of the didactic in biography, his major concern was with the devastating effects of fashion on taste and discrimination. His most energetic efforts were always, as in the satiric poetry, directed against the sentimentalists, the Della Cruscans, and the structure of fashion that supported them. "I ask for elegant wit," he says in Letter XLV, "and they hand me Peter Pindar — I inquire for sublimity, and they present me Della Crusca" (p. 179). This is placed at the end of the book to recall the reader to a brilliant passage at the beginning that sums up the criticism, social as well as literary, of the whole work:

Then, my dear Chum, if you wish an introduction, carry with you no letter of civility, but hasten to your ink-pot, tag me a hundred lines to some languishing Anna Matilda, or dying Dorinda; spangle them well with bland metaphors and love-lorn similies; drop a word or two in some lines, and insert others in capital letters, so as to render the meaning unintelligible, and then, of course, you know it must be sublime: or write a lugubrious sonnet to some captive mouse, or pretty pathetic ode to a sportive mouser,

Essayist

Who on the bosom of the spangled eve,
With velvet step and deeply dulcet breath,
PURS for his attic love! —

select some sweet fanciful name . . . such as Valentina Orsona,
Assenella Crusca, or Idiotilla, or any other name more significant
of the attributes of your muse; carry the soft effusions of your
melancholy muse to the editors of the most fashionable magazine;
and, after you have *love-lorned* enough to make a little volume of
verse, publish your works, boldly, under your own name . . .
and then inscribe your volume to the honourable, or right honourable, Mrs. ———, the patroness of some blue-stocking club,
beginning your dedication thus: — "Madam, your exalted genius,
correct taste, and elegant knowledge of ancient and modern
learning, so richly displayed in that incomparable poem, your
devine ode to the sleeping Cicada," &c. &c. &c. . . . Then, if you
are not the most unfortunate wight of a poet who ever attempted
the temple of fame, you will be invited to the club, be enrolled as
a member, and, perhaps, have your name immortalized in the
next Ladies' Day. (pp. 12–14)

The reader is provided at the outset with a frame of reference,
a set of values, and all the succeeding letters fall in place. The
arrangement of material may seem casual, as it should in a
book of letters, but a plan is there.

When one reads of wits as "the cicada of literature, who
chirp away the summer and starve in the winter of life" (p.
79), the word "cicada" has taken on added associations from
the opening passage; and when one hears a politician "point
out this defective plank in the vessel of the commonwealth,
and drag from their lurking-holes those pestiferous worms
who are gnawing the foundations of the constitution" (p. 24),
one knows that Della Crusca has become a statesman. There
is not a great deal of formal organization of the individual
essays, and like actual letters they may introduce secondary
subjects, more briefly treated, near the end; the over-all arrangement, too, from government through books to clothing
and back to literary matters and national character, is in-

tended to suggest the random order of selected letters rather than formal argument. What is carefully planned, however, is that the seeming casualness shall add up to something in the end: all the letters do contribute toward a consistent and coherent point of view. The book's brevity is part of its effectiveness, for the letter writer's attitude has been so firmly established in those pages that one can infer what his reactions would be to other topics not discussed.

In this process, the style, no less than the attitudes themselves, is central. Some of Tyler's best flights of humorous fancy, with brisk and lively movement, occur in these pages. Every letter unobtrusively furnishes its epigram or flash of wit: "After a while [in the House of Commons] something like silence (which, however, would be called an uproar in any decent assembly) was produced" (pp. 25–26); the Lords discussed "a subject abstruse in itself, and rendered more so by the eloquence of the learned counsel" (p. 40); "let precedents govern if justice is trampled upon" (pp. 42–43); in regard to biographies of prostitutes, Constantia Philips is "the mistress of this school," but her followers have gone so far that "her infamous memoirs may be considered, in a comparative view, as an ethical work written expressly for the promotion of virtue" (p. 65). Tyler's similes are fresh and occasionally arise from his own interests — the theater and the law. The House of Lords, compared to the House of Commons, is "what the Opera-house is to Drury-lane theatre. . . . but, then, even an opera is not without its absurdities. . . . [exhibiting] heroes in recitative, dancing princes, and British lions" (p. 34). Boswell's inclusion of trivial details reminds Tyler of the question of immaterial facts in court: "Were a man called to testify to a contract . . . he would not be guilty of perjury should he omit to relate that one of the contracting parties, on his way to the court, had fallen into a jakes" (p. 56). Tyler's literary knowledge appears in classical allusions (as on pp. 26, 78, 112) and quotations from Pope (pp. 29, 88, 105), Stern (p. 78), Addison (p. 4), Shakespeare (pp. 49, 86), and other English authors. That the style is functional the letter writer himself suggests in Letter VIII, describing lords speaking:

> If the first was Somnus, the second was father Nox himself; — eldest night — ere Satan, that Brindsley of Milton, had canalled chaos, and built a bridge and rail-way o'er the "wide abyss," for the transportation of original sin into paradise. — Pardon the magnificence of my metaphor, my excellent friend; remember I am in training for the honours of a blue-stocking club. (p. 39)

If a dull and imitative style is indicative of a lack of taste and judgment, reflecting ultimately on the character of a whole people, then a series of letters addressed to a young republic must be particularly careful, not simply to assert, but to demonstrate what is good and what is bad. For that reason, the letter writer more effectively expresses the same ideals as Jonathan, Manly, and Updike, and his book deserves the labels which have been applied to it: "tour de force" and "minor classic." [25] The style and content of *The Yankey in London* are one.

"The Bay Boy"

If *The Yankey in London* illustrates Tyler's perennial experimentation with ways of revealing the native American character, one of his unfinished manuscripts gives even greater evidence of his progression toward a more direct portrayal of the American experience. Entitled "The Bay Boy," this work is a revision of the early chapters of *The Algerine Captive*, making more extensive use of details drawn from Tyler's own youth in Boston. Such a book had been promised in the sixteenth chapter of *The Algerine Captive*:

> The remarks I made upon this hospitable, busy, national, town born people; my observations upon their manners, habits, local virtues, customs, and prejudices; the elocution of their principal clergymen; with anecdotes of publick characters, I deal not in

private foibles; and a comparative view of their manners, at the beginning, and near the close of the eighteenth century, are pronounced, by the partiality of some friends, to be original, and to those who know the town, highly interesting. If this home-spun history of private life, shall be approved, these remarks will be published by themselves in a future edition of this work. (I, 124–125)

An accurate description of the content of "The Bay Boy," this passage also suggests that at least parts of it were already written in 1797. But it was this manuscript which occupied much of Tyler's time during his last years, and whether his labors were then revision or original composition is difficult to say. Tyler's wife, in her diary entry for 22 April 1825, wrote, "Began copying *Bay Boy* for the press." [26] The version which survives is not complete, consisting of thirteen main sections (119 pages) and five smaller fragments, only roughly arranged into chapters and often without transitions between them. Much of the material presented in *The Algerine Captive* in short chapters is consolidated, much reappears verbatim (chapters 5–11), some (the first four chapters, for example) is omitted, and a great deal (in local detail) is added. [27] Whatever the course of composition, Tyler recognized the greater value of volume I of *The Algerine Captive* and saw in it the only path that a native literature could take.

"The Bay Boy" perhaps should be considered a novel rather than an essay, for it does repeat episodes from an earlier novel and presents a larger number of characters. But it is more accurately an autobiography written in the third person — "this home-spun history of private life." Updike is still the hero, but the focus is not so much on what he does as on what he sees; the account is descriptive first and narrative second. The reader remembers, not the activities Updike engages in, but the flavor of a New England Sunday, the celebrations of Thanksgiving and Christmas, a Twelfth Night ball, a Commencement Day, a Revolutionary political discussion, and the hazards of early theatrical productions in Boston; he remembers detailed portraits of historical figures, like Dr. Sylvester Gardiner or the Reverend Henry Caner,[28] and vivid sketches of types, such as the young boy in love or the hypochondriac old lady. Satire is still present, but there are two additional elements which mark an advance over *The Algerine Captive*. One is deeper characterization, involving both psychological insight and precise detail; the other, possibly the result of Tyler's late revisions, is a mellowness and warmth, a nostalgia mixed with amusement. Updike's mother, for example, before her marriage "began to show evident signs of veteran maidenhood, was more and more attentive to her Parrot, made daily assignations with the tabby cat, and could not abide the noise of children." Another woman, Mrs. Diaway (whose parlor is described in concrete detail) spent her time in bed, "her head covered by mob caps tier over tier and the whole surmounted by a cambrick handkerchief which she occasionally shifted, as if to guard against the rude contact of some wandering zephyr"; she "languidly pointed" to a chair and "ordered the servant with a shiver to close the door immediately" when Updike visited her on his first professional call as a physician.

Tyler retains the fictional thread of a physician-hero, which gives the account an emotional distance that might have been difficult in a straight autobiography. The nostalgic passages are by no means sentimental: witness the description of the drowsy congregation at a Sunday afternoon service (quoted in Chapter 1) or of the young hero when he thinks he is in love. Updike watches a girl each Sunday in church, only to find when he returns home to eat that "the first mouthful of goose stuck in my throat, could no more swallow than if a whole dumpling was sticking in my gullet — could not think what ailed me, never suspected I was in love." But soon he visits the family that employs the girl and sees her in old clothes, "her hair unkempt and the big drops of perspiration occasioned by her labors, standing upon her forehead or trickling in dingy channels down her neck. . . . The charm of first love was broken." This realism is constantly present, and it rests on a solid foundation of physical details, set forth in language full of colloquialisms.[29] These fragments suggest that Tyler was well on his way toward producing an organically American work, native in content, attitude, and expression. It is entirely possible that "The Bay Boy," if completed as begun, would have ranked with *The Contrast* in reputation; at any rate it represented the next step. Tyler knew where *The Contrast* was leading, even if he never arrived there.

One reason for the relative success of "The Bay Boy" is undoubtedly that it was revised late in Tyler's life and could benefit from a more mature point of view, a knowledge of human nature gleaned from several decades in the courtroom; but another reason is that it was revised at all. Most of Tyler's work was hastily written, dashed off at a moment's notice. The legend of Tyler's speed in composing *The Contrast*, and Nancrede's reference to the "Moral Tales" as "eight days' amusement," are suggestive of a central fact about Tyler's literary labor. Dennie, no deliberate worker himself, continually admonished Tyler to be less hasty:

You appear to proceed in any literary undertaking with a lover's ardor. Be not too impatient; hurry in writing and over-weening zeal with the fair, are both dangerous. Horace, and the rest of those dull fellows, advise slowness in composition; but I know thy pride, and the naughtiness of thy heart. . . . you shall give me your Royal word not to write a play in less time than I have dictated this sentence. If you are determined to Lope-de-vega it, and write 100 lines upon one leg — why then, to conclude dramatically with Capt. Cape, "Dam'me, I'm off."

In another of his charming letters, Dennie referred to Tyler's "galloping consumption of ink." [30] The productions of Tyler's pen, it is all too evident, are not the carefully wrought creations of a painstaking craftsman, and it is both superfluous and irrelevant to criticize them for failing to meet the highest tests of literary art. Their importance lies elsewhere, and it is the very speed of their composition, curiously enough, which points the direction.

Tyler's writings are the products of brief idle moments between the rounds of circuit-riding and legal business. "The Bay Boy" is instructive because it shows the older man with leisure changing the proportions and emphases of what he had written hastily in his younger years. Tyler's whole career is similarly instructive because it epitomizes the position of the writer in the early years of the republic. Dennie put the problem in these terms: "I think it hard, Royall, when I am actually industrious & disposed to exercise regularly peculiar talents, that I can not obtain bread and wine." [31] Tyler was more successful than Dennie in solving the dilemma, since he was more willing to put writing in second place and devote his energies to interpreting "unintelligible law to Green Mountain jurors"; but this solution was hard-won, and more doubts crossed his mind than Mary Tyler was ever aware of. He did find time to write fiction, drama, verse, and essay, but he was not a man of letters. He was an intelligent man, however, with an active and vigorous mind, and when he wrote he expressed the spirit of his own time and place. To such a man, it seemed only the natural thing to do, but for that reason he could not fully comprehend that his Jonathan and his Updike were of greater significance for the cultural development of the nation than all the self-conscious pleas for a native literature which he, and others before him, had uttered. If his "abilities . . . in this wooden world" are to be "esteemed above mediocrity," it is precisely because of those "sonnets to rustic loves, and tales for children" which he disparaged. He could not avoid speaking in the idiom of the age, but he instinctively sensed what lay beyond it. In this is his proper praise.

Chronology

1757 Royall Tyler born in Boston on 18 July, second son and fourth child of Royall and Mary Steele Tyler; originally named William Clark Tyler.

1776 Graduated from Harvard; also received B.A. from Yale. Began study of law with Francis Dana.

1778 Served as aide to General Sullivan, with rank of Major, in the Battle of Rhode Island, August.

1779 Received M.A. from Harvard.

1780 Admitted to bar, 19 August.

1785 Love affair with Abigail Adams ended.

1787 Served as aide to General Lincoln in the attempt to capture the insurgents in Shays' Rebellion, January–March; arrived in New York on this mission, 12 March.
The Contrast performed at John Street Theatre, New York, 16 April.
May Day in Town performed, 19 May.

1790 *The Contrast* published, May.
Moved to Vermont, settling in Guilford in 1791.

1793 *The Origin of Evil* published.

1794 Became State's Attorney for Windham County (through 1801). Married Mary Hunt Palmer at Framingham, Massachusetts, May.
Literary partnership with Joseph Dennie, as "Colon & Spondee," began, July; contributions to Dartmouth *Eagle* and *Federal Orrery*.

1796 Contributions to *Newhampshire and Vermont Journal* began.

1797 *The Algerine Captive* published, August.
The Georgia Spec performed in Boston, 30 October.

1800 *Oration* on George Washington published, March.

1801 Moved to Brattleboro, 3 March.
Became an Assistant Judge of Vermont Supreme Court.
The Spirit of the Farmers' Museum published, containing many of Tyler's periodical contributions.

Chronology

1806   Contributions to *Polyanthos* began.

1807   Became Chief Justice of Vermont Supreme Court (through 1813).

1808   *The Trial of Cyrus B. Dean* published.

1809   *The Yankey in London* published, October.
Vermont Supreme Court *Reports* (volume I) published, December (the second volume coming out in 1810).

1811   Became Professor of Jurisprudence, University of Vermont (through 1814).

1815   Became Register of Probate for Windham County (through 1822).

1826   Died at Brattleboro, 26 August, after suffering from cancer for several years.

1931   *The Chestnut Tree* published (written in 1824).

1941   *Four Plays* published (*The Island of Barrataria; The Origin of the Feast of Purim; Joseph and His Brethren; The Judgement of Solomon*).

1967   *The Verse of Royall Tyler* published.

Selected Bibliography

PRIMARY SOURCES

Books, Pamphlets, and Broadsides

The Contrast. A Comedy. Philadelphia: Prichard & Hall, 1790. Reprinted by the Dunlap Society (New York, 1887), with an introduction by Thomas J. McKee, and in a limited edition (Boston: Houghton Mifflin, 1920), edited by James B. Wilbur, with an introduction by Helen Tyler Brown (reviewed by H. S. Wardner in *Vermonter*, XXVI [February 1921], 40–41). Reprinted also in Arthur Hobson Quinn, *Representative American Plays* (New York: Appleton, 1917); Montrose J. Moses, *Representative Plays by American Dramatists* (New York: Dutton, 1918); Robert E. Spiller, *The Roots of National Culture* (New York: Macmillan, 1933); Allan G. Halline, *American Plays* (New York: American Book Company, 1935); Edwin H. Cady, *Literature of the Early Republic* (New York: Rinehart, 1950); Alan S. Downer, *American Drama* (New York: Crowell, 1960); Milton R. Stern and Seymour L. Gross, *Viking Portable Library American Literature Survey*, volume I (New York: Viking, 1962); and Richard Moody, *Dramas from the American Theatre 1762–1909* (Cleveland: World Publishing Company, 1966).

The Origin of Evil. An Elegy. N.p., 1793.

A Christmas Hymn . . . Sung at Claremont, N.H. 1793. Broadside.

The Algerine Captive; or, the Life and Adventures of Doctor Updike Underhill: Six years a prisoner among the Algerines. 2 vols. Walpole, N.H.: David Carlisle, 1797. Reprinted in two volumes by G. and J. Robinson (London, 1802); in the *Lady's Magazine* (London), XXXV (1804); and in one volume by Peter B. Gleason (Hartford, 1816).

Convivial Song, Sung at Windsor, on the Evening of the Fourth of July. Broadside, 1799.

An Oration, Pronounced at Bennington, Vermont, . . . In Commemoration of the Death of General George Washington. Walpole, N.H.: Printed for Thomas & Thomas by David Carlisle, 1800.

The Trial of Cyrus B. Dean, For the Murder of Jonathan Ormsby and Asa Marsh. Burlington, Vt.: Samuel Mills, 1808.

2 1 3

Selected Bibliography

The Yankey in London, Being the First Part of a Series of Letters Written By an American Youth, During Nine Months' Residence in the City of London. New York: Isaac Riley, 1809.

Reports of Cases Argued and Determined in the Supreme Court of Judicature of the State of Vermont [1800–1803]. 2 vols. New York: Isaac Riley, 1809–1810. Reprinted, with annotation, by the West Publishing Company (St. Paul, Minn., 1888).

A Valedictory Address . . . at the Quarterly Examination of Miss Peck's Select School. Broadside, 1823.

The Chestnut Tree, Or a Sketch of Brattleborough (East Village) At the Close of the Twentieth Century, Being an Address to a Horse Chestnut Presented to the Author by the Rev. A. L. Baury. North Montpelier, Vt.: Driftwind Press, 1931.

Four Plays, ed. Arthur Wallace Peach and George Floyd Newbrough (volume 15 of "America's Lost Plays," ed. Barrett H. Clark). Princeton: University Press, 1941. Reprinted by the Indiana University Press (Bloomington, 1965), bound with volume 16 of the series.

The Verse of Royall Tyler, ed. Marius B. Péladeau. Charlottesville: University Press of Virginia, 1967. Issued also in the *Publications of the Colonial Society of Massachusetts,* XLIV (1967).

Contributions to Periodicals

Because Tyler's many poems and essays appeared anonymously in scattered newspapers and magazines over a number of years, no entirely satisfactory record of them has yet been compiled. The fullest is the list of Tyler's poems in the Péladeau thesis (pp. 266–272), or its revised version in his 1967 edition. Periodical references to the poems and essays mentioned in the present study are given in the Notes. The principal periodicals to which Tyler contributed (with the years, roughly, of his original contributions) are as follows: *Eagle, or Dartmouth Centinel* (1794); Boston *Federal Orrery* (1794–1795); Boston *Tablet* (1795); Walpole (N.H.) *Newhampshire and Vermont Journal, or The Farmer's Weekly Museum* (1796–1799); *Port Folio* (1801–1804); *Polyanthos* (1806–1807).

A large selection of Tyler's poems and essays (particularly in the "Colon & Spondee" column) is reprinted in *The Spirit of the Farmers' Museum* (Walpole: Printed for Thomas & Thomas by D. & T. Carlisle, 1801). Periodical pieces have also been included in the following: Samuel Kettell, *Specimens of American Poetry* (3 vols.; Boston: S. G. Goodrich, 1829); Joseph T. Buckingham, *Specimens of Newspaper Literature* (2 vols.; Boston: Redding, 1850); E. A. and G. L. Duyckinck, *Cyclopaedia of American Literature* (2 vols.; Philadelphia: Rutter, 1855); A. M. Hemenway, *Poets and Poetry of Ver-*

Selected Bibliography

mont (Rutland: Tuttle, 1858); E. C. Stedman and E. M. Hutchinson, *A Library of American Literature*, volume IV (New York: Webster, 1888); Burton E. Stevenson, *Poems of American History* (Boston: Houghton Mifflin, 1908); Walter J. Coates, *Favorite Vermont Poems, Series One* (North Montpelier: Driftwind, 1928), *Series Five* (1934); W. J. Coates and Frederick Tupper, *Vermont Verse: An Anthology* (Brattleboro: Stephen Daye Press, 1932); Louis Untermeyer and Carter Davidson, *Poetry: Its Appreciation and Enjoyment* (New York: Harcourt, Brace, 1934); Louis Untermeyer, *Early American Poets* (New York: Library Publishers, 1952); Karl Kroeber and John O. Lyons, *Studying Poetry* (New York: Harper & Row, 1965); George F. Horner and Robert A. Bain, *Colonial and Federalist American Writing* (New York: Odyssey Press, 1966).

Manuscripts

The only extensive collection of manuscript material relating to Royall Tyler is the Tyler family papers at the Vermont Historical Society. The Royall Tyler Collection (Gift of Helen Tyler Brown) consists principally of ten boxes, some of the contents of which are as follows:

Box 45 — typescripts of "The Bay Boy," the sacred dramas, the Washington oration, a Christmas sermon, "Utile Dulci," and miscellaneous poems, along with correspondence about *Grandmother Tyler's Book* and *The Chestnut Tree*, Mary Tyler's later diary, and copies of some Tyler letters.

Box 46 — material gathered by Helen Tyler Brown in her research, and letters from Mary Tyler to Royall.

Box 47 — notebooks and scrapbooks of Thomas P. and Gertrude Tyler.

Boxes 48–49 — mainly printed material.

Box 50 — letters and papers of Helen Tyler Brown, a typescript of *The Island of Barrataria*, and a handwritten copy of Thomas P. Tyler's memoir of his father.

Box 51 — galley proofs and other material connected with the publication of *Grandmother Tyler's Book*, and Tyler family correspondence of the nineteenth century.

Box 52 — Brown family papers.

Box 77 — Helen Tyler Brown's Boston researches, and another typescript of "The Bay Boy."

Box 78 — correspondence of Helen Tyler Brown in the 1910's and 1920's.

The Vermont Historical Society has certain other Tyler material — notably a typescript of the T. P. Tyler memoir, a handwritten copy of *The Chestnut Tree*, a group of documents relating to Shays' Rebellion, and numerous photostatic copies of relevant papers.

Other libraries have a few Tyler letters or documents:

The Boston Public Library — four letters from Tyler (to John S. Tyler, May 1814, 1 December 1814; two others to unidentified correspondents, probably of 1807); ten letters to Tyler (from Joseph T. Buckingham, 14 March 1820; Stephen R. Bradley, 27 January 1810; Martin Field, 28 October 1816; Samuel L. Knapp, 7 January 1820; Jonathan Robinson, 31 January 1811; David Tracy, 25 October 1808, 19 July 1812; J. S. Tyler, 11 December 1811; Mary Tyler, 30 December 1810, 28 January 1811); four juvenile poems in manuscript; four legal documents signed by Tyler (November 1796, 15 October 1807, 30 July 1808, 25 October 1810).

William L. Clements Library — two documents signed by Tyler (11 February 1808, 1–2 February 1809).

Columbia University Library — one letter from Tyler (to Jonathan Robinson, 5 June 1812); one letter to Tyler (from Jonathan Robinson, 1 December 1811); two documents signed by Tyler (March 1794, 5 March 1802).

Dartmouth College Library — one letter from Tyler (to Jonathan Hunt, 24 December 1798).

Haverford College Library — one letter from Tyler (to an unidentified correspondent, 21 February 1787).

Houghton Library, Harvard University — one document signed by Tyler (2 August 1808).

Massachusetts Historical Society (Adams Papers) — four letters from Tyler (to Abigail Adams, 13 October 1785; to John Adams, 13 January, 27 August 1784, 15 October 1785); three letters to Tyler (from Abigail Adams, 4 January 1785; John Adams, 3 April 1784, 12 December 1785).

Massachusetts State Archives — one letter from Tyler (to Benjamin Lincoln, 18 February 1787); three reports by Tyler about Shays' Rebellion (13, 17 February, 6 March 1787).

New Hampshire Historical Society — two letters from Tyler (to Joseph Dennie, 9 September [1794], 7 October 1795); one letter to Tyler (from Jonathan Robinson, 21 July 1811).

The New-York Historical Society — one letter to Tyler (from Russell Fitch, 15 January 1811); one document signed by Tyler, about "The Touchstone" (26 January 1818).

New York Public Library — one letter from Tyler (to Israel Tefft, 24 November 1820); one document signed by Tyler (30 October 1804).

Pennsylvania Historical Society — two letters from Tyler (to David G. Barnet, 12 February 1810; to Mary Tyler, 9 October 1807); one

letter to Tyler (from Jonathan Robinson, 8 January 1810); three documents signed by Tyler (26 October 1802; 3, 4 February 1809).
University of Vermont Library — one letter to Tyler (from Jonathan Robinson, 25 April 1809); eight documents signed by Tyler (23 October 1798; 2 June 1803; August 1805; June, 27 September 1806; 28 May, August, 29 August 1812).
University of Virginia Library — four letters from Tyler (to William Griffith, 18 May 1824; Jonathan Jones, 16 February 1812; P. C. Merril, 26 March 1810; Cornelius S. Vanness, 23 November 1812); one document signed by Tyler (22 February 1808).
Still other manuscript material is in private collections; for example, the present writer has one document signed by Tyler (26 January 1810).

SECONDARY SOURCES

Bibliographies

There has been no full bibliography. The principal checklists are those in the 1920 edition of *The Contrast*; in *Driftwind*, VI (March 1932), 27–31 (by Walter J. Coates); in the bibliography volume of the *Literary History of the United States* (New York: Macmillan, 1948); and in the Péladeau thesis. A descriptive bibliography of Tyler's works, prepared by the present writer, is "Some Uncollected Authors XLII: Royall Tyler, 1757–1826," *Book Collector*, XV (1966), 303–320.

Biographical and Critical Studies

Listed here are articles exclusively on Tyler and books which devote entire sections or chapters to him; other works, with briefer comment on Tyler, are referred to in the Notes.

Burnham, Henry. *Brattleboro, Windham County, Vermont*, ed. Abby Maria Hemenway. Brattleboro: D. Leonard, 1880. A pioneer effort to publish the facts of Tyler's life (pp. 83–101); draws heavily and uncritically on the manuscript Tyler memoir; the most important and comprehensive early account, and the source for most later sketches.

Butterfield, L. H., Wendell D. Garrett, and Marc Friedlaender. "Introduction" to *The Earliest Diary of John Adams* (Cambridge: Harvard University Press, 1966), pp. 1–42. Includes an account of Tyler's relations with the Adamses ("The History of the Manuscript Reconstructed," pp. 16–32).

Cabot, Mary R. *Annals of Brattleboro 1681–1895*. 2 vols. Brattleboro: E. L. Hildreth, 1921–1922. Contains a general sketch of Tyler (I, 251–271), often repeating Burnham verbatim.

Selected Bibliography

Chapman, Bertrand William. "The Nativism of Royall Tyler." Master's thesis, University of Vermont, 1933. A discussion principally of *The Algerine Captive* and "The Bay Boy," useful for its examination of sources.

Cowie, Alexander. *The Rise of the American Novel*. New York: American Book Company, 1948. The most extensive critical discussion of *The Algerine Captive*, stressing its satire and "crisp, classic prose" (pp. 60–68).

Crane, Charles Edward. *Pen-drift: Amenities of Column Conducting*. Brattleboro: Stephen Daye Press, 1931. Contains a general summary of Tyler's career based on secondary sources ("Royall Tyler," pp. 118–125).

Halline, Allan Gates. "Main Currents of Thought in American Drama." Ph.D. dissertation, University of Wisconsin, 1935. Includes, in chapter I ("Nationalism: Royall Tyler," pp. 15–30), a discussion of the historical background and importance of *The Contrast*.

Lauber, John. "*The Contrast*: A Study in the Concept of Innocence," *English Language Notes*, I (September 1963), 33–37. An analysis of the play as a precursor of the Jamesian international theme, with American innocence opposed to European sophistication.

Nethercot, Arthur H. "The Dramatic Background of Royall Tyler's *The Contrast*," *American Literature*, XII (1941), 435–446. Carefully examines Tyler's sources and preparation as a dramatist.

Newbrough, G. F. "Mary Tyler's Journal," *Vermont Quarterly*, XX (1952), 19–31. A selection of entries (between 1821 and 1826) from Tyler's wife's journal, important for an understanding of Tyler's last years.

Péladeau, Marius B. "The Verse of Royall Tyler: Collected and Edited." Master's thesis, Georgetown University, 1962. A valuable attempt to establish the canon of Tyler's poetry, with extensive annotations and bibliographical citations; the introduction (pp. 1–38) includes a general survey of Tyler's career. (For the published edition, see the list of primary materials above.)

Quinn, Arthur Hobson. *A History of the American Drama from the Beginning to the Civil War*. Second edition. New York: Appleton-Century-Crofts, 1943. The standard discussion of *The Contrast* (pp. 64–73).

———— "Royall Tyler," *Dictionary of American Biography*, XIX (1936), 95–97. A scholarly account, based on the Tyler manuscripts as well as the published material.

Riese, Teut. *Das englische Erbe in der amerikanischen Literatur: Studien zur Entstehungsgeschichte des amerikanischen Selbstbewusstseins im Zeitalter Washingtons und Jeffersons* ("Beiträge zur

Selected Bibliography

Englischen Philologie," 39). Bochum-Langendreer: Heinrich Pöppinghaus, 1958. Concentrates, in the section about Tyler (pp. 139–149), on *The Algerine Captive* and its relation to the English picaresque tradition.

Rourke, Constance. *The Roots of American Culture and Other Essays*, ed. Van Wyck Brooks. New York: Harcourt, Brace, 1942. Contains an important evaluation of Tyler's concern with the Yankee character (pp. 114–124).

Seilhamer, George O. *History of the American Theatre*. 3 vols. Philadelphia: Globe Printing House, 1888–1891. Includes a detailed account of the reception of *The Contrast* (II, 225–239), largely unfavorable to Tyler.

Stein, Roger B. "Royall Tyler and the Question of Our Speech," *New England Quarterly*, XXXVIII (1965), 454–474. A suggestive analysis of *The Contrast* as an early treatment of the search for an authentic native idiom — a search that continues to the present, fluctuating in its emphases between the Jonathan and Manly types.

Taft, Russell. "Royall Tyler," *Green Bag*, XX (January 1908), 1–5. A general biographical sketch, with emphasis on Tyler's legal career (cf. *Green Bag*, VI [1894], 72–74).

Tanselle, G. Thomas. "Early American Fiction in England: The Case of *The Algerine Captive*," *Papers of the Bibliographical Society of America*, LIX (1965), 367–384. A collation of the various editions of the novel, showing the care with which the text was treated in England.

Tupper, Frederick. "Royall Tyler, Man of Law and Man of Letters," *Proceedings of the Vermont Historical Society*, IV (1928), 65–101. An estimate of Tyler's entire career, giving biographical facts but emphasizing his literary productions.

Tyler, Mary Palmer. *Grandmother Tyler's Book: The Recollections of Mary Palmer Tyler*, ed. Helen Tyler Brown and Frederick Tupper. New York: Putnam, 1925. The autobiography of Tyler's wife, of obvious importance for first-hand information about the family. Reviewed by H. S. Wardner in *Vermonter*, XXIX (1924), 181–182; by G. H. Busey in New York *Tribune*, 10 May 1925; in *Saturday Review of Literature*, I (28 March 1925), 633; in Boston *Transcript*, 16 December 1925.

Tyler, Thomas Pickman. "Royall Tyler," *Proceedings of the Vermont Bar Association*, I (1878–1881), 44–62. A general survey of Tyler's life, based on his son's long memoir.

White, Pliny H. "Early Poets of Vermont," *Proceedings of the Vermont Historical Society, 1917–1918* (1920), pp. 93–125. The earliest substantial commentary on Tyler's verse (pp. 108–119), originally read on 18 October 1860.

Notes

I. *Lawyer and Wit*

1. The best account of this Royall Tyler (1724–1771) is in Clifford K. Shipton, *Sibley's Harvard Graduates*, XI (Boston, 1960), 313–318. His standing (determined mainly by the social position of the family) was sixteenth in a class of thirty-nine (p. 176); he received his Master's degree in 1746 and a degree from Yale *ad eundem* in 1750 (see the Quinquennial Catalogues). After graduation he studied law for a time with the great Edmund Trowbridge (1709–1793); cf. Shipton, *Harvard Graduates*, and *Commonwealth History of Massachusetts*, ed. Alfred B. Hart (New York, 1928), II, 179. For more information on the pamphlet episode, see *Extract from the Journal of the Honorable House of Representatives . . . Relating to the Imprisonment of Daniel Fowle and Royall Tyler* [Boston, 1756]; for an unfavorable estimate of his character, see *The Conversation of Two Persons under a Window on Monday Evening the 23rd of March* [Boston, 1765]; for his relationship to Otis, see William Tudor, *Life of James Otis* (Boston, 1823), p. 92, and Shipton, *Harvard Graduates*, XI, 254–255; for his activities in demanding withdrawal of British troops, see Edward L. Pierce, ed., "Diary of John Rowe," *Proceedings of the Massachusetts Historical Society*, 2nd ser., X (1895–96), 67 (entry for 14 June 1768), and George G. Wolkins, "The Seizure of John Hancock's Sloop *Liberty*," *ibid.*, LV (1921–22), 250n (the *Romney* affair, 16 June 1768); for his later services to Harvard, see Josiah Quincy, *The History of Harvard University* (Boston, 1860), II, 101, 488; for the repercussions of his remarks after the Boston Massacre, see *Proceedings of His Majesty's Council . . . Relative to the Deposition of Andrew Oliver* (Boston, 1770) and William Gordon, *The History of the Rise, Progress, and Establishment of the Independence of the United States of America* (London, 1788), I, 288–289; and for a detailed account of his last hours, told by his physician Thomas Young, see the Boston *Evening Post*, 3 June 1771. He is also mentioned, as Shipton indicates, in the Massachusetts *Archives* (see especially XXIV, 303, and XXVI, 213), the *Records* of the Province Council (XV, XVI), and John Adams' *Works* (Boston, 1850–1856), II, 247. Specific dates of his numerous offices and committee appointments can be ascertained in

the *Reports of the Record Commissioners of the City of Boston* (39 vols.; Boston, 1876–1909), XIV, XVI, XVIII, XIX, XX, XXIII (his marriage is recorded in XXVIII, 265); and in *The Acts and Resolves, Public and Private, of the Province of Massachusetts Bay* (21 vols.; Boston, 1869–1922), III, IV, V, XV, XVI, XVII, XVIII. He is listed as one of the Sons of Liberty who dined at the Liberty Tree, Dorchester, on 14 August 1769, in *Proceedings of the Massachusetts Historical Society*, XI (1869–70), 142. Henry Burnham, in *Brattleboro, Windham County, Vermont* (Brattleboro, 1880), says (p. 87) that Tyler went into the mercantile business with his brother-in-law, Samuel Phillips Savage (husband of his sister Sarah). In the Boston Public Library there are two letters (1760, 1761) written to Tyler in his capacity as a member of the committee to look after victims of the Boston fire.

2. The most detailed treatment of the genealogy is in *Grandmother Tyler's Book*, ed. Frederick Tupper and Helen Tyler Brown (New York, 1925), esp. pp. 327–357, with charts on pp. 329, 331, 333; see also Thomas Bridgman, *Memorials of the Dead in Boston . . . Inscriptions on the Sepulchral Monuments in the King's Chapel Burial Ground* (Boston, 1853), pp. 288–291, and the *New England Historical and Genealogical Register*, VIII (1854), 102. Thomas Tyler's name appears in the list of inhabitants of Boston in 1695 in the *Reports of the Record Commissioners*, I, 169; his sons, besides William, were named Thomas (born 15 August 1685), John, and Andrew (who married the sister of Sir William Pepperell), and they appear in the Boston records, VIII–XII, XIV–XVII (the source for the dates in the text). These records suggest (IX, 167, 182) that Thomas, not William as in *Grandmother Tyler's Book*, was the eldest of the brothers. William's portrait, painted by John Smibert, was presented to the New England Historic, Genealogical Society in 1874; see its *Register*, XXIX (1875), 119. William's children, besides Royall, included another Thomas, William, Joseph, and Sarah. See further references to the Tylers in the Boston records, XXII, XXV, XXVIII, XXX. Willard I. Tyler Brigham's *The Tyler Genealogy* (Plainfield, N.J., and Tylerville, Conn., 1912) deals with an entirely separate line of Tylers, though it mentions Thomas Tyler (and the "Thomas Tyler Boston Line") on p. v, in pointing out the number of original Tyler immigrants in the Boston area.

3. "An Act to change the Christian name of William Clark Tyler from William Clark to Royall," passed 23 April 1772 (*Acts and Resolves . . . of the Province of Massachusetts Bay*, VI, 213, and see further references given there; the act is also listed at V, 181, where the date is reported as 25 April 1772).

4. Quoted from p. 9 of an unpublished memoir of Tyler by one of his sons, Thomas Pickman Tyler, now in the Vermont Historical

Society (Royall Tyler Collection, gift of Helen Tyler Brown). Page references will be made to a typewritten copy consisting of 233 pages (numbered 1–232, with one page skipped), then a brief gap, followed by 69 more pages (with new pagination, from 47 to 115, hereafter prefixed with a superscript 2 to distinguish them from earlier pages with the same numbers); though Helen Tyler Brown did not finish her renumbering of this copy, it is still more convenient for reference than the handwritten fair copy. The memoir has been drawn upon extensively for several published accounts, notably Burnham's. It is here quoted by permission of the Tyler heirs and the Vermont Historical Society.

5. For this reconstruction I am indebted to the researches of Bertrand W. Chapman, "The Nativism of Royall Tyler" (master's thesis, University of Vermont, 1933), pp. 55–61. For information about the Latin School at this period, see Henry F. Jenks, *Catalogue of the Boston Public Latin School* (Boston, 1886), esp. pp. 35–40 (a letter from Harrison Gray Otis describing the school in the 1770's); references to Tyler and to his father (who had entered in 1732) are on pp. 87, 47. Cf. Arthur W. Brayley, *Schools and Schoolboys of Old Boston* (Boston, 1894), esp. pp. 33–35; and Kenneth B. Murdock, "The Teaching of Latin and Greek at the Boston Latin School in 1712," *Publications of the Colonial Society of Massachusetts*, XXVII (1932), 21–29 (Tyler's father, p. 26). A typescript of "The Bay Boy" is in the Vermont Historical Society, Box 45, Envelope 29.

6. Details of this period of Harvard history are drawn from Samuel Eliot Morison, *Three Centuries of Harvard* (Cambridge, Mass., 1936), pp. 133–163; Quincy, *Harvard University*, II, 148–181; Samuel F. Batchelder, *Bits of Harvard History* (Cambridge, Mass., 1924), pp. 37–76, 243–258; Albert Matthews, "Harvard Commencement Days, 1642–1916," *Publications of the Colonial Society of Massachusetts*, XVIII (1916), 354–355; *The Cambridge of 1776*, ed. Arthur Gilman (Cambridge, Mass., 1875); and George Gary Bush, *History of Higher Education in Massachusetts* (Washington, 1891), esp. pp. 60–61, 71, 80.

7. Reprinted in the *Publications of the Colonial Society of Massachusetts*, XXXI (1935), 358; the earlier quotation from the laws occurs on p. 347.

8. Tyler is listed on p. 32 (and his father on p. 19) of the *Catalogus eorum qui in Collegio Harvardino, quod est Cantabrigiae Nov-anglorum, ab Anno MDCXLII, ad Annum MDCCLXXVI* (Boston, 1776) and also on the 1776 broadside *Proceribus Politiae Massachusettensis Honoratissimis*; for his Yale degree, see p. 22 of *Catalogus eorum qui in Collegio-Yalensi . . . ab anno MDCII ad Annum MDCCLXXVIII, alicujus Gradus Laurea donati sunt* (New Haven, 1778).

9. Tyler's father died intestate, and the size of the estate is generally

reported as £4100 (cf. Shipton, *Harvard Graduates*); however, Abigail Adams in 1782 declared Tyler's patrimony to be £7000, though he could not then realize more than half that amount because of the depreciation of the paper currency; he was his mother's favorite, she says, and his mother insisted that the elder brother John Steele share equally with Royall (letters from Abigail to John Adams, 23 and 30 December 1782, Adams Papers Microfilms, Reel 359).

10. Tyler memoir, p. 10; Burnham, *Brattleboro*, p. 87.

11. According to Francis Dana, Tyler had studied with him "but a short time, two or three months" and then continued his study with Hichborn; see letter from Dana to Adams, 23 May 1783, Adams Papers Microfilms, Reel 360 (in answer to Adams' letter of 24 March 1783, inquiring about Tyler's character). Abigail Adams, however, in her letter to her husband on 30 December 1782 (Reel 359), says that Tyler studied with Angier after Dana left. Another tradition makes him one of the pupils of John Adams himself — an impossibility since it is clear from the extensive correspondence relating to Tyler's courtship of Adams' daughter (1782–1786) that Adams had never met Tyler (see, for example, letters from Abigail to John Adams, 23 and 30 December 1782, Reel 359; from Richard Cranch to Adams, 20 January 1784, Reel 362; from Tyler to Adams, 15 October 1785, Reel 366). Cf. *Legal Papers of John Adams*, ed. L. Kinvin Wroth and Hiller B. Zobel (Cambridge, Mass., 1965), I, lxxxi, note 182. Adams had, however, known Tyler's father and on one occasion in 1770 had borrowed some books he recommended; see the *Diary and Autobiography of John Adams*, ed. L. H. Butterfield (Cambridge, Mass., 1961), I, 362.

12. The group occasionally asked distinguished outsiders to join them; when Dr. Korant, "a man of extensive learning," came to Boston from South America, they felt impelled to become acquainted with his views on government. See *The Autobiography of Colonel John Trumbull*, ed. Theodore Sizer (New Haven, 1953), pp. 44–46, 56–57. Biographical sketches and further references for Francis Dana (1743–1811), William Eustis (1753–1825), and Rufus King (1755–1827), as well as John Trumbull (1756–1843), may be found in the *Dictionary of American Biography*; Thomas Dawes (1757–1825), Aaron Dexter (1749–1829), and Christopher Gore (1758–1827) are less well-known. Trumbull painted portraits of some members of the group, and he described one as "Head of Royal Tyler, with both hands — a respectable portrait." This portrait, like the one of Dawes, is now lost; but, according to family tradition, it hung for years in the office of Tyler's brother at the Boston Custom House and was either burned in a Custom House fire or destroyed when removed at the time of the fire (Tyler memoir, p. 13). Trumbull's autobiography also includes information about his friendship with John Steele Tyler

in France in 1780 and about the danger the two found themselves in after the André affair (pp. 58–59, 63–72).

13. See the Records of the College Faculty, IV, 70, 74–75 (in the meetings for 20 October and 18 November 1777). The Quarter Bill Books show that Tyler did not remain in residence at Harvard as a tutor after his graduation, but Sewall did (through the quarter ending 12 December 1777); in any case the faculty had announced that "Bachelors of Arts in particular, whether residing at the College or not, who are guilty of any Scandalous immorality, are accountable therefor, whenever they come to ask for their Second Degree" (Records, IV, 70). Two years later (at the meeting of 10 July 1779) the faculty reaffirmed its stand, insisting that the three men could not be awarded their masters' degrees unless they apologized (IV, 110–111). Cf. *The Earliest Diary of John Adams*, ed. L. H. Butterfield *et al.* (Cambridge, Mass., 1966), p. 23, note 50. The only other references to Tyler in the faculty Records occur at III, 207 (entered as a freshman in July 1772), 225 (fined seven shillings on 15 March 1774 for absence from recitation), 228 (excused from commons for a brief period, recorded 1 April 1774); IV, 11 (fined sixpence on 4 April 1775 for abusing a library book; excused from commons for half a week, recorded 7 April 1775). See also Corporation Records, II, 481 (petitioned to use the college library in 1777). It should be noted that references to "Tyler 1^{mus}" during this period are to Tyler's classmate Dean Tyler, two years older, and that Royall Tyler is "Tyler 2^{dus}"; in the 1777 episode the chief basis for equating "Sr Tyler" with Royall rather than Dean is that King and Sewall are known to have been friends of Royall. Quotations from material in the Harvard Archives are made by permission of Clifford K. Shipton for the Harvard University Library.

14. Jeremiah Mason, *Memoir and Correspondence* (Cambridge, Mass., 1873), p. 32.

15. This statement occurs in the manuscript Private Journal of the antiquarian John Langdon Sibley (now in the Harvard Archives). His entry for 15 October 1856 (p. 109) begins, "Mr Royal Morse, (illegitimate son of a woman who was sweeper for very many years in the college buildings by a student, Royall Tyler)." The woman, one year older than Tyler (she was born 24 October 1756 — see *Records of the Church of Christ at Cambridge in New England, 1632–1830*, ed. Stephen P. Sharples [Boston, 1906], p. 165), was Katharine Morse, who for over forty years worked in the Harvard dormitories, as her mother had before her; she was a familiar figure in Cambridge, mentioned in Augustus Peirce's *The Rebelliad* (1842; written in 1819), eulogized in verse by B. D. Winslow (1835), and depicted with her broom in a cartoon — see Batchelder, *Bits of Harvard History*, pp.

278–280. Her mother may be the Mrs. Morse reported to have "2 Rooms" available at the time Burgoyne's men were in town (Samuel F. Batchelder, *Bits of Cambridge History* [Cambridge, Mass., 1930], p. 58). Her son Royal was born 6 June 1779, according to his obituary in the Cambridge *Press* on 10 February 1872 (signed with Sibley's initials); he was baptized on 12 January 1782 (at which time his mother was admitted to full communion), according to Sharples, *Records*, pp. 240, 243, and *Vital Records of Cambridge, Massachusetts, to the Year 1850*, ed. Thomas W. Baldwin (2 vols.; Boston, 1914–15), I, 502. Royal Morse, during his long life of nearly ninety-three years, was a prominent and respected figure in Cambridge. It was Morse to whom James Russell Lowell referred in his sketch of "Cambridge Thirty Years Ago" in *Fireside Travels* (Boston, 1864): "Long may R.M. be spared to us, so genial, so courtly, the last man among us who will ever know how to lift a hat with the nice graduation of social distinction!" (p. 35). (This identification is made by Thomas Wentworth Higginson in "Life in Cambridge Town," in *The Cambridge of Eighteen Hundred and Ninety-Six*, ed. Arthur Gilman [Cambridge, Mass., 1896], p. 40.) In 1792 Katharine Morse bought the Lamson-Francis-Gamage-Richardson house, and Royal continued to live there for many years — cf. *An Historic Guide to Cambridge* (rev. ed.; Cambridge, Mass.: Hannah Winthrop Chapter of the Daughters of the American Revolution, 1907), p. 158. He married Hannah Rand on 25 May 1800 (Sharples, *Records*, p. 491), and at least two children are recorded in the *Vital Records*, in 1800 and 1803 (Baldwin, I, 501; II, 668); his mother died on 23 February 1835 (Baldwin, *Vital Records*, II, 669; William Thaddeus Harris, *Epitaphs from the Old Burying-Ground in Cambridge* [Cambridge, Mass., 1845], p. 165). He became a well-known auctioneer (listed, for example, as one of five in the *Cambridge Directory for 1848*), and he was an assessor for a time (Lucius R. Paige, *History of Cambridge, Massachusetts* [Boston, 1877], p. 468; cf. pp. 231, 450). In his later years he was a fund of information about earlier days in Cambridge, and he contributed his recollections both to Sibley (for use in his biographies of Harvard graduates) and to Paige (for his history of Cambridge); according to Paige, his "memory of events which occurred during his life was remarkably comprehensive and accurate," and his "traditional lore was almost equivalent to authentic history" (p. 413). In regard to Tyler's paternity of Morse, it seems highly unlikely that Sibley, himself a student of local history and a friend of Morse, would be incorrect; at the same time, an extensive search has failed to produce any corroboration of Sibley's remark.

16. Mercy Otis Warren, *History of the . . . American Revolution*

(Boston, 1805), II, 45–46; see also Batchelder, *Bits of Cambridge History*, pp. 3–113.

17. *Massachusetts Soldiers and Sailors of the Revolutionary War* (17 vols.; Boston, 1896–1908), XVI, 240; *Acts and Resolves . . . of the Province of Massachusetts Bay*, XIX, 710–711. In the fall of 1779 John Steele Tyler and others resigned because of the depreciation of currency and petitioned for their payment (*Acts and Resolves*, XXI, 130, 254).

18. Tyler memoir, pp. 14–15; Burnham, *Brattleboro*, p. 86. Information about the Newport campaign may be found, among other places, in Francis Vinton Greene, *The Revolutionary War and the Military Policy of the United States* (New York, 1911), pp. 150–154 (which includes a map).

19. A copy of Tyler's admission to the bar is in the Tyler Papers, Box 45, Envelope 20. It had been voted, upon Hichborn's motion, at the 18 July 1780 meeting, according to George Dexter's transcript of the "Record Book of the Suffolk Bar," *Proceedings of the Massachusetts Historical Society*, XIX (1881–82), 154. See also note 29 below.

20. William Willis, *A History of the Law, the Courts, and the Lawyers of Maine* (Portland, 1863), p. 105; repeated in Burnham, *Brattleboro*, p. 88. Willis dates Tyler's arrival in Falmouth as 1779 and says that the privateer episode took place during Tyler's practice in Cumberland.

21. Abigail to John Adams, 30 December 1782, Adams Papers Microfilms, Reel 359. Abigail dates Tyler's "excursion" to Falmouth as "18 months ago." According to her letters of 23 December 1782 and 10 January 1783, he had then been in Braintree for nine months. All quotations, here and below, from the Adams Papers (microfilm edition) are made by permission of the Adams Manuscript Trust.

22. Abigail to John Adams, 23 December 1782, Adams Papers Microfilms, Reel 359. This letter also quotes from a reply Tyler made to a note of Abigail's informing him that he was not yet well enough established in business to think of marriage.

23. Abigail to John Adams, 30 December 1782, Adams Papers Microfilms, Reel 359. She added that Tyler had "opened his mind" to her and "declared his attachment" for her daughter.

24. Abigail to John Adams, 10 January 1783, Adams Papers Microfilms, Reel 360.

25. His letters to Abigail of 8 April–9 June 1783 and 11 April 1783 (Adams Papers Microfilms, Reel 360) and of 13 July 1783 (Reel 361) contain further anxious allusions to the affair.

26. Abigail to John Adams, 7 April 1783, Adams Papers Microfilms, Reel 360.

27. Abigail to John Adams, 7 May 1783, Adams Papers Microfilms, Reel 360. She had expressed the same opinion more briefly in a letter to Adams on 28 April 1783.

28. Abigail to John Adams, 20 June 1783, Adams Papers Microfilms, Reel 361. A few days earlier, on 14 June, she had written to Tyler an encouraging but restrained letter, giving him advice on how to overcome a tendency toward dissipation (see Tyler memoir, pp. 20–23; Tyler Papers, Box 45, Envelope 4).

29. His admission to the Supreme Judicial Court was recommended in February 1783 (Records of the Supreme Judicial Court, 1783, f. 29, in Suffolk County Court House); the action was approved on 30 July 1783, according to the "Record Book of the Suffolk Bar," *Proceedings of the Massachusetts Historical Society*, XIX (1881–82), 156. Tyler is also listed as being present at the quarterly meetings of the bar on 12 October 1784, 11 January 1785 (p. 160), and 12 July 1786 (p. 161).

30. According to Abigail Adams' letter of 27 December 1783 (Adams Papers Microfilms, Reel 362), the farm included fifty acres of wooded land and the best collection of fruit trees in Braintree; according to Joseph Palmer's letter of 16 June 1784 (Reel 363), Tyler paid £1000 for it. The "Vassall-Borland" farmhouse was later owned by the Adamses (1788–1927) and is now the Adams National Historic Site in Quincy. (See note 55 below.)

31. Cf. Abigail's letters of 20 June and 19 October 1783 (Adams Papers Microfilms, Reel 361), 27 December 1783 (Reel 362), and 3 January 1784 (Reel 362).

32. Quoted in Adams' *Diary*, III, 156n.

33. John to Abigail Adams, 25 January 1784, Adams Papers Microfilms, Reel 362.

34. *Diary*, III, 160–161, in a passage taken from Abigail's diary (entry for 1 July 1784). In *Grandmother Tyler's Book* we are told that "Mrs. Adams appeared as much afflicted as her daughter" (p. 79).

35. *Grandmother Tyler's Book*, p. 80. Cf. the account given by Mary Cranch in her letter to Abigail Adams of 8 October 1786 (Adams Papers Microfilms, Reel 369).

36. Cranch to Adams, 20 January 1784, Adams Paper Microfilms, Reel 362. Another testimonial to Tyler's character came from General Joseph Palmer, writing on 16–18 June 1784: "Previous to his coming to Braintree, I knew not any thing of him, but 'tis said that he scattered some wild Oats; be this as it may, since he came hither, his conduct, so far as I know, has been unexceptionable, & he is generally respected, & has, I believe, his full share of business" (Reel 363).

37. Adams to Tyler, 3 April 1784, Adams Papers Microfilms, Reel 362.

38. Tyler to Adams, 27 August 1784, Adams Papers Microfilms, Reel 363.

39. Mary Cranch to Abigail Adams, 16 January 1785, Adams Papers Microfilms, Reel 364. Cf. the references to Tyler in her letters of 7 August, 10 October, 6 November 1784 (Reel 363), and 25 April 1785 (Reel 364), and in her daughter's letter of 6 November 1784 (Reel 363).

40. Mary Cranch to Abigail Adams, 4 June 1785, Adams Papers Microfilms, Reel 364.

41. For Abigail had been making inquiries on her own into Tyler's conduct; see, for example, her letters to her uncle, Dr. Cotton Tufts, on 2 May 1785 (Adams Papers Microfilms, Reel 364) and to her son John Quincy on 26 June 1785 (Reel 364) and 23 August 1785 (Reel 365).

42. *Grandmother Tyler's Book*, p. 76. This note and the letters were delivered by Charles Storer, a friend of Tyler's and a cousin of young Abigail's, who, with Colonel Smith, escorted the Adams ladies frequently during their stay in Europe; *Grandmother Tyler's Book*, p. 81, gives at second hand Storer's account of Abigail's making her final decision. Her mother and Storer exchanged numerous letters commenting on Tyler — such as those of 12 February, 23 March, 13 April 1786 (Adams Papers Microfilms, Reel 367); 22 May, 15 August, 12 September 1786 (Reel 368). Cotton Tufts (who looked after the Adamses' business affairs in their absence) was appointed to collect Nabby's letters and other Adams possessions from Tyler, but it was not until late summer of 1786 that he succeeded in getting a part of them (Tufts to Adams, 15 August 1786, Reel 368; cf. his letter of 13 April 1786, Reel 367, and Mary Cranch's letter, 28 September 1786, Reel 368). Whether or not Tyler kept the Adams letters, his memory of their detailed descriptions of life in England no doubt served him well in making the national contrasts which are so important in *The Contrast* and *The Yankey in London*.

43. The connection between Tyler and the Adamses was given national publicity in the summer of 1965, when John Adams' Harvard diary (beginning in June 1753, earlier than any previously known diary of Adams) was discovered among the Tyler Papers. Presumably Tyler had picked it up in Adams' library (which Adams had invited him to use) and had never returned it; he could have found it either before Abigail's departure (for her letter of 23 December 1782, on Reel 359 of the Adams Papers Microfilms, shows the freedom with which he removed items from the library) or after she had sailed for Europe (since she included among her last instructions the stipulation that only Tyler and Richard Cranch were to be given access to the library

—see her letter of 18 June 1784 in the Clements Library). Wendell
D. Garrett, an associate editor of The Adams Papers, made the discovery; his own account appeared in the *Boston Sunday Globe*, 4 July
1965, p. 7, accompanied by an article on the Tyler love affair by Mary
Meier (pp. 1, 7). The news release was widely reprinted all over this
country and abroad. This "diary" (containing lecture notes, notes on
legal cases, and the like) has been published as *The Earliest Diary of
John Adams*, ed. L. H. Butterfield *et al.* (Cambridge, Mass., 1966),
with an introduction tracing the relationship of Tyler with the
Adamses (pp. 16–32). It is possible that this document had been un-
knowingly mentioned in print thirty years earlier, for among the lists
of gifts received, in the *Proceedings of the Vermont Historical Society* for 1936, occurs this statement: "Nearly three-fourths of the
Royall Tyler diary, written in 1753 while he was a student at Harvard,
has been typed as far as it could be deciphered" (IV, 39). Neither
Tyler nor his father was at Harvard in that year, and no Tyler diary
is now known.

44. The Tyler account occurs in *Grandmother Tyler's Book*, pp.
75–82; a retelling based on it is in Katharine Metcalf Roof's *Colonel
William Smith and Lady* (Boston, 1929), pp. 33, 35, 46–50 (chapter
9), 90–101 (chapter 14), 132–133, 308 (including the "suspicion that
Mr. Adams found himself exhilarated by denunciation"). Accounts
based on the Adams Papers are found in Adams' *Diary*, III, 192–193n,
and *Earliest Diary*, pp. 18–28; Janet Whitney, *Abigail Adams* (Boston,
1947), pp. 167–171; Page Smith, *John Adams* (New York, 1962), pp.
531–532, 559–560, 572–573, 591–593, 614–615, 658–662, 665–666 (emphasizing Tyler's "disconcerting instability," his "streak of morbidity
and melancholy introspection," and his "reputation for being fast");
Lida Mayo, "Miss Adams in Love," *American Heritage*, XVI (February 1965), 36–39, 80–89; and Irving Stone, *Those Who Love* (New
York, 1965), pp. 387–393, 398–402, 404–406, 409, 429, 446, 457, 463–
464, 469–470, 481, 484. According to the Tyler version, even Tyler's
participation in the balloon craze was enough to cause a report about
his frivolous behavior to reach Adams' ears (*Grandmother Tyler's
Book*, pp. 80–81; Roof, *Smith*, pp. 98–100). It is also claimed that
Tyler, to prove the Cranches responsible for the malicious gossip,
once planned with the Adamses to give exclusive attention to the
Cranch girls for a few days, whereupon Tyler, in the eyes of the
Cranches, became a model of virtuousness — but, understandably, all
the more wicked when the trick was discovered (*Grandmother Tyler's
Book*, pp. 78–79; Roof, *Smith*, pp. 46–50).

45. Tyler to Adams, 15 October 1785, Adams Papers Microfilms,
Reel 366. Tyler's letter to Abigail is dated 13 October 1785. Adams
replied on 12 December 1785 with a friendly letter, which did not

mention his daughter's prospective union with Smith but did allude to a change in circumstances (Reel 107, pp. 447–448). According to Abigail's letter to Mary Cranch on 15 August 1785 (in the American Antiquarian Society), Tyler had written young Abigail only four letters.

46. On 9 February 1786, for example, she wrote, "I am more thankful than ever that I have been so cautious in what I said about him." This letter and those of 10 January and 22 March–9 April 1786 are on Reel 367 of the Adams Papers Microfilms; those of 8 November and 10 December 1785 are on Reel 366.

47. John Quincy to Abigail Adams, 28 December 1785, Adams Papers Microfilms, Reel 366. Cf. his letter of 15 May 1786 and Abigail's to him of 13 June 1786 (Reel 368). Letters from John Quincy (who had returned to the United States to study at Harvard) to his sister occasionally refer to his associations with Tyler — as those of 29 August–7 September, 8–18 September, and 19–30 September 1785 (Reel 365).

48. Eliza Shaw to Abigail Adams, 18 June 1786, Adams Papers Microfilms, Reel 368. She had earlier expressed dissatisfaction with Tyler's conduct, on 6 November 1785 (Reel 366); more favorable references are in her letters of 12 June 1785 (Reel 364) and 22 July 1786 (Reel 368).

49. Mary Cranch to Abigail Adams, 7 May 1786, Adams Papers Microfilms, Reel 368. That the Cranch daughters delighted in tormenting Tyler is suggested by Betsy Cranch's account of their posting, by the side of a letter for Tyler, the calling card of "Mr. and Mrs. Smith"; see her letter to Abigail, 20 May 1786 (Reel 368).

50. Mary Cranch to Abigail Adams, 2 July 1786, Adams Papers Microfilms, Reel 368.

51. See her letters of 8 July (Tyler neglecting the Cranches' invitations) and 28 September 1786 (Tyler in debt for £200 and speaking slightingly of Colonel Smith) on Reel 368 of the Adams Papers Microfilms; 8 October (Tyler defending himself at the Cranches' expense) and 9 October 1786 (Tyler criticizing Smith and encouraging Negroes to stay in the Adams house) on Reel 369. Her remark on 21 December 1786 (Reel 369) makes it clear that Abigail had asked her not to discuss Tyler further; Abigail had made the same request over a year earlier, on 15 August 1785 (letter in the American Antiquarian Society). Tyler's name did briefly recur in their correspondence at the time of the production of *The Contrast*: Mary Cranch alluded disapprovingly to his play-writing (22 April–20 May 1787, Reel 369), and Abigail thought that the contrast was probably between his own character and that of Smith (16 July 1787, privately owned, and quoted in Adams' *Earliest Diary*, p. 29).

52. Mary Cranch to Abigail Adams, 8 July 1786, Adams Papers Microfilms, Reel 368; cf. her letter of 22 March–3 April 1786, Reel 367.

53. Tyler to Abigail Adams, 13 October 1785, Adams Papers Microfilms, Reel 366; *Grandmother Tyler's Book*, p. 96.

54. This chronology is based on a letter from Mary Cranch to Abigail Adams, 2 July 1786, Adams Papers Microfilms, Reel 368; it differs somewhat from Mary Tyler's retrospective account in *Grandmother Tyler's Book*. For references to Tyler's positions on committees or as moderator of Braintree town meetings, between 1784 and 1786, see *Records of the Town of Braintree*, ed. Samuel A. Bates (Randolph, Mass., 1886), pp. 547, 549, 552, 553, 558–560, 564, 565.

55. See especially Mary Cranch's letter to Abigail Adams, 28 September 1786, Adams Papers Microfilms, Reel 368. The house and farm reverted to the Borlands in 1787, and the Adamses, upon the advice of Mary Cranch, purchased it (Mary Cranch to Abigail Adams, 22 April–20 May 1787, Reel 369).

56. See the accounts of Lincoln in the *Dictionary of American Biography* and in Francis Bowen, *Life of Benjamin Lincoln* (in the *Library of American Biography*, ed. Jared Sparks, 2nd ser., XIII [1847], 207–434), which mentions Tyler on p. 404. See also J. G. Holland, *History of Western Massachusetts* (Springfield, 1855), I, 230–302; Joseph Parker Warren, "The Confederation and the Shays Rebellion," *American Historical Review*, XI (1905–06), 42–67; and John H. Lockwood *et al.*, *Western Massachusetts: A History 1636–1925* (New York, 1926), I, 113–206.

57. Tyler memoir, p. 29; Burnham, *Brattleboro*, p. 89; *Grandmother Tyler's Book*, p. 105.

58. Letter in the Vermont Historical Society; printed in Burnham, *Brattleboro*, p. 90.

59. Burnham, *Brattleboro*, p. 91; *Records of the Governor and Council of the State of Vermont*, ed. E. P. Walton (8 vols.; Montpelier, 1873–1880), III, 119, 125, 375–376 (with pp. 357–380, an appendix on "Vermont at the Period of Shays's Rebellion — 1784 to 1787"). A few months later, on 28 August 1787, Ethan Allen wrote Tyler, pointing out that amicable relations now existed between Vermont and Massachusetts in regard to fugitives and asking whether Tyler could procure enough subscriptions for the publication of the appendix to Allen's *Reason the Only Oracle of Man* (Burnham, *Brattleboro*, p. 92). Tyler apparently could not, for it was not published until 1873 (in the April through August issues of the *Historical Magazine*); see John Pell, *Ethan Allen* (Boston, 1929), p. 264.

60. Letter of 17 February 1787, in Tyler memoir, pp. 44–45.

61. The "Memorial" of 6 March 1787, read in the Massachusetts

House and Senate on 7 March, is now in the Archives of the Secretary of State, Boston, along with a letter to Lincoln of 18 February 1787 and some earlier reports about Shays.

62. Tyler memoir, p. 51.

63. Burnham, *Brattleboro*, pp. 89–92, and Tyler memoir, pp. 29–57, give detailed accounts of Tyler's role in Shays' Rebellion and quote documents written by Tyler and Lincoln. There are also documents relating to Shays' Rebellion in the Tyler Papers at the Vermont Historical Society, including Tyler's letter to Governor Chittenden, 23 February 1787. Some of the state histories, like Ira Allen's *The Natural and Political History of the State of Vermont* (London, 1798), p. 248, allude to Tyler's place in the Shays affair. Further information and references can be found in the sketches of Shays (c. 1747–1825), Shepard (1737–1817), Bowdoin (1726–1790), Sedgwick (1746–1813), Allen (1738–1789), and Chittenden (1730–1797) in the *Dictionary of American Biography*.

64. *Grandmother Tyler's Book*, p. 107; Burnham, *Brattleboro*, p. 93.

65. Burnham, *Brattleboro*, p. 92; Tyler memoir, p. 58.

66. "Biographical Sketch of Gen. Joseph Palmer," *New Englander*, III (January 1845), 2; this article (pp. 1–23), in a magazine edited by one of Tyler's sons, Edward Royall Tyler, is one of the most detailed treatments of Palmer, printing a number of letters and documents, especially in connection with the Rhode Island affair.

67. See Samuel A. Bates, ed., *Records of the Town of Braintree* (Randolph, Mass., 1886), esp. pp. 453–454, 511–512; William S. Pattee, *A History of Old Braintree and Quincy* (Quincy, 1878), esp. pp. 475–482 (purchase of land in Germantown), 486–490 (biographical sketch of Palmer, with a portrait), 490–492 (sketch of Cranch). In addition to the *New Englander* article and the sketch in *DAB*, references to Palmer's work in the Provincial Congress may be found in the *Journals of the Provincial Congress of Massachusetts* (Boston, 1838), *passim*, and the New Hampshire *Provincial Papers*, ed. Nathaniel Bouton, VII (Nashua, 1873), 457. He is also alluded to in the sketch of Robert Treat Paine in George A. Ward, *The Journal and Letters of Samuel Curwen* (4th ed.; Boston, 1864), p. 586. Background for the Rhode Island incident is in Alden Bradford, *History of Massachusetts*, II (Boston, 1825), 125–137, 160–166. It is undoubtedly Palmer's glassworks that Edwin Atlee Barber is referring to in *American Glassware* (Philadelphia, 1900) when he says that thick greenish bottles were made in Germantown in 1760 (p. 12).

68. Adams, *Diary*, I, 233 (1 February 1763).

69. For genealogical trees setting forth these relationships, in both the Palmer and Hunt families, see *Grandmother Tyler's Book*, p. 329. The Palmers are discussed in that book on pp. 20–110 *passim* and in

such books about later branches of the family as Julian Hawthorne, *Nathaniel Hawthorne and His Wife* (Boston, 1884), I, 39–81, and Louise Hall Tharp, *The Peabody Sisters of Salem* (Boston, 1950), pp. 11–19, 341–342. A sketch of J. P. Palmer, as a member of the Boston Tea Party, is included in Francis S. Drake's *Tea Leaves* (Boston, 1884), pp. cxxxviii–cxxxix. For the Hunts, see *Grandmother Tyler's Book*, pp. 5–19, and citations in T. B. Wyman, Jr., *Genealogy of the Name and Family of Hunt* (Boston, 1862–1863), pp. 286–287. The Hunt daughters formed other interesting associations, since Katherine had Elbridge Gerry as a suitor and Mary's second husband (Richard Perkins) was earlier married to John Hancock's sister. Since John Hunt (as well as three of his sons) graduated from Harvard (1734), a sketch appears in Shipton, *Harvard Graduates*, IX (1956), 414–418. One of the sons, Samuel, was for thirty years Master of the Boston Latin School, following John Lovell (see Jenks, *Latin School*, p. 7).

70. The chronology here is confused and is partly a matter of conjecture, for the dates in *Grandmother Tyler's Book* are not always consistent. A comparison of the published book with the manuscript of Mary Tyler's memoirs (in the possession of Edward Royall Tyler — a microfilm copy in the Library of Congress and a handwritten copy in the Vermont Historical Society) shows that numerous small omissions were not indicated by ellipsis marks; but the confusion in dates is in the original as well, the natural result of the tricks of memory after sixty years.

71. This visit to New York is fully described in chapter 4 of *Grandmother Tyler's Book*, pp. 111–137. Mary Tyler mistakenly says that *The Contrast* "was acted every night for some weeks" in 1789 (p. 118).

72. The move to Framingham is described in *Grandmother Tyler's Book*, pp. 138–157. J. H. Temple, in his *History of Framingham, Massachusetts* (Framingham, 1887), says that William and John Hunt operated a tavern at the Phinehas Rice (Nat. Hardy) place, which Joseph P. Palmer took over about 1789 and which his wife kept until 1797 (p. 360).

73. *Grandmother Tyler's Book*, p. 151.

74. *Grandmother Tyler's Book*, p. 180. Constance Rourke, in *The Roots of American Culture* (New York, 1942), comments on Tyler's "obscure and complicated inner life" — reflected in his moodiness, his formality, and his secrecy — and remarks, "Surely he was not in love with little Mary Palmer" (pp. 120–121).

75. According to the *Gazetteer and Business Directory of Windham County, Vermont, 1724–1884*, comp. Hamilton Child (Syracuse, N.Y., 1884), p. 304 (the source also for the figures on Brattleboro

below). The population of Guilford had been only 436 twenty years earlier, in 1771, and it was to fall from its 1791 population to 2256 by 1800. Tyler is mentioned in the sketch of Guilford in Zadock Thompson's *History of Vermont* (Burlington, 1842), III, 83.

76. Burnham, *Brattleboro*, pp. 94–95. In the June term of 1793, Tyler had 62 cases, 32 of them new; in November 48 cases, 22 of them new.

77. The New Lebanon visit is taken up in *Grandmother Tyler's Book*, pp. 157–176, and an incident involving the bracelet on pp. 201–203.

78. This is another point at which the chronology is difficult. The relevant passage of *Grandmother Tyler's Book* (pp. 177–192) first suggests that the proposal came during Tyler's visit just after Mary's return from New Lebanon in the winter of 1792–93; but when Tyler left, after the proposal, he took Mary's father with him, and Joseph Palmer's letters en route to Vermont are dated February 1794. Either Tyler did not propose quite so soon after Mary's return or else Mary is combining her memories of two separate occasions.

79. For the story of the secret marriage, the months of waiting, and the eventual entry into Guilford, see *Grandmother Tyler's Book*, pp. 204–232. The house in which the Tylers lived in Guilford was on land bought by James Fosdick from James and Edward Houghton; see *Official History of Guilford, Vermont*, ed. Broad Brook Grange No. 151 (Guilford, 1961), pp. 196, 368. Other references to Tyler's activities in Guilford are on p. 110 (report of the December town meeting in 1794, when Tyler received eleven votes, more than the other candidates, for the position of representative to the legislature) and pp. 159–160 (brief biographical sketch). See also *Vermont Historical Gazetteer*, V (1891), part 3, pp. 42, 46 (where John Phelps is named as a "warm friend and admirer of Judge Tyler" in Guilford).

80. Joseph Pearse Palmer, who spent his last years away from home, tutoring in Woodstock and Windsor, Vermont, was killed on 25 June 1797, when he fell from a bridge that was under construction at Woodstock. Edward Palmer, through Tyler's influence, had been apprenticed to the Brattleboro printer Benjamin Smead; on 2 July 1797 he drowned and caused the friend who was trying to save him to drown, too. William Wells, the pastor of Christ's Church in Brattleboro, delivered the funeral sermon, which was printed in 1798 by Smead as a twenty-page pamphlet: *A Sermon, Preached at Brattleborough, Vermont, July 3, A.D. 1797 . . . at the Interment of Mess. Pardon Taylor and Edward Palmer, Who the Day Before Were Drowned in Connecticut River*. The story of the drowning is recounted in a four-page preface; the sermon takes Job 1:21 as its text. Tyler's mother was declining in health during the winter of 1799–

1800, and John Steele had written urging Tyler to visit her, but he did not go; see *Grandmother Tyler's Book*, pp. 244–245, 270–271.

81. The letter, written on 18 March 1801, appears in *Grandmother Tyler's Book*, pp. 278–282, in Burnham, *Brattleboro*, p. 97, and in Mary R. Cabot, *Annals of Brattleboro* (Brattleboro, 1921–1922), I, 265–267. Because of its associations (as site of the first meetinghouse in Brattleboro and home of Micah Townsend, first lawyer in the state), the history of this property has been described by Martha Votey Smith in "On Meeting-House Hill," *Vermonter*, XXVI (January 1921), 22–25. See also the *Records of the Council of Safety and Governor and Council of the State of Vermont*, I, 519.

82. The Brattleboro years are described in more detail on pp. 272–326 of *Grandmother Tyler's Book*.

83. Tyler, in the course of his correspondence with Riley about *The Yankey in London* and the Vermont *Reports*, mentioned his wife's work, on 22 May 1810: "Captain Holbrook will show you the manuscript of a little Treatise upon the nurture and management of Infants. You will please not to mention through what channel this work comes to you; but if you incline to print a first edition, upon such terms as Captain Holbrook and you can agree upon, you can keep the manuscript, and the remainder, which will be about as much more, shall be sent to you by the middle of June. I have no doubt it will sell, as it is upon an interesting topic, and written by an American Lady. It must, however, be printed tastily as it is calculated for sale in cities. You can show it to any of your medical friends" (Tyler memoir, p. 280). According to the memoir (p. 286), Mary Tyler refused to have her name on the title page, even though Riley was willing to pay more if the work were signed. There are a few internal hints of her authorship: the preface is signed "Mary"; on p. 17 the author says she has brought up eight children, the number the Tylers had in 1811; on p. 170 she refers to "little Joseph," and Joseph Dennie Tyler would have been not quite seven at the time. The book is discussed briefly by Frederick Tupper in "Royall Tyler, Man of Law and Man of Letters," *Proceedings of the Vermont Historical Society*, IV (1928), 99–100; Tupper originally made the suggestion that Tyler may have supplied his wife with the poetical quotations.

84. *American Modern Practice* (2nd ed.; Boston, 1826), pp. 706, 726, 706, respectively.

85. Mary Tyler died at the age of ninety-one on 7 July 1866, having outlived four of her children. An obituary appears in the *Vermont Phoenix* for 13 July 1866; see also Cabot, *Annals*, I, 271–272, where "Madam Tyler" (as the village called her) is described as "a light and center to society, giving warmth and enjoyment to all who came within her sphere."

86. For example, in a letter to Jonathan Hunt on 24 December 1798 (now in the Dartmouth Library), Tyler mentions that a Mr. Smead has just begun to study in his office.

87. Jacob served as Assistant Judge with Tyler from October 1801 to September 1803, when he was replaced by Theophilus Harrington. In October 1807, when Tyler became Chief Justice, the third place was filled by Jonas Galusha (later Governor), who was replaced in 1809 by David Fay. Tyler was succeeded as Chief Justice by Nathaniel Chipman. James Benjamin Wilbur, in *Ira Allen: Founder of Vermont* (New York, 1928), says that Tyler had been since 1787 an "intimate friend" of Isaac Tichenor, "to whom he undoubtedly owed his appointment" to the Supreme Court (II, 357). For the report of Tyler's election (and taking of the oath — pages given below in parentheses) each October from 1801 through 1812, see the *Records of the Governor and Council of the State of Vermont*, IV, 293 (299), 337, 373; V, 12, 71 (73), 108, 155 (157), 205 (212), 248–249, 286–287, 321 (325), 353 (375); other duties of Tyler are recorded at IV, 97; V, 192, 298, 316; VI, 16, 25.

88. Stephen Row Bradley wrote to Tyler on 27 January 1810, suggesting the possibility that Tyler take over his Senate seat; the letter is in the Boston Public Library and has been published in the Library's *Bulletin*, VII (1903), 70–71. See also the letter (in the Columbia Library) from Jonathan Robinson to Tyler, 1 December 1811.

89. Evidence of one of Tyler's University services is the manuscript copy of the University laws, dated 28 July 1811 and compiled by Tyler and William Czar Bradley; see *UVM Notes*, XVII (December 1920), 8. Jonathan Robinson wrote Tyler on 21 January 1811, congratulating him on his new position as Professor of Law and praising him for his attitude that the law is not infallible and often needs correction (letter in New Hampshire Historical Society). The minutes of the corporation show that Tyler attended meetings on 12 June 1802, 13 October 1804, 11 September 1807, six meetings in October 1810, 2 January 1811, 12 July 1812, and 21 October 1813, and that his main function was to represent the University at the state legislature; his Vermont M.A. was granted 30 June 1811. (See record in Tyler Papers, Box 46). Julian I. Lindsay, in *Tradition Looks Forward: The University of Vermont, A History* (Burlington, 1954), points out that Tyler, soon after he took the oath as trustee (2 January 1811), was asked, on 14 January, to work with President D. C. Sanders in preparing a public address to announce the new administration (pp. 91–92).

90. *Grandmother Tyler's Book*, pp. 183–184. When Thomas P. Tyler tells the incident in his memoir, he says that Tyler's method in the sermons was one of logical argumentation, as if he were presenting a case to a jury; the memoir also suggests that the Reverend Mr.

Wollage was angry upon discovering that Tyler had spoken in his absence.

91. Tyler's connection with the ministry can be overemphasized if, as sometimes happens, he is confused with another Royal [S.] Tyler (1763–1826), who was pastor at Andover, Connecticut, from 4 July 1792 to 20 May 1817 (see Brigham, *Tyler Genealogy*, I, 184–185). This Tyler published *A Family Discourse* (Boston, 1817), which has at times been attributed to the dramatist, as has a letter (17 December 1792) now in the Dartmouth Library, despite the fact that it is signed as "Pastor" of the church at Andover.

92. *Grandmother Tyler's Book*, p. 105.

93. Tyler memoir, pp. 112–114. In the memoir the letter is dated at Bennington, January 1800, but, according to the title page of the *Oration*, the speech was delivered on 22 February. Furthermore, Tyler writes that he wishes his wife were present, but she says, in *Grandmother Tyler's Book* (p. 105), that the only occasion on which she ever heard him speak in public was to deliver the Washington oration. It is perhaps possible that he gave the speech twice, just after Washington's death in December and again on Washington's birthday.

94. The oration has also been discussed by Tupper, "Royall Tyler," pp. 98–99.

95. The two passages are, respectively, from letters of 4 February 1810 and 15 June 1812 (Burnham, *Brattleboro*, pp. 99, 100). From the time Robinson first went to the Senate in 1807 he wrote frequent letters, often weekly, to Tyler describing the political situation in Washington, valuable for their first-hand accounts of events leading up to the War of 1812. See the Tyler memoir, pp. 174–203, 209–220, ^{2}49–54, ^{2}93–115; Robinson's letters to Tyler may also be found at the Boston Public Library, New Hampshire Historical Society, Pennsylvania Historical Society, University of Vermont, and Vermont Historical Society.

96. John A. Graham, *A Descriptive Sketch of the Present State of Vermont* (London, 1797), pp. 154–155. An illustration of one of the traits mentioned here, championing the underdog, is furnished in the correspondence of Roger Vose and Joseph Dennie; it seems that, in a 1789 case in which two of Dennie's Harvard classmates were accused of assault, Tyler was counsel for the defense — see H. M. Ellis, *Joseph Dennie and His Circle* (Austin, Tex., 1915), p. 66; and *The Letters of Joseph Dennie*, ed. Laura G. Pedder (Orono, Me., 1936), p. 57n. Though Graham calls Tyler a resident of Ryegate, there is no mention of Tyler in Edward Miller and Frederic P. Wells, *History of Ryegate, Vermont* (St. Johnsbury, Vt., 1913).

97. Tyler memoir, pp. 107–108.

98. A series of Tyler's letters to Riley is included in the Tyler

memoir (pp. ²54–81 *passim*). The correspondence seems to have begun (on Riley's part) on 10 October 1808, and Tyler first replied on 8 November. On 22 July 1809 he sent the last batch of material for the first volume, and on 13 December 1809 Riley wrote: "The Reports are out, and will be shipped to Mr. Fessenden on Monday." Tyler sent the copy for 360 pages of volume II on 22 May 1810. The copyright deposit date for volume I is 27 October 1809; for volume II, 30 November 1810.

99. A similar attitude is reflected in Tyler's own comment that "at a not far distant period the bar of *Vermont* will be viewed in a light not unfavourable by the more eminent of the profession in the elder States" (2 Tyl. 135). The reception of the *Reports* is discussed in the Tyler memoir, p. 81; these two letters, of 21 July and 3 August 1810, are quoted from that source.

100. The People v. Douglass, 4 Cowen 26 (1825); he made the remark in connection with a citation of 1 Tyl. 252. The comment is repeated by John William Wallace in *The Reporters, Chronologically Arranged* (3rd ed.; Philadelphia, 1855), p. 343. Nine small corrections of Tyler's work are listed in Guy B. Horton, *Notes on the Vermont Reports* (Montpelier, 1941), pp. [5–6]. Perhaps it was Savage's remark which lay behind the comments in the Boston *Courier* obituary of Tyler: "The two volumes of reports which bear his name, were prepared with almost as much haste and lack of labor as his light literary articles, and are of course meagre abstracts of Decisions, the majority of which are of no permanent value."

101. Statements by Tyler appear in the reports of the following cases: Pearse v. Goddard, 1 Tyl. 373 (1802); Adams v. Brownson, 1 Tyl. 452 (1802); Robbins v. Windover and Hopkins, 2 Tyl. 11 (1802); Harris v. Huntington *et al.*, 2 Tyl. 129 (1802); Selectmen of Windsor v. Jacob, 2 Tyl. 192 (1802); Rich v. Trimble, 2 Tyl. 349 (1803); State v. White, 2 Tyl. 352 (1803); Browne *et al.* v. Graham, 2 Tyl. 411 (1803). Tyler is listed as *dubitante* or *hesitante* in the following: Doe v. Whitlock, 1 Tyl. 305 (1802); Sherwood v. Pearl, 1 Tyl. 319 (1802); Hawley v. Clerk and Hazletine, 2 Tyl. 20 (1802); Wallace v. Farnsworth, 2 Tyl. 297 (1803); Cushenden and Rutherford v. Harman *et al.*, 2 Tyl. 431 (1803). Tyler did not sit for the case of Houghton v. Jewett and Martin, 2 Tyl. 183 (1802), because he was counsel for the plaintiff.

102. 1 Tyl. 454; 2 Tyl. 141.

103. See H. S. Wardner, "Judge Jacob and His Dinah," *Vermonter*, XIX (May–June 1914), 80–88. The case is one of the few that Horton singles out for brief comment in *Notes on the Vermont Reports* (no pagination). It is also referred to in two biographical sketches by Russell Taft which emphasize Tyler's legal career: *Green Bag*, VI

(1894), 72–74 (part of a series on the Supreme Court of Vermont, V, 553–564; VI, 16–35, 72–91, 122–141, 176–192); and "Royall Tyler," *Green Bag*, XX (1908), 1–5. Tupper ("Royall Tyler," p. 67) assigns to Tyler the famous statement that the only valid claim to a slave is "a quit-claim deed of ownership from the Almighty," but Horton attributes the remark to Tyler's fellow-judge Theophilus Harrington. (Tupper's main discussion of Tyler's legal career is on pp. 79–82.)

104. The denial of the appeal for Dean is on pp. 36–48 of the pamphlet; the quotation from the jury charge is taken from the Tyler memoir, pp. 228–232. In addition to these sources, two detailed accounts of the affair are in Walter Hill Crockett, *Vermont: The Green Mountain State* (New York, 1921), III, 3–15, and *Vermont Historical Gazetteer*, ed. A. M. Hemenway, II (1871), 342–347 (which includes another passage from the jury charge). Less complete are Walter Hill Crockett, *A History of Lake Champlain* (Burlington, 1909), p. 237, and Ralph Nading Hill, *The Winooski: Heartway of Vermont* (New York, 1949), pp. 127–132 (which quotes from a ballad on the subject). Mary Tyler wrote to her husband on 3 March 1809, "Mr. Buckingham has sent us the *great trial*" (Tyler Papers, Box 46).

105. This chronology of the circuit is derived from Tyler's *Reports*.

106. These letters are included in the Tyler memoir, pp. 138–151. The specific quotations given here are, respectively, from the letters of 2 February, 8 February, 11 January, and 11 February 1802. A similar sentiment occurs in a letter of January 1800: "I enjoy myself as well as I could wish or expect away from you" (p. 114); in the same letter he tells of declining an invitation because "I have religiously resolved never to participate in the evening social circle without the presence of my wife." The Pennsylvania Historical Society has a three-page letter from Tyler to his wife, written at Woodstock on 9 October 1807. It expresses the same concern with the health of his family, gives advice about the tenant, and promises money. Some letters to Tyler from his wife, during these years, are in the Tyler Papers, Box 46.

107. The salary of the Vermont Chief Justice was $1000 and of the Assistant Judges $900 (the Governor received only $750), according to *Walton's Vermont Register and Farmer's Almanack* for 1819 (Montpelier), p. 97. Graham (*Descriptive Sketch*, p. 179) gives the salary for 1792 as 27 shillings per day on the circuit for the Chief Justice and 22 shillings for the Assistant Judges. After Tyler's retirement from the bench, he no longer had any right to the state's collection of statute books, and the *Records of the Governor and Council of the State of Vermont* report that George Worthington was asked, on 8 November 1814, to move these volumes from Tyler's house in Brattleboro to the statehouse in Montpelier (VI, 99–100).

108. Burnham, *Brattleboro*, p. 101. Burnham credits the story to Justice Daniel Kellogg, who was a young law student at the time and who was present in the courtroom.

109. Letter of 22 May 1810, in Tyler memoir, p. 79.

110. The fullest account of the accomplishments of Tyler's children is in appendix B of *Grandmother Tyler's Book*, pp. 337–357. For Edward Royall, see also the obituary notice in the *New Englander*, VI (October 1848), 603–608, which lists his articles and published sermons; for Amelia, see also Cabot, *Annals*, I, 382–384. Royall (Charles) published a legal work, *A Book of Forms*, in Brattleboro in the early summer of 1845; George Palmer wrote an elegy on Lincoln, *The Successful Life* (Brattleboro, 1865), and revised the *Encyclopedia of Religious Knowledge* in 1858.

111. Denison's son Henry, a classmate of young Royall's, wrote an elegy on his friend's death; he, too, was to die as a young man (in October 1819). Undoubtedly it was this association which made Denison one of the few persons to whom Tyler would talk in the months just after the tragedy (*Grandmother Tyler's Book*, p. 325). For a fuller account of Henry Denison, see the *Official History of Guilford, Vermont*, pp. 171–172. Twenty-six of Denison's poems (with a biographical sketch) are included in *The Columbian Lyre* (Glasgow, 1828), pp. 245–284; the "Elegy on the Death of Royall Tyler, jun." (pp. 280–282), in forty-eight iambic pentameter lines, contains a reference to Tyler's grief: "That eve, that saw a hapless father weep." There is a letter in the New York Public Library, from Tyler to Israel Tefft (editor of the Savannah *Georgian*), 24 November 1820, which shows that Tyler had agreed to contribute to a biography of young Denison (for an edition of his works), and was doing research into Denison's ancestry; in the letter, he apologizes for not having finished his part, and he quotes from a letter of James Rousseau which discusses the whereabouts of Denison's manuscripts. Tefft was responsible for getting Denison's poems into *The Columbian Lyre*, and he wrote an explanation of the delay in publication to be inserted at the front of the volume; the Boston Public Library copy is inscribed to his son, Henry Denison Tefft. See G. T. Tanselle, "*The Columbian Lyre*, 1828," *Transactions of the Edinburgh Bibliographical Society*, IV (1966), 159–165.

112. The moves to five different Brattleboro houses, after the family left the farm, are recorded in *Grandmother Tyler's Book*, p. 326, note 1. *Walton's Vermont Register* for 1819 lists the Register of Probate fees: the charge for recording or copying a will was eight cents; for drawing up an administration bond, thirty-four cents; and for drawing the probate of a will thirty-four cents (for estates up to $166), and forty-two cents (over $166). Tyler is listed as Register of

Probate from 1815 to 1821 in Leonard Deming's *Catalogue of the Principal Officers of Vermont* (Middlebury, 1851), pp. 81–83. Though Tyler was not able to transact much legal business in his last years, he was listed in the *Vermont Register* as one of the attorneys in Brattleboro to the very end of his life; see, for example, the *Registers* for 1819 (p. 82), 1820 (p. 63), 1822 (p. 87), 1824 (p. 69), 1826 (p. 99).

113. This journal begins on 2 December 1821 and continues until 1843, providing a contemporary record for the years following those covered in the retrospective *Grandmother Tyler's Book* (written 1858–1863). Selections for the years 1821–1826 have been published by G. F. Newbrough in "Mary Tyler's Journal," *Vermont Quarterly*, XX (1952), 19–31, from which the present quotations are taken (cf. Tyler Papers, Box 45, Envelope 10). The continually recurring motif is faith in God despite adversity; the journal is important for its detailed references to current prices (apples at 10¢ a bushel, a quarter of beef at $3.25), household chores (such as making pies, knitting, mending shirts), social activities (visits from Judges Denison and Whitney, games of backgammon), and medical knowledge, as well as to Tyler's decline. There are letters of Mary Tyler's from this period mentioning financial difficulties (12 January 1823) and the low state of Tyler's health (10 August 1825), in the Tyler Papers, Box 46.

114. According to Dr. Gordon N. French of the Green Mountain Clinic, Northfield, Vermont, Tyler's disease was melanosarcoma, tumor of the choroid layer of the eye (Newbrough, "Journal," p. 31).

115. Burnham, *Brattleboro*, p. 101.

II. *Dramatist:* The Contrast

1. Quoted from Tyler's unpublished and unfinished work, "The Bay Boy," from a section entitled "First Theatrical Presentation in Boston," describing an amateur production of *Cato*; quoted, by permission of the heirs and the Vermont Historical Society, from a typescript in the Tyler Papers, gift of Helen Tyler Brown.

2. Constance Rourke, "Rise of Theatricals," *The Roots of American Culture* (New York, 1942), pp. 88–108. The standard history of the early American theater is Arthur Hobson Quinn's *A History of the American Drama from the Beginning to the Civil War* (2nd ed.; New York, 1943), pp. 1–135; for greater detail see the first volume of George C. D. Odell's *Annals of the New York Stage* (New York, 1927) and Hugh F. Rankin's *The Theater in Colonial America* (Chapel Hill, N.C., 1965).

3. Dunlap, *History of the American Theatre* (New York, 1832), p. 71. The 1786 date is repeated by (among others) Benrimo (referred

to below); Henry A. Beers, *Initial Studies in American Letters* (New York, 1895), pp. 63–64; Julian W. Abernethy, *American Literature* (New York, 1902), pp. 98–99; William B. Cairns, *A History of American Literature* (New York, 1912), pp. 138–139.

4. See *Argus and Patriot*, n.s. XXIX (5 November 1879), 1; M. D. Gilman, *The Bibliography of Vermont* (Burlington, 1897), p. 282; Tyler memoir (cf. Chapter 1, note 4, above), p. 60. This date is followed by (among others) Henry Burnham, *Brattleboro, Windham County, Vermont* (Brattleboro, 1880), p. 93; and Walter Hill Crockett, *Vermont* (New York, 1921), V, 73.

5. Joseph Ireland, *Records of the New York Stage* (New York, 1866), I, 76. Among the early historians, George O. Seilhamer also gives the correct date, in his *History of the American Theatre* (New York, 1888–1891), II, 215, as does Oscar Wegelin, in *Early American Plays 1714–1830* (New York, 1900); but T. Allston Brown, in *A History of the New York Stage* (New York, 1903), I, 9, dates the first performance as 18 April 1787.

6. Because the reviewer refers to the performance "last evening," Barnard Hewitt, in *Theatre U.S.A.: 1668 to 1957* (New York, 1959), p. 34, gives the opening date as 17 April 1787. However, one must assume, I think, that the reviewer was doing the actual writing of the review on the day after the performance and that it did not get printed until the second day. It seems safer to rely on the advertisements. If a performance were to be held on the 17th, it is unlikely that the notice on the 17th would mention only the one for the following evening, when the issue for the 16th does say "This Evening."

7. The companion piece on 18 April was O'Keeffe's *The Poor Soldier*; on 2 May, Colman's *The Deuce Is in Him*; and on 12 May, Inchbald's *The Widow's Vow*. See the advertisements in the *Independent Journal*; this paper also reports the 18 April performance as "with some alterations." There is no evidence for a 5 May performance of *The Contrast*, as listed by Seilhamer (*History*, II, 215) and Odell (*Annals*, I, 255): no such performance is announced in the New York newspapers; 5 May 1787 was a Saturday, and plays were normally presented only on Monday, Wednesday, and Friday; and the play for Friday, 4 May, was *Romeo and Juliet*.

8. Quoted by Montrose J. Moses, *Representative Plays by American Dramatists* (New York, 1918), p. 436. After the publication of the play in 1790, it was given a number of unauthorized productions in Southern cities by Charles McGrath, who continually pirated copyrighted works; in 1790 and 1791 audiences in Alexandria, Frederick, Georgetown, Hagerstown, Williamsburg, and perhaps other cities saw *The Contrast*. It was performed in the first regular Boston season, on 29 October 1792; in Alexandria in 1793; in Charleston on 25 Feb-

ruary 1793 and 11 February 1794; in Boston again on 11 May 1795; and in Philadelphia on 27 June 1796. Cf. Thomas C. Pollock, *The Philadelphia Theatre in the Eighteenth Century* (Philadelphia, 1933), pp. 45, 141, 158, 303; and Eola Willis, *The Charleston Stage in the XVIII Century* (Columbia, S.C., 1924), pp. 163, 196. In Charleston the play was advertised as by "Major Tyler," and it was given the subtitle, "The American Son of Liberty."

9. See the article on *Androboros* and text by Lawrence H. Leder, *Bulletin of the New York Public Library*, LXVIII (1964), 153–190. As early as 1894 Paul Leicester Ford, in "The Beginnings of American Dramatic Literature," *New England Magazine*, n.s. IX (1894), 673–687, tried to correct the misconceptions about *The Contrast* by pointing out some of these other firsts.

10. A. Benrimo, "The First American Play," *Dramatic Magazine*, I (May 1880), 57–59; Andrew P. Peabody, "The Farmer's Weekly Museum," *Proceedings of the American Antiquarian Society*, n.s. VI (1889), 115; "Early American Dramatists," *Theatre*, XXIV (October 1916), 208, 250; *Official History of Guilford, Vermont* (Guilford, 1961), p. 160. Katharine Metcalf Roof, in *Colonel William Smith and Lady* (Boston, 1929), declares, "*The Contrast* was the first play by an American dramatist to be produced in the American theatre" (p. 133n); but she also assigns its production to 1786 (p. 133) and its composition to Tyler's stay with his mother at Jamaica Plain, where "between outbursts of despair he unquestionably wrote dramas" (p. 132).

11. Dunlap, *History*, p. 71; Ireland, *Records*, I, 76.

12. Hewitt, *Theatre U.S.A.*, p. 36; Rourke, "Rise of Theatricals," p. 115.

13. See Evert A. and George L. Duyckinck, *Cyclopaedia of American Literature* (New York, 1855), I, 432; and Joseph T. Buckingham, *Specimens of Newspaper Literature* (Boston, 1850), II, 203. Thomas P. Tyler, in giving the 1789 date for the production of the play, sets the winter of 1788–89 as the time of its composition (see note 4 above).

14. This whole argument is set forth clearly by Arthur H. Nethercot in "The Dramatic Background of Royall Tyler's *The Contrast*," *American Literature*, XII (1941), 435–446.

15. Frederick Tupper, "Royall Tyler, Man of Law and Man of Letters," *Proceedings of the Vermont Historical Society*, IV (1928), 71.

16. *Worcester Magazine*, III (May 1787), 61; Seilhamer, *History*, II, 234–235; *Independent Chronicle*, 30 October 1797.

17. Dunlap, *History*, pp. 71–72; Duyckinck, *Cyclopaedia*, I, 432; Odell, *Annals*, I, 256; Oral Coad and Edwin Mims, *The American Stage* (New Haven, 1929), p. 33; Robert E. Rogers, "Our Dramatic

Past," *New Republic*, X (21 April 1917), 10–11 sup. (review of Quinn's anthology); Moses, *Representative Plays*, pp. 435, 437; Grenville Vernon, *Yankee Doodle-Doo* (New York, 1927), p. 23; Russell Blankenship, *American Literature* (New York, 1931), pp. 703–704; Quinn, *History*, pp. 294–303; Glenn Hughes, *A History of the American Theatre* (New York, 1951), pp. 57–58.

18. Arthur Hornblow, *A History of the Theatre in America* (Philadelphia, 1919), I, 171. Some of the other roles were taken by prominent actors also: Manly by John Henry, Dimple by Lewis Hallam, Van Rough and Charlotte by Mr. and Mrs. Morris, Jessamy and Maria by Mr. and Mrs. Harper. In the Baltimore cast (followed in the 1789 New York performance) Hallam took the role of Manly and Harper of Dimple. For information about the casts see Odell, *Annals*, I, 257, 274; Seilhamer, *History*, III, 211, 250. On Wignell, see W. B. Wood, *Personal Recollections of the Stage* (Philadelphia, 1854).

19. Perley Isaac Reed, *The Realistic Presentation of American Characters in Native Plays Prior to Eighteen Seventy* (Columbus: *Ohio State University Bulletin*, May 1918; Contributions in Language and Literature, No. 1), p. 136. He points out further that after the years 1787–1789 the Yankee type rarely appears for twenty years, but particularly after 1815 it becomes very prominent.

20. Reed, *Realistic Presentation*, pp. 136–137.

21. See Albert Matthews, "Brother Jonathan," *Publications of the Colonial Society of Massachusetts*, VII (1901), 94–122; "Brother Jonathan Once More," XXXII (1935), 374–386. Matthews reports the story that the term originated as a friendly nickname applied by Washington to Governor Jonathan Trumbull of Connecticut but rejects the account because it can be traced back no farther than 1846.

22. The discovery of this first Jonathan play was announced by Marston Balch in "Jonathan the First," *Modern Language Notes*, XLVI (1931), 281–288. Balch points out a number of parallels between Tyler's figure and Atkinson's and believes that in both cases the Yankee "remains at the end the most clearly defined figure of all." Atkinson's play would have attracted more attention if it had been played in London, but Mrs. Inchbald's version of Patrat's work was already established there (as well as in America, where Tyler could have seen it on 23 March 1787).

23. This is not to disagree with Constance Rourke in considering Tyler's depiction of Jonathan an event of prime historic significance, but only to change the emphasis. When she asserts that the Yankee sprang "almost full blown" from *The Contrast*, with not even a prose sketch preceding it ("Rise of Theatricals," p. 117), she is speaking,

I take it, of the appearance of a satisfactory literary embodiment of a particular attitude, not the appearance of the attitude itself — though, of course, the nature of a literary symbol is such that it often makes this kind of separation difficult. Reed has the same point in mind when he says that Jonathan was "reproduced fundamentally from the very substance of American civilization" (*Realistic Presentation*, p. 46); Allan G. Halline, however, in his anthology *American Plays* (New York, 1935), finds the nationalism of the play a much greater contribution than the creation of Jonathan (pp. 4–6). For further discussion of Yankee characters, see Walter Blair, *Native American Humor* (New York, 1937), pp. 17–37; Richard M. Dorson, "The Yankee on Stage," *New England Quarterly*, XIII (1940), 467–493; James J. Quinn, "The Jonathan Character in American Drama" (unpub. diss., Columbia, 1955).

24. Vernon, in *Yankee Doodle-Doo* (pp. 23–24), says that *The Contrast* "gave to us the version of 'Yankee Doodle' which most of us know"; Reed (*Realistic Presentation*, p. 48) considers it the first dramatic use of the text; Balch ("Jonathan the First," p. 287n) traces the "authentic" version, not printed until 1815, to Edward Bangs, a Harvard undergraduate with Tyler. See also *Living Age*, LXX (10 August 1861), 382–384; and O. G. T. Sonneck, *Report on "The Star Spangled Banner," "Hail Columbia," "America," "Yankee Doodle"* (Washington, 1909), pp. 79–156.

25. This tradition (including "Alknomook") has been discussed by Frank Edgar Farley, "The Dying Indian," in *Anniversary Papers by Colleagues and Pupils of George Lyman Kittredge* (Boston, 1913), pp. 251–260.

26. Thomas J. McKee in his introduction to the Dunlap Society edition of *The Contrast* (New York, 1887), p. x; Quinn, *History*, p. 71n. Richard Moody, in *America Takes the Stage* (Bloomington, Ind., 1955), mentions a "*Death Song of a Cherokee Chief* (1790)" as one of Tyler's works (p. 86).

27. *The Poems of Philip Freneau*, ed. F. L. Pattee (Princeton, 1903), III, 313–314; Pattee did append a note saying, "The authenticity of a poem suspected to be Freneau's may always be gravely doubted if it is not found to be included in his collected works, for he hoarded his poetic product . . . with miserly care." It was still credited to Freneau by W. B. Cairns in *Early American Writers* (New York, 1909), p. 440, and Annie Russell Marble, *Heralds of American Literature* (Chicago, 1907), pp. 95–96, among others. But Harry Hayden Clark did not include it in his 1929 edition, and Lewis Leary, in *That Rascal Freneau* (New Brunswick, N.J., 1941), says that the *American Museum* "mistakenly" attributed the song to Freneau (p. 152).

28. Anne Home Hunter, *Poems* (London, 1802), pp. 79–80; *British*

Critic, XX (1802), 409–413; *Gentleman's Magazine*, XCI (part 1; January 1821), 89–90. She says that the lyrics were suggested by a man who had resided among the Cherokees. The song appeared in Joseph Ritson's *Select Collection of English Song* (London, 1783), I, ii, and in sheet music of the early 1780's. In America, after the *American Museum* appearance (I, 90), it was included in *The Philadelphia Songster* (Philadelphia, 1789), p. 8; the American sheet music came later, about 1800. The songs from *Tammany* are reprinted in *Magazine of History*, XLIII (1931), 59–69. McKee noted its use in a British play, John Scawen's *New Spain*, but the date he gave, 1740, is a misprint for 1790. For further discussion, see *Musical Antiquary*, III (1912), 166–170; Tom Peete Cross's review of Henry A. Burd's *Joseph Ritson* (1916) in *Modern Philology*, XVII (1919), 233–238; and G. T. Tanselle, "The Birth and Death of Alknomook," forthcoming in the *Newberry Library Bulletin*.

29. All quotations are from the first edition of 1790. Act and scene (rather than page) numbers are given to facilitate reference to later editions (which are not always, however, very accurate; a dependable one, despite a few changes in punctuation, is in Arthur Hobson Quinn's anthology *Representative American Plays* [New York, 1917]). The first edition used inverted commas around lines and passages "omitted in the representation"; within the passages quoted in this chapter, then, single quotation marks indicate words not spoken on the stage.

30. The reading of a letter (III.i) is a common device to accomplish the same ends, but at least it makes the exposition more plausible in a framework that emphasizes externals.

31. Herbert R. Brown, in "Sensibility in Eighteenth-Century American Drama," *American Literature*, IV (1932), 47–60, discusses *The Contrast* in terms of the sentimentality, the didacticism, the sympathy for humanitarian reform, and the "prevailing moral tone" characteristic of both the drama and the fiction of the time; he shows some parallels between Manly and Bevil in Steele's *The Conscious Lovers* (1722). Nethercot ("Dramatic Background," pp. 444–446) suggests a possible influence in Hugh Kelly's *False Delicacy* (1768), which exposes excesses of sentiment and has a character similar to Maria; he also points to George Colman's *Polly Honeycombe* (1760) for its references to the circulating libraries. For a fuller discussion of the sentimental tradition, see Ernest Bernbaum, *The Drama of Sensibility* (Boston, 1915).

32. Nethercot ("Dramatic Background," p. 442) suggests possible sources for some of the names: Manly in Vanbrugh's *Provoked Husband* (1728) and Wycherley's *Plain Dealer* (1677); Transfer in Samuel Foote's *The Minor* (1760).

33. Van Rough's phrase, however, is not so much a speech habit as an expression of a ruling philosophy with him.

34. Marie Killheffer, in "A Comparison of the Dialect of 'The Biglow Papers' with the Dialect of Four Yankee Plays," *American Speech*, III (1928), 222–236, analyzes Jonathan's language in *The Contrast*, particularly III.i. Tyler's method, she says, is to use "a few localisms against a background of standard English" (pp. 230–231); *The Contrast*, among the plays she studied, "shows the slightest attempt to indicate dialect but by far the largest proportion of dialect words used are localisms" (p. 235). She gives a summary of the traits of the Jonathan-figure on p. 222. Another discussion of the language in *The Contrast* is in George H. McKnight and Bert Emsley's *Modern English in the Making* (New York, 1928), pp. 479–480; one of the contrasts in the play is shown to be the difference between "the American countrified mode of speech and the refinements of speech in American urban life" — for Jonathan uses older forms no longer current in cultivated conversation. That the play is "thematically concerned with questions of language" has been perceptively argued by Roger B. Stein, in "Royall Tyler and the Question of Our Speech," *New England Quarterly*, XXXVIII (1965), 454–474. He suggests that the heart of the drama is a satiric exposure of the weakness or falsity of various speech patterns, which become masks to hide character; the search for an honest, authentic native speech produces an unresolved dilemma, he says, from which Tyler is forced to extricate himself by resorting to a conventional plot line in the last part of the play.

35. "Rantipole," first used about 1700, appears in Vanbrugh's *Provoked Husband* and provides a further reason for believing that this play may have influenced Tyler; it was performed in New York two weeks before *The Contrast*, on 29 March 1787. Tyler's use of "penseroso" is discussed by B. Sprague Allen in *Tides in English Taste, 1619–1800* (Cambridge, Mass., 1937), II, 176.

36. The idea that the play is important as an early treatment of the "international theme," contrasting American innocence with Old World corruption, is discussed by John Lauber, "*The Contrast*: A Study in the Concept of Innocence," *English Language Notes*, I (1963), 33–37. He compares the Dimple-Maria-Manly relationship with that of Osmond-Isabel-Goodwood in *The Portrait of a Lady*; in Manly, he says, Tyler almost provides an instance of R. W. B. Lewis' "American Adam." The first American play with international contrasts, according to Halline's *American Plays*, is John Leacock's *The Fall of British Tyranny* (1776).

37. *Daily Advertiser*, 18 April 1787; *Independent Journal*, 5 May 1787; *Worcester Magazine*, III (1787), 61; *Pennsylvania Herald*, 13 November 1787 (see Seilhamer, *History*, II, 233).

38. The *Pennsylvania Journal*, after the Baltimore production, also praised the sentiments of the play, speaking of the "vices it corrects" and the "pernicious maxims of the Chesterfieldian system" which it exposes (Seilhamer, *History*, II, 233).

39. The volume was advertised for sale by Thomas & Andrews' Bookstore in the *Massachusetts Centinel*, 22 May 1790; it was entered for copyright in the Pennsylvania district court on 15 June 1790. The subscription list in the published volume contains 371 names, including Aaron Burr, David Humphreys, Isaiah Thomas, Jonathan Trumbull, and George Washington; some persons subscribed for more than one copy, and the list thus accounts for 658 copies, 311 of which were to go to persons in Maryland. See Seilhamer, *History*, II, 234–237, for a discussion of the list and for an exposition of the theory that publication was held up because of jealousy aroused by Wignell's success as Jonathan.

40. *Universal Asylum and Columbian Magazine* (Philadelphia), V (August 1790), 117–120.

41. "Scenes from the Contrast," *Massachusetts Magazine*, II (October 1790), 581–583.

42. Dunlap, *History*, pp. 71–72; Buckingham, *Newspaper Literature*, II, 203; Duyckinck, *Cyclopaedia*, I, 432.

43. Charles F. Richardson, *American Literature 1607–1885*, II (New York, 1888), 18; *A Library of American Literature*, ed. Edmund C. Stedman and Ellen M. Hutchinson, IV (New York, 1888), 92–97. Other late nineteenth-century references to the play, besides Seilhamer (1889), *History*, II, 225–239, are in Washington Frothingham and Charlemagne Tower, *Our Book*, 2nd ed. (New York, 1892), pp. 380–382; Donald G. Mitchell, *American Lands and Letters* (New York, 1897), pp. 220–224; Katherine Lee Bates, *American Literature* (New York, 1898), pp. 82–83 (" Dull, trivial, and shapeless"); Henry A. Beers, *An Outline Sketch of American Literature* (New York, 1887), p. 79 ("very low comedy").

44. Despite the myth that only one or two copies survive, there are at least a dozen copies of the first edition now in institutional collections. George Washington's copy sold for $2800 in the Avery sale of 1919 and for $3100 in the Wilbur sale of 1933. See Wilbur's preface to his 1920 edition of *The Contrast*, pp. v–xviii; L. E. Chittenden, *Personal Reminiscences* (New York, 1893), pp. 288–293; and G. T. Tanselle, "Some Uncollected Authors XLII: Royall Tyler, 1757–1826," *Book Collector*, XV (1966), 303–320.

45. For example: Marble (1907), *Heralds*, pp. 238–242; Carl Holliday, *The Wit and Humor of Colonial Days* (Philadelphia, 1912), pp. 295–301; William J. Long, *American Literature* (Boston, 1913), p. 93 (Tyler's "crude plays"); William P. Trent *et al.*, *Cambridge History of American Literature* (New York, 1917), I, 218–219; Hornblow

(1919), *Theatre in America*, I, 170–172; Quinn (1923), *History*, pp. 64–73; Mary Caroline Crawford, *The Romance of the American Theatre* (Boston, 1925), pp. 91–94; Montrose J. Moses, *The American Dramatist* (Boston, 1925), pp. 72–74; Odell (1927), *Annals*, I, 255–257; Coad and Mims (1929), *American Stage*, p. 33; Charles Angoff, *A Literary History of the American People* (New York, 1931), II, 372–376 ("worthless as drama"); Fred Lewis Pattee, *The First Century of American Literature 1770–1870* (New York, 1935), pp. 218–221; Van Wyck Brooks, *The World of Washington Irving* (New York, 1944), pp. 148, 160; Robert E. Spiller *et al.*, *Literary History of the United States* (New York, 1948), pp. 186–187; Hughes (1951), *History*, pp. 57–58; A. H. Quinn *et al.*, *Literature of the American People* (New York, 1951), pp. 198–200; Walter F. Taylor, *The Story of American Letters* (rev. ed.; Chicago, 1956), pp. 60–61; Hewitt (1959), *Theatre U.S.A.*, pp. 34–37.

46. Some of these performances are as follows: 6–8 June 1912: Brattleboro pageant; 16, 18 January 1917: Players of the University of Pennsylvania; 22–23 January 1917: Drama League of America (New York); 7 April 1917: Drama League of Boston; 19–21 November 1925 and 11–12 June 1926: Cornell Dramatic Club; 30 October 1926: Columbia Laboratory Players (reviewed in *Billboard*, XXXVIII [October–December 1926], 39); 7–19 March 1927: Pasadena Community Playhouse; 1932: Marquis Players of Lafayette College (Easton, Pa.); 15–17 December 1937: Bennington College Theatre Guild; 25 March 1940: Dock Street Theatre, Charleston (version arranged by Charles H. Meredith); 11–16 November 1940: Senior Players, Pasadena; 5–6 December 1941: Curtain Callers, Manse Barn, Tappan, N.Y. (Meredith version); 3–12 November 1943: Catholic University of America (directed by Walter Kerr); 20 July 1948: On-Stage, New York Academy of Vocal Arts (reviewed by Richard Watts in New York *Post*, 22 July; by William Hawkins in *World Telegram*, 23 July); July 1954: Hyde Park (N.Y.) Players; 26–27 March 1958: Boston University Division of Fine Arts (directed by Priscilla Bussan); 17 February–8 March 1959: Fair Park Arena Theatre, Dallas; December 1960: Hofstra College Drama Department; July 1966: O'Neill Conference, Waterford, Conn. (produced and directed by Worthington Minor). Photographs of productions appear in *Theatre Arts*, XVI (July 1932), 570; XXIII (July 1939), 526; XXXVIII (September 1954), 31; and in *Life*, XXXVII (2 August 1954), 73.

47. The articles by Killheffer (1928), Balch (1931), Brown (1932), Nethercot (1941), Lauber (1963), and Stein (1965) have already been referred to, as has the dissertation by Reed (1918). Among the other relevant dissertations are Allan G. Halline, "Main Currents of Thought in American Drama" (Wisconsin, 1935), and Josef A. Elfenbein,

"American Drama 1782–1812 as an Index to Socio-Political Thought" (New York University, 1952).

48. See, for example, "Our First Truly National Play: How a Young Harvard Graduate Was Inspired to Create 'Brother Jonathan,'" *Delineator*, LXXXV (July 1914), 7; J. L. Hornibrook, "America's First Comedy," *Landmark*, XIV (1932), 391–392.

49. Anthologies edited by Quinn (1917), Moses (1918), Spiller (1933), Halline (1935), Cady (1950), Downer (1960), Stern and Gross (1962), and Moody (1966) — see Bibliography. Excerpts from the play have been reprinted in numerous biographical sketches of Tyler and in other anthologies.

50. Before its publication in the 1790 volume, the prologue had been published in the New York *Daily Advertiser* on 20 April 1787.

III. *Dramatist: Later Plays*

1. New York *Daily Advertiser*, 19 May 1787. The prologue was to be spoken by Mrs. Morris.

2. The New York *Journal and Weekly Register* of 17 May 1787, for example, advertised the play for "tomorrow"; but the New York *Packet* the next day was still announcing it for "tomorrow," with a note about its unavoidable postponement. Cf. George C. D. Odell, *Annals of the New York Stage* (New York, 1927), I, 259.

3. Odell, *Annals*, I, 259. Arthur Hornblow, in his *History of the Theatre in America* (Philadelphia, 1919), similarly says that the play "probably had little merit" (p. 172).

4. The letter is in volume VII of the Madison Papers, Library of Congress; it has been published by Worthington C. Ford, in "The Federal Constitution in Virginia, 1787–1788," *Proceedings of the Massachusetts Historical Society*, 2nd series, XVII (1903), 461; and it is quoted by Helen Tyler Brown in her introduction to the 1920 limited edition of *The Contrast* (p. xxx).

5. *The Letters of Joseph Dennie*, ed. Laura G. Pedder (Orono, Me.: University of Maine Studies, 2nd series, no. 36, 1936), pp. 150–151; the five letters from Dennie to Tyler given in this edition are taken from the Tyler memoir (cf. Chapter 1, note 4, above).

6. Tyler memoir, p. 84; T. P. Tyler says that a fragment of the play was found among his father's papers. For announcements of the play, see Boston *Columbian Centinel*, 4 May 1796, and *Independent Chronicle*, 5 May.

7. Dennie to Tyler, 14 April 1797, in *Letters*, p. 156.

8. See also, for other announcements, *Massachusetts Mercury*, 27 October 1797; *Columbian Centinel*, 28 October; Boston *Gazette*, 30 October.

9. See *Columbian Centinel*, 12 March 1796, where part of the poem

is quoted; this speculation, it is said, "has been made the sport of wit, in prose and verse."

10. See, for example, *Massachusetts Mercury*, 3 October 1797.

11. *Columbian Centinel*, 28 October 1797; quoted by Frederick Tupper in "Royall Tyler, Man of Law and Man of Letters," *Proceedings of the Vermont Historical Society*, IV (1928), 82.

12. See the notices in the New York *Time Piece*, 20 December 1797 and 12 February 1798; *Daily Advertiser*, 19, 20, 22, 23 December 1797. Although there is no evidence that the play was ever printed, it is treated as a published volume (octavo, Boston, 1797) in Evans entry 32946 and Sabin 97618.

13. John Steele Tyler to Royall Tyler, 11 December 1811 (letter in Boston Public Library). For information about J. S. Tyler as manager of the Boston theater, see W. W. Clapp, *A Record of the Boston Stage* (Boston, 1853), pp. 24–35; Clapp says that he took over "more from a desire to advance the cause of the drama than from any pecuniary motives." Tyler's 1795 poetical "Address" is in the *Federal Orrery*, 9 November 1795 (see Chapter 4, below). The *Vermont Historical Gazetteer*, I (1867), 559, in a list of Tyler's works, includes "An Author's Evenings — a Comedy repeatedly performed in Boston," but the writer is seemingly confusing Tyler's newspaper columns with a play.

14. Tyler, writing to Dennie on 7 October 1795, quoted from a letter he had received from his brother John Steele, commenting that Tyler's "Mock Doctor" would probably be a success in Boston (letter in New Hampshire Historical Society). Perhaps both Tyler and one of his sons wrote a play on this subject, for Julian I. Lindsay, in *Tradition Looks Forward* (Burlington, 1954), reports that Royall Tyler, Jr., wrote an adaptation of Molière (entitled "Quackery") while he was attending the University of Vermont (pp. 102–103).

15. Stanley T. Williams, in *The Spanish Background of American Literature* (New Haven, 1955), traces the influence of Cervantes in America, at its height near the turn of the century (I, 44–46); he dates Tyler's play at about 1800 (I, 408). Quotations from *Four Plays* are by permission of Norbert Towne, attorney for Mrs. Arthur Peach.

16. Though it is superfluous to find a source for this in Cervantes, Sancho in chapter 45 does ridicule the affectation of nobility immediately upon his arrival in Barataria, when he learns that "Don" has been attached to his name.

17. Although episodic, Sancho's adventures in Barataria in *Don Quixote* are set in the larger framework of the plot devised by the Duke and Duchess, and the Sancho chapters alternate with those about Don Quixote. Whether or not Tyler expected his audience to fill in the background of the trick on Sancho from a knowledge of

Don Quixote is a debatable question that does affect the texture of the play. In Cervantes the reader knows how Sancho got to be governor and enjoys watching him outwit those who expected him to look more foolish than ever; in Tyler this dimension is lacking, for Sancho seems to be presented as a legitimate governor, possibly to make stronger the satire on unqualified rulers. Perhaps the two references to "Duke Don Cosmo Jokeley" indicate that we are to assume the *Don Quixote* background; on the other hand, the battle at the end is more realistic than in Cervantes — Tyler's stage directions do not indicate that the soldiers are performing purely for the effect to be produced on Sancho.

18. This speech is foreshadowed by Sancho's last one in III.i: "I can but marvel why so many men wish to be Governour when they get nothing but abuse for their pains — but the world will never lack Sancho's."

19. In the same conversation Sancho makes a number of other puns: "a word for your private ear" — "Which ear is that?"; "the belle of Barrataria" — "Hope she has a short clapper." In III.ii a Courier is announced, and Sancho says, "I'll curry him . . ." (p. 26). He also engages in more elaborate plays on words: Don Formal refers to the preceding governor who was called "the Skeleton of the Law & the Shadow of Justice"; Sancho answers, "I had rather be called the fat squab of the Law and the Substance of Justice. Let him have all the Honour — and let me have the Dumpling" (p. 10). Like Jonathan, he often has unusual exclamations, sometimes related to the meaning of the statement, such as "Snuff my peepers — how it vanished!" (p. 23).

20. It seems safe to take this as a reference to the American Presidency, though of course such a comment is dramatically inappropriate in the play; if this reading is correct, then the *terminus a quo* can be pushed forward to the time of Washington's death in 1799.

21. Tupper, "Royall Tyler," p. 101.

22. Quoted, by permission, from a typed introduction to the sacred dramas in the Tyler Papers (Box 45, Envelope 33) in the Vermont Historical Society, the gift of Helen Tyler Brown. This brief introduction, another statement of American literary independence, asserts, "The unrivaled excellence of the parent Country in any art or science should not be permitted to confound us into inactivity, but should rather excite to emulation."

23. For example, the King James version reads, "I believed not the words, until I came, and mine eyes had seen it; and, behold, the half was not told me. . . . Happy are thy men, happy are these thy servants, which stand continually before thee, and that hear thy wisdom" (10:7–8). In Tyler this becomes:

Slow was I to believe, but now I've come
And with mine eyes thy glory do behold.
Well may I say that not one half was told.
Happy the men, thrice happy they who stand
Before thee, and continually do hearken
To thy wisdom. (p. 119)

24. Baanah was one of Solomon's twelve commissariat officers (cf. I Kings 4:12 and 4:16); Chalcol was noted for his wisdom (as in I Kings 4:31); Shimei, of the house of Saul, cursed and stoned David (II Samuel 16:5–8), later begged forgiveness (II Samuel 19:16–23), and was eventually executed by Solomon (I Kings 2:8–9, 36–46); "Liba" is an error (whether made by Tyler or a later copyist) for Ziba, to whom David gave the possessions of Mephiboseth (II Samuel 9:1–13; 16:1–4); Solomon's daughters, Taphath and Basmath, and their husbands, Abinadab and Ahimaaz, both among Solomon's twelve officers (all mentioned near the beginning of Act II), are referred to, respectively, in I Kings 4:11 and 4:15. The name Maachah, which Tyler assigns to the scheming mother, does occur in the Bible but not in that connection; sometimes a male name (I Kings 2:39), it is given as the name of a king's mother in I Kings 15:2. Belkis (or Balkis), though not Biblical, is the name sometimes ascribed to this particular Queen of Sheba; for a discussion and further references, see A. J. Wensinck and J. H. Kramers, *Handwörterbuch des Islam* (Leiden, 1941), under "Bilkis," p. 81.

25. For a rare example of alliteration, see Esther's soliloquy at the end of III.iii in *The Origin of the Feast of Purim* (pp. 57–58).

26. The first epigraph is Proverbs 16:18: "Pride goeth before Destruction and a haughty spirit before a fall"; the second is Psalms 58:11, which asserts that "there is a reward for the righteous"; and the third is Proverbs 31:30, stating that "a woman that feareth the Lord, she shall be praised."

27. Compare, for example, Haggai 2:6–7, 22 ("For thus saith the Lord of hosts; Yet once, it is a little while, and I will shake the heavens, and the earth, and the sea, and the dry land; And I will shake all nations. . . . And I will overthrow the throne of kingdoms") with Tyler's chorus on p. 36 ("Thus saith the Lord: / 'Yet once — and yet it is a little while / And I — the Heavens, and the earth — the sea / And the dry land will shake; before my face / The nations of the earth shall quake and fear. / The thrones of kingdoms I will overthrow' ").

28. Though Tyler says in the first stage direction that the "Time chorus" is composed of women (as opposed to the group labeled simply "Chorus," which is made up of men), at the end of the play

he has a "Chorus of Jewish Women" alternate with the "Time Chorus." The male Chorus is listed in the dramatis personae as "Elam Chorus."

29. The names in this play are again Biblical, but (as with Liba-Ziba in the Solomon play) someone has had trouble reading Tyler's z's: the name of Haman's wife should be Zeresh (see Esther 5:10, 14), not Geresh, and the leader of the returning Jews, referred to in Act I on p. 35 and twice on p. 38 as Gerababel, should be Zerubbabel (see Haggai 1:12; 2:2, 4, 21, 23). Carshena, who speaks in III.i, is one of the seven princes of Ahasuerus mentioned in Esther 1:14, as is Memucan, referred to in I.ii (p. 39). Meres, another of the seven princes, is identified in the cast as "friend of Haman"; though no speech is assigned to him, perhaps the short one on p. 55, labeled "One of Haman's Friends," is his. Harbonah and Carcas are two of Ahasuerus' seven eunuchs (Esther 1:10), and Hatach is another eunuch appointed to attend Esther (Esther 4:5). Luzzi and Elam, who speak in I.ii, are not listed in the cast. Elam is the head of a family that returns to Palestine (see Ezra 2:7; Nehemiah 7:12), and Luzzi, not a Biblical name, is perhaps related to the town of Luz (Bethel), close to Jerusalem. Shushan is the Biblical name of Ahasuerus' palace (Esther 1:2). Haggai appears four times on p. 35 as "Haggia," but, though there is a Biblical Haggiah (I Chronicles 6:30), obviously the prophet Haggai is meant throughout.

30. There is no division marked "Act III" in the printed text, but it may be assumed that Act III begins on p. 85; the preceding scene is labeled "Act Second — Scene Third," and the one following ends with "End of the Second Scene," presumably of Act III — thus the intervening scene must be the first of Act III. The editors point out (p. 63) that, in the case of this one play, they have not found the original manuscript and have based their text on "what seems to be a carefully made copy."

31. Of the eleven brothers of Joseph, enumerated in Genesis 49:3–27, those who have speaking parts in the play are Simeon, Levi, Reuben, Zebulon, Issachar, Judah, Dan, and Benjamin. The only other characters, besides Joseph and Jacob, are Jacob's wife Leah, Joseph's steward, and his interpreter. As in the Bible, Reuben is the brother who defends Joseph from the others' anger, but Tyler describes his efforts in much greater detail.

32. For example, Genesis 42:13 reads: "Thy servants are twelve brethren, the sons of one man in the land of Canaan; and, behold, the youngest is this day with our father, and one is not." The Tyler passage (p. 80) is as follows: "Thy servants, O my Lord, are brethren twelve, / Sons of one man, who in Canaan dwells / And behold the

youngest with our Father / Is this day — and one is not." Not only single speeches but large passages are taken almost verbatim from Genesis — cf. Genesis 43:1–13 with II.ii (pp. 82–84).

33. There are times, however, when Tyler's elaboration of a sentiment is less successful because it does not blend in with the diction and syntax of the paraphrased verse. An example is Joseph's praise of home, "where first he felt a Mother's kiss / And a fond Father's love" (p. 80).

IV. Poet

1. There had been virtually no scholarly work on Tyler's poetry before Marius B. Péladeau wrote his master's thesis at Georgetown University in 1962, entitled "The Verse of Royall Tyler: Collected and Edited." Though I do not always come to the same conclusions as he does about the attribution of particular poems, I wish to express my gratitude to Mr. Péladeau for generously allowing me to consult both his thesis and a revised version of it which he prepared for publication. Walter Muir Whitehill of the Boston Athenaeum very kindly offered to let me examine the galley proofs of the Péladeau edition, prior to its appearance in the *Publications of the Colonial Society of Massachusetts*. These proofs, however, did not become available before the time when the page proofs of the present book had to be returned. I have therefore not seen the Péladeau edition in its final form and am not able to give page references to it for the poems discussed in this chapter.

2. H. Milton Ellis, *Joseph Dennie and His Circle* (Austin: University of Texas Studies in English No. 3, 1915), p. 43. Ellis' work is the most detailed source of information about Dennie. But of particular interest is Tyler's own memoir of Dennie's courtroom manner in the *New England Galaxy*, 24 July 1818.

3. A brief account of the *Eagle* is in John King Lord, *A History of the Town of Hanover, N.H.* (Hanover, 1928), pp. 265–266; see also Clarence S. Brigham, *History and Bibliography of American Newspapers 1690–1820* (Worcester, 1947), I, 462.

4. See, e.g., *Port Folio*, II (19 June, 14 August, 9 October 1802), 191, 249, 313. Cf. "Conserves from the Cookshop of Adeona," *Farmer's Weekly Museum*, 16 January and 15 May 1798.

5. See the *Port Folio*, I (14 March 1801), 87: "When the Editor [Dennie] and a literary friend first projected the scheme of writing miscellaneous essays in conjunction, the prose was generally understood to be the province of the Editor, and the poetry that of his associate." Earlier, on 28 February 1801 (I, 69), Dennie had referred to the work of his "associate and *principal*" as "the *poetry* of *Spondee*."

6. However, Dennie did occasionally contribute poetry and Tyler prose; in some of the early columns, for example, there are poems signed "C."

7. For further information about the *Orrery*, see Joseph T. Buckingham, *Specimens of Newspaper Literature* (Boston, 1850), II, 221–250; cf. Brigham, *American Newspapers*, I, 296.

8. On the *Tablet*, see Ellis, *Joseph Dennie*, pp. 69–83.

9. See George Aldrich, *Walpole as It Was and as It Is* (Claremont, N.H., 1880), pp. 76–82. The *Farmer's Museum* has been discussed in various places; see, especially, Andrew P. Peabody, "The Farmer's Weekly Museum," *Proceedings of the American Antiquarian Society*, n.s. VI (1889), 106–129; Ellis, *Joseph Dennie*, pp. 84–109; Buckingham, *Newspaper Literature*, II, 174–220; Brigham, *American Newspapers*, I, 486–489. Jeremiah Mason's *Memoir and Correspondence* (Cambridge, Mass., 1873) includes a first-hand account of the Walpole group (esp. pp. 28–32) and suggests that in Walpole was "more motion, life, and bustle" because it was in transition between the "rude and boisterous manners" of the original settlers and a more "civilized, orderly" condition.

10. Buckingham (*Newspaper Literature*, II, 179) says, "For three years . . . , the Museum was more richly supplied with original communications of a literary character than any other paper, that had then, or has since, been published in the United States." Peabody asserts that "it is not too much to say that this paper had a larger amount and variety of original matter of a high character than there has been in the same number of issues of any American paper before or since" ("Farmer's Weekly," p. 109).

11. The most extensive account of the *Port Folio* is by John Queenan, "*The Port Folio*: A Study of the History and Significance of an Early American Magazine" (unpub. diss., University of Pennsylvania, 1955). See also Frank Luther Mott, *A History of American Magazines 1741–1850* (New York, 1930), pp. 223–246; Albert H. Smith, *The Philadelphia Magazines and Their Contributors* (Philadelphia, 1892), pp. 86–151 (which credits Tyler with all the "Colon & Spondee" papers, p. 125); and Ellis P. Oberholtzer, *The Literary History of Philadelphia* (Philadelphia, 1906), pp. 168–188.

12. Some writers, including Péladeau in his thesis, assign much more poetry in the *Port Folio* to Tyler on the ground that all the contributions signed "S." are his. I am inclined to be more cautious. To begin with, we have a reasonably reliable basis for attributing ten items to Tyler in the annotations in the file that belonged to John E. and Harrison Hall, the later editor and publisher of the *Port Folio*; see Randolph C. Randall, "Authors of the *Port Folio* Revealed by the Hall Files," *American Literature*, XI (1940), 379–416. Of the ten items

there recorded for Tyler, five are prose (either signed "Colon & Spondee" or not signed at all) and two are "Colon & Spondee" poems reprinted from the *Museum*; only three original poems are left, and these are unsigned. To these we may obviously add "Love and Liberty" (IV, 336), which is signed in print with Tyler's name. But the Hall file provides no justification for associating all "S." work with Tyler; Dennie's own comments in his editorial column would furnish better justification, since he is still (in 1801 and 1802) referring to Tyler as "S.", but his remarks all have to do with the fact that "S." has been neglecting his poetry and sending nothing in. The two early poems (I, 24, 39) which have prefatory notes signed "S." may be by Tyler despite what the notes say, but in view of the fact that Dennie soon after laments Tyler's absence, they may very well not be his. Dennie's next comment on Tyler comes at the same time that he reprints an old "Spondee" poem; and his three pleas in 1802 begin two months after the last 1802 contribution marked as Tyler's in the Hall files. The one poem in 1803 (Hall files) and the one in 1804 (Tyler's signature) cause little trouble. But early in 1804 there is indication that "S." may no longer stand for Tyler, even in Dennie's mind. His message to "S." on 11 February 1804 (IV, 48) is a curt dismissal, in sharp contrast to his earlier tone when addressing Tyler; and prose contributions signed "S." begin to appear under the "Samuel Saunter" heading (IV, 57). Poems signed "S." occur with some frequency in the early part of 1805, but again Dennie's note does not lend credence to the equation of "S." with Tyler, for on 20 April 1805 he writes, " 'S,' whose penmanship is not familiar, but whose poetry is of a character so agreeable to us, that we wish for farther specimens, is, we are convinced, a writer, endowed with such ability, that we shall always welcome him in the shape of a contributor to our poetical stock" (V, 118). As for the second series of the *Port Folio*, if "S." is not automatically assumed to be Tyler, the kinds of poems signed "S." do not seem characteristic of him; in at least one case (n.s. V, 64) the "S." might be an abbreviation of "Stanley," the signature of the poem just above, and on 15 August 1807 (n.s. IV, 110–111) "S." is identified as the author of political essays in the Boston *Gazette*. By the time of these later "S." poems, Dennie's health was not allowing him to spend as much time with the magazine as before, and Tyler was at the height of his legal activity — both circumstances lessening the chances of Tyler's poetry appearing in the *Port Folio*. In the Tyler Papers at Montpelier is a file of the *Port Folio*, but the numerous markings in it are not contemporary and represent only later guesses at what may conceivably have been Tyler's work. All this is not to say that Tyler may not have contributed a great deal to the *Port Folio*; it is only that we do not yet have a firm way of knowing. If one is looking for items of Tyler's, it seems to me that such remarks by Dennie as the following carry more weight than the letter "S.": "The well-known wit, who favoured us with the sensible satire against 'Fanaticism,' published in vol. IV. No. 50, is sure to be always warmly welcomed by his affectionate friend. We shall omit no opportunity of doing honour to a man for whose head and heart we entertain a well-founded partiality" (V, 7). The poem "Fanaticism" (IV, 400), though unsigned, may possibly be Tyler's.

13. Joseph T. Buckingham, *Personal Memoirs and Recollections of Editorial Life* (Boston, 1852), I, 56; Tyler memoir (cf. Chapter 1, note 4, above), p. 169. Buckingham seems to have kept up a contact with Tyler; Mary Tyler wrote to her husband on 3 March 1809 saying that Buckingham had sent a letter "in which he seems to anticipate *more good things in the Spring*" (Tyler Papers, Box 46).

14. On the *Centinel*, see Buckingham, *Newspaper Literature*, II, 58–117.

15. These have been published, respectively, in Mary R. Cabot, *Annals of Brattleboro* (Brattleboro, 1921–22), II, 834; *Favorite Vermont Poems, Series One*, ed. W. J. Coates (North Montpelier, 1928), p. 6 (and in *Driftwind*, September 1926); *ibid.*, p. 5; *Series Five* (1934), p. 19. Another poem, "A Valedictory Address," was published only as a broadside during Tyler's lifetime (the unique copy is in the possession of Marius B. Péladeau) but was reprinted in Henry Burnham, *Brattleboro, Windham County, Vermont* (Brattleboro, 1880), pp. 84–85; it is a poem of 160 tetrameter lines (based on the metaphor of children as flowers in a garden) written for his son, Thomas Pickman, to recite at the closing of Rebecca Peck's school for the summer of 1823.

16. In the Tyler Papers are typed copies of many poems, some of them apparently unpublished (before Péladeau's edition); Box 45, Envelope 36, contains "The Inimitable Fair" (36 anapaestic lines), "Say is it height, or shape, or air" (36 iambic lines), and "The Colt" (16 lines, dated 1796), among others. In the Boston Public Library are four manuscript poems, supposed to be juvenilia of Tyler: a 16-line jingle (plus a 6-line "chorus") about a "jolly cobler," with the inevitable pun on mending soles; an 8-line "Song" about a merchant anxiously looking to sea; 8 lines beginning "Oh, like a storke among the Rush"; and 8 lines on "Our old Moll" who hands out "a Mug of foaming Flip." The copy of "The Bay Boy" in the Tyler Papers (Box 45, Envelope 29; cf. Box 77, Envelope 13) contains original epigraphs, not included in *The Algerine Captive*, at the beginnings of most sections; three of them, amounting to more than 60 lines of tetrameter couplets, are labeled as from "The Doggerel Romaunt," and one (of

8 lines) is said to be from "The Pleasures of Pain." Other verses appear in the typescript of "Utile Dulci" (Box 45, Envelope 35), particularly a 111-line poem on the wisdom of Darius.

17. "Anacreontic to Flip," *Eagle*, 11 August 1794 (signed "Colon & Spondee"; 36 lines); reprinted in *Newhampshire and Vermont Journal*, 5 September 1794, and *Columbian Centinel*, 4 October 1794. All quotations are from the earliest publication of each poem.

18. *Eagle*, 25 August 1794 (signed "S."; 56 lines); reprinted in *Tablet*, I (19 May 1795), 4, and in *Port Folio*, I (14 March 1801), 87–88. Though this poem praises the "rural beauty," Tyler at other times celebrates the city, as in "The Town Eclogue," *Polyanthos*, II (June 1806), 181–184 (54 lines of tetrameter couplets), where he says, "Her rustick coz let others sing, / But let me taste the town bred Spring."

19. "A Reputation Vindicated," *Farmer's Weekly Museum*, 11 April 1797 (16 lines); reprinted in *Port Folio*, I (24 October 1801), 339. Another poem about marital relations with an unsentimental — even bitter — conclusion is "The Test of Conjugal Love," *Eagle*, 29 December 1794 (36 lines), reprinted in *Farmer's Weekly Museum*, 27 March 1798, and in *The Spirit of the Farmers' Museum* (Walpole, N.H., 1801), pp. 258–259. All poems which were reprinted in this anthology and are here credited to Tyler have been endorsed with a "T" or "Tyler" by Joseph Dennie in the copy (now in the Boston Public Library) which he presented to James Abercrombie on 26 December 1801. See also Chapter 6, note 10, below.

20. "Epigram," *Farmer's Weekly Museum*, 25 September 1797 (14 lines).

21. "The Mechanick Preferred: An Epigram Founded on a Recent Fact," *Polyanthos*, II (April 1806), 56 (signed "S."; 12 lines).

22. *Polyanthos*, V (April 1807), 49–50 (signed "S."). Another "Epigram" on clothes and poverty is in the *Eagle*, 17 November 1794 (6 lines), reprinted in the *Federal Orrery*, 27 November 1794 (signed "S.").

23. *Farmer's Weekly Museum*, 1 May 1798 (44 lines); reprinted in *Spirit*, pp. 227–228.

24. See Mark Longaker, *The Della Cruscans and William Gifford* (Philadelphia, 1924); Roy B. Clark, *William Gifford: Tory Satirist, Critic, and Editor* (New York, 1930), pp. 36–80; Edward E. Bostetter, "The Original Della Cruscans and the *Florence Miscellany*," *Huntington Library Quarterly*, XIX (1956), 277–280, 288–290, 293–300. For the influence of the Della Cruscans in America, see Fred Lewis Pattee, *The First Century of American Literature 1770–1870* (New York, 1935), pp. 107–115, and M. Ray Adams, "Della Cruscanism in America," *PMLA*, LXXIX (1964), 259–265 (which quotes 46 lines of Tyler's "Address to Della Crusca"). Adams suggests that the reference

to "Criticus," who "bids instructed taste to scorn / The sound of Della Crusca's horn," in the *Farmer's Weekly Museum* of 2 January 1798, may be to Tyler (p. 262).

25. Reprinted in *Spirit*, pp. 223–225.

26. *Farmer's Weekly Museum*, 16 May 1797 (signed "Della Yankee" in a "Colon & Spondee" column); reprinted in *Spirit*, pp. 221–223.

27. *Farmer's Weekly Museum*, 11 September 1797.

28. *Farmer's Weekly Museum*, 1 April 1799; reprinted in *Spirit*, pp. 289–292, and in *Port Folio*, I (24 October 1801), 339. The prose comment which introduces the poem announces that Messrs. Colon & Spondee "Have, at a great expense, erected an Epithet Jenny, with which they card, spin, and twist all kinds of epithets" and with which, therefore, they may be able to compete against European productions.

29. *Farmer's Weekly Museum*, 15 April 1799; reprinted in *Spirit*, pp. 311–314.

30. *Farmer's Weekly Museum*, 20 May 1799; reprinted in *Spirit*, pp. 218–219.

31. *Newhampshire and Vermont Journal*, 14 March 1797 (24 lines); reprinted in *Spirit*, p. 234, with the heading "Fond Frederick to Fanny, False Fair." On p. 186 of *Spirit* is an epigram written in reply, entitled "Frighted Fanny's Faithful Friend, to Frederic, Fictitiously Fond."

32. *Farmer's Weekly Museum*, 3 June 1799 (64 lines); reprinted in Haverhill *Federal Gazette*, 28 June 1799, and in *Spirit*, pp. 243–245. The poem also contains some good descriptions of contemporary scenes, such as farmers sending vegetables to Boston. Other poems have literary sources, like the popular "Spondee's Mistresses," which refers at the beginning to Cowley's description of his mistresses and then takes up Miss Conduct, Miss Chance, Miss Take, and so on; *Farmer's Weekly Museum*, 15 April 1799 (42 lines), reprinted in *Port Folio*, I (28 March 1801), 104, in *Spirit*, pp. 225–227, in *Farmer's Museum*, 5 January 1802, and in Brattleboro *Reporter*, 12 September 1803. Another is "The Widower," which has as its subtitle "A Parody on Pope's Ode to Solitude" (actually a serious poem praising marriage); *Eagle*, 24 November 1794 (signed "S."; 20 lines), reprinted in *Newhampshire and Vermont Journal*, 5 December 1794.

33. *Farmer's Weekly Museum*, 25 April 1797; reprinted in *Spirit*, pp. 229–232.

34. *Farmer's Weekly Museum*, 2 October 1797; reprinted in *Spirit*, pp. 239–243.

35. *Eagle*, 6 January 1794; the unique copy of the later broadside version (with a revised last stanza) is at Dartmouth (cf. Vermont Historical Society *News and Notes*, II [December 1950], 1–2).

36. Another occasional religious poem, "Hymn to the Supreme

Being," written for Good Friday 1803, contains the line, "A nation's voice we raise"; *Port Folio*, III (21 May 1803), 168 (identified in the Hall file).

37. Besides the original publication, the poem has appeared in *Spirit*, pp. 235–236; in the anthologies edited by Kettell (1829), Stedman and Hutchinson (1888), Stevenson (1908), Coates (1928), Coates and Tupper (1932), and Untermeyer (1952) — see Bibliography; and in *Theatre Arts*, XXIX (July 1945), 417, and *Collier's*, CXXVIII (7 July 1951), 20.

38. *Port Folio*, IV (20 October 1804), 336; reprinted in the *Columbian Centinel*, 24 July 1805. Cf. Thomas Paine's poem "The Great Republic; Or, The Land of Love and Liberty" in the *Columbian Centinel*, 13 July 1796.

39. The first on 29 July 1799, and the second on 5 August 1799 (reprinted in Haverhill *Federal Gazette*, 8 August 1799, and as a broadside, the unique copy of which is in the University of Vermont library).

40. *Federal Orrery*, 29 December 1794 (signed "R. Tyler, Esq."); reprinted in *Newhampshire and Vermont Journal*, 10 February 1795.

41. *Federal Orrery*, 9 November 1795 (signed "By a Gentleman of Vermont"); the poem is quoted by W. W. Clapp, *A Record of the Boston Stage* (Boston, 1853), in his account of the opening of the third season (p. 26).

42. *Polyanthos*, II, 62–70, 197–202. For the literary context, see Agnes Marie Sibley, *Alexander Pope's Prestige in America 1725–1830* (New York, 1949).

43. The line between occasional verse and reflective poetry is of course not clear-cut. Tyler's "Elegy: Occasioned by the Death of the Rev. Samuel Stillman, D.D., Pastor of the First Baptist Church in Boston," in the *Polyanthos*, V (April 1807), 45–49, is both occasional and reflective; it also illustrates the degree to which Tyler sometimes echoed English poetry, for its twenty-six iambic pentameter quatrains continually remind one of Gray's "Elegy": "Mute is that warning voice, whose power awoke / The sleeping conscience from its dread repose" (lines 17–18); "The sculptured urn, let polished Europe raise" (line 26); "What though no massy fanes his dust inclose, / No brass or marble his loved form supply; / Yet, not forgotten shall his dust repose, / Nor yet unhonoured shall the good man die" (lines 33–36).

44. *Eagle*, 21 July 1794 (signed "T."); eleven stanzas reprinted as "The Cave of Chastity" in *Columbian Centinel*, 2 August 1794.

45. *Tablet*, I (11 August 1795), 50–51 (signed "S."; 88 lines); reprinted in *Newhampshire and Vermont Journal*, 14 February 1797, and in *Farmer's Museum*, 26 January 1801.

46. *Polyanthos*, V (May 1807), 127–132 (signed "S."; 162 lines).

Tyler quotes this poem in one of the fragments of "The Bay Boy," where he has Updike submit it for inclusion in the poets' corner of the *Massachusetts Spy*.

47. *Farmer's Weekly Museum*, 6 May 1799; reprinted in *Port Folio*, I (14 November 1801), 368. See also "Fluttering lovers, giddy boys," *Newhampshire and Vermont Journal*, 6 December 1796 (30 lines), reprinted in *Spirit*, pp. 219–220.

48. *The Algerine Captive* (Walpole, N.H., 1797), I, 49.

49. Respectively, II, 21, 69, 130, 141, 227. The blank verse passages appear as epigraphs to chapters 2, 4, 10, and 29 in the first volume (I, 37, 49, 94, 182) and chapters 2, 9, 15, 16, 19, 22, 23, and 35 in the second (II, 21, 69, 97, 117, 130, 141, 150, 227). Two other epigraphs are by Tyler: an iambic quatrain at chapter 20 of the second volume (II, 132) and eight lines of iambic tetrameter couplets (paraphrasing Horace) at chapter 21 (II, 135).

50. *Polyanthos*, II (April 1806), 52–53.

51. Though the lines are not numbered in the Driftwind edition, the line numbers here and below are based on that text. It should be pointed out, however, that this numbering will not serve for references to the manuscript copy of the poem (not in Tyler's hand) at the Vermont Historical Society (the copy from which the Driftwind edition was taken), for there are a great many differences between the two versions. In the printed edition there is a note explaining that line 23 has been altered from "Thy homely sarcophagus burst" to "Shall burst thy rough sarcophagus" because of "false accent on word 'sarcophagus.'" But there is no indication that the poem has been silently changed for publication at nearly a hundred other points as well. There are three kinds of editorial alteration involved: (1) omission of stanzas — four stanzas are omitted in the published version, following lines 376, 456, 468, and 644; (2) rearrangement of stanzas — three stanzas originally following line 600 are inserted (along with one other) in the published version after line 692 (thus becoming lines 693–708); (3) revision of single words or phrases — ninety lines contain substantive variants, ranging from insignificant errors (such as *ah-oh* in line 33) and minor changes (e.g., *which-that*, 124, 162) to revisions in diction (as *view-see*, 36; *whim-chance*, 38; *immense-dull*, 55; *bounding-bouncing*, 147; *boisterous-roistering*, 301; *drive-send*, 308; *walls-halls*, 345; *path-task*, 350; *barb'rous-cruel*, 586; *sweat-brow*, 591), changes in number of noun, verb, and pronoun (99, 132, 150, 518, 520, 574, 677), and the recasting of an entire stanza (the last, 741–744). In some cases the changes are no doubt correct (as in lines 486 and 513, where lost rhymes are restored), but in others they produce inferior readings (as in line 328, where *As* replaces *And*). If these revisions do not greatly affect a total evaluation of the poem, one

should at least be aware of their existence. Quotations from this poem are made by permission of Mrs. Dorothy Sutherland Melville and Dr. Allan D. Sutherland.

52. Donald G. Mitchell, *American Lands and Letters* (New York, 1897), p. 221.

V. Novelist

1. *Independent Chronicle*, 24, 31 August 1797. Part of this chapter was read at a meeting of the Midwest Modern Language Association in Normal, Illinois, on 8 May 1964.

2. It was advertised in the *Farmer's Weekly Museum* on 31 July and 7 August 1797 as "Now in press"; as "Just published" on 14, 21, 28 August, 4 September, and 2, 9 October. It was also labeled as "just published" in the advertisement for Blake's Book Store, in the Boston *Independent Chronicle*, 28 September and 5 October. The price was $1.50. The source for the size of the edition is a preface Tyler later wrote for a proposed new edition, quoted in the Tyler memoir (cf. Chapter 1, note 4, above), pp. 98–100. Two excerpts appeared in the *Farmer's Weekly Museum* on 14 August 1797 (volume I, chapter 18) and on 21 August (volume II, chapter 14).

3. Nancrede's advertisement is dated 21 September 1797 and appears in the *Independent Chronicle* for 5, 12, 19, 26 October and in the *Columbian Centinel* for 27 September and 4 October. Knowledge of Tyler's identity underlies a statement in the *Columbian Centinel* for 25 October 1797: "It is said that the presumptuous editor of the Walpole paper [Dennie] is helped to all his native poetry by Dr. Updyke Underhill, who was six years a prisoner among the Algerines." As late as 1937, W. Roberts could write to *Notes and Queries* (CLXXII, 282) asking who the author of *The Algerine Captive* was; he deduced that the author was American from the reference to Dilworth's *Spelling Book*. Roberts' query was answered twice, first briefly by Albert Matthews (p. 374) and then in more detail the following week by Robert S. Forsythe (pp. 389–390). Many readers must have taken the book as a true account of adventure: William Czar Bradley, in a letter of 7 December 1857 (now in the Vermont Historical Society), tells of "an honest Westmoreland farmer" who came into his father's office soon after the publication of the book, talking about "Dr. Underhills adventures"; when the truth was explained, the "indignation of the farmer on hearing what he called the gross imposition was almost uncontrollable and would have delighted the author." The letter also gives indication that Pliny White at this time was planning to prepare a new edition of *The Algerine Captive*.

4. Dennie to Tyler, 30 August 1797, in *The Letters of Joseph Dennie*, ed. Laura G. Pedder (Orono, Me.: University of Maine Studies, 2nd series, no. 36, 1936), p. 165.

5. Coleman to Tyler, 24 September 1797, in Tyler memoir, pp. 103–104.

6. See *Farmer's Weekly Museum*, 17, 24, 31 July, 6 August, 1 October 1798.

7. Tyler memoir, pp. 98–99.

8. For a detailed account, see especially Gardner W. Allen, *Our Navy and the Barbary Corsairs* (Boston, 1905), pp. 11–58; Ray W. Irwin, *The Diplomatic Relations of the United States with the Barbary Powers 1776–1816* (Chapel Hill, N.C., 1931), pp. 1–81; and H. G. Barnby, *The Prisoners of Algiers: An Account of the Forgotten American-Algerian War 1785–1797* (London, 1966). (I am indebted to Richard Colles Johnson for assistance with this documentation.)

9. The *Newhampshire and Vermont Journal*, which Tyler certainly read, devoted much space in the issue of 29 March 1796 to the text of the 1795 treaty with Algiers and letters of Humphreys and Washington about it. As examples of the various kinds of attention given to Algiers in the newspapers, see the issues of this paper for 23 August 1796, 29 October 1798, 4 February 1799, and 25 August 1800; see also the Boston *Independent Chronicle*, 20 October 1785, 27 April 1786, 16 October 1788; the Hanover (N.H.) *Eagle*, 13, 20 January 1794, 9 February, 27 August 1795; the Boston *Federal Orrery*, 26, 29 January, 30 November 1795.

10. There were other poetic references, if not whole poems, as in David Humphreys' *On the Happiness of Americans* (1786) and Joel Barlow's *Columbiad* (1807).

11. In *The Algerine Captive* Tyler himself refers to such authorities as Shaw (II, 100), Sales, and Prideaux (II, 141–142). For further discussion of several possible sources and of the book's historical accuracy, see Bertrand W. Chapman, "The Nativism of Royall Tyler" (master's thesis, University of Vermont, 1933), pp. 24–26, 32–47.

12. This pamphlet of twenty-four pages, printed in Boston for N. Coverly, does not usually quote from Tyler verbatim but is often extremely close, especially in the "Concise Description of Algiers" (pp. 18–22) — compare, for example, the sixth sentence of chapter 16 of Tyler's second volume (II, 118) with the opening of Nicholson's description ("Algiers is situated in the bay of that name, and built upon the sea shore an eminence, which rises above it"); or the concluding anecdote of chapter 25 (II, 164) with Nicholson's version. The beginning of the pamphlet is based on the first chapter in Tyler's second volume; the phrase "Six Years a Prisoner among the Algerines"

appears in the titles of both works. For other books about Algerine captivity, after 1797, see the bibliographies in Allen, *Our Navy* (pp. 305–311), and Irwin, *Diplomatic Relations* (pp. 205–214).

13. *Port Folio*, II (16 January 1802), 8.

14. See Dorothy Blakey, *The Minerva Press* (London, 1939), p. 196. Cf. *Anti-Jacobin Review*, VI (1800), 451.

15. Roland L. Shodean, in "English Editions of American Authors 1801–1863" (master's thesis, University of Chicago, 1958), says that only eight American novels of the 1801–1820 period were published in England before 1863 (p. 26); the Robinsons published only one American work during that time (p. 180).

16. Tyler memoir, p. 99.

17. It is unlikely that the changes in punctuation are authorial, nor is it characteristic of Tyler to make the kind of careful verbal revision reflected in the Robinson edition; and in 1802 he was occupied with legal matters. On the other hand, Tyler was interested later in revising the work, and perhaps he made some revisions as early as 1802. The tradition of asserting that the English edition grossly altered the book began with Dennie, who commented on the treatment of American novels in England in the *Port Folio*, IV (1 September 1804), 277; of *The Algerine Captive* he said, "Some London *Lethe* had washed away every American trace," and he assured his readers that he "actually sat by the American author, while he was writing the above adventures, and know, that, *at this present writing*, he neither prescribes nor compounds in the city of London, but administers the justice of his country from the supreme courts of Vermont." For a more detailed collation of the various editions, see G. T. Tanselle, "Early American Fiction in England: The Case of *The Algerine Captive*," *Papers of the Bibliographical Society of America*, LIX (1965), 367–384.

18. *Lady's Magazine*, XXXV (1804), 37–43, 68–75, 134–142, 198–204, 247–254, 289–296, 345–352, 401–408, 457–465, 513–521, 569–577, 625–639, 681–690.

19. *The Algerine Captive* (Walpole, N.H., 1797), I, 35–36. All quotations are from the first edition.

20. *Monthly Review*, XLII (September 1803), 86–93.

21. *Port Folio*, III (4 June 1803), 181; IV (28 April 1804), 134. Tyler is here referred to as "a favourite friend of the Editor of the Port Folio."

22. *Monthly Anthology and Boston Review*, IX (November 1810), 344–347. The review was written by Nathaniel Appleton Haven, according to the entry for 13 November 1810 in the *Journal of the Proceedings of the Society Which Conducts the Monthly Anthology &*

Boston Review, introd. M. A. DeWolfe Howe (Boston, 1910), p. 242.

23. The text was set from a copy of the Robinson 1802 edition, but further changes — usually omitted letters or words — were made accidentally. Typographical errors, for example, appear on pp. 70, 82, 87, 101, 108, 164, 197.

24. It has been reissued in Publication No. 64 of the Augustan Reprint Society, *Prefaces to Three Eighteenth-Century Novels*, ed. Claude E. Jones (Los Angeles, 1951); the editor says that the preface and dedication may well be the most important parts of *The Algerine Captive*. The preface was also reprinted by Frederick C. Prescott and John H. Nelson in *Prose and Poetry of the Revolution* (New York, 1925), pp. 253–255. Attention was drawn to the preface from time to time in the nineteenth century — for example, by G. P. Lathrop, "Early American Novelists," *Atlantic Monthly*, XXXVII (April 1876), 404–405, and by W. J. Fletcher, "An Early Call for 'the American Novel,'" *Critic*, XVI (15 February 1890), 83.

25. Cf. Tremaine McDowell, "Sensibility in the Eighteenth-Century American Novel," *Studies in Philology*, XXIV (1927), 383–402. Lillie D. Loshe, in *The Early American Novel* (New York, 1907), contrasts the romantic and sentimental approach of *Fortune's Football* (which also involves Algerine piracy) with the "iconoclastic realism" of *The Algerine Captive* (pp. 24–25).

26. A wholly fictitious genealogical tree has grown up around Tyler's invention of the names Benoni and Updike, and certain persons have claimed their descent through this line, asserting that Updike had three children after his return from captivity. But these two names were inventions of Tyler's, and the Benoni line has no authenticity, as shown by Josephine C. Frost in *Underhill Genealogy* ([Boston]: Underhill Society, 1932), II, 43–50. On p. 50 of that work is a letter from E. R. Tyler, equating the captured ancestor with Tyler's great-grandfather; but the chart in *Grandmother Tyler's Book* (New York, 1925) labels the great-uncle as the "Algerine Captive" (p. 331). The Underhill family owned the house in Stratford which Shakespeare bought in 1597; see J. H. Morrison, *The Underhills of Warwickshire* (Cambridge, 1932), pp. 31, 76–77, and Mark Eccles, *Shakespeare in Warwickshire* (Madison, Wis., 1961), pp. 88–89. The activities of John Underhill are recounted in Belknap's *History of New-Hampshire* (rev. ed.; Dover, N.H., 1831), I, 23–27, in *Underhill Genealogy*, I, 28–33, and in H. C. Shelley's *John Underhill* (New York, 1932); Whittier's poem on Underhill appears in the *Atlantic Monthly*, XXXII (December 1873), 668. *Newes from America* was reprinted in the *Collections of the Massachusetts Historical Society*, 3rd series, VI (1837), 1–28. The first three chapters of *The Algerine*

Captive were reprinted as "An Account of Captain John Underhill" in the *Marvellous and Entertaining Repository* (Boston), II (1827), 229–238.

27. Chapter and page numbering begins anew with volume II.

28. Paine argues that the minority should always govern; Peter Pindar replies that, since most of the crowd present had been swayed to Paine's viewpoint, it automatically is defeated, by Paine's own reasoning. Paine, pictured as a moody man, then "retired from the presence of triumphant wit, mortified with being foiled at his own weapons" (I, 181). Updike finds it hard to understand why Paine wrote such a book as *The Age of Reason* unless as a "sacrifice to save his life from the devouring cruelty of Robespierre" or as an outlet for his "passion for paradox" (I, 183); yet he did not recant. In this, Tyler's most vehemently hostile portrait, there is also reference to Paine's drinking; and a Peter Pindar epigram is quoted (said to have been written in a copy of *The Age of Reason* and not included in Peter Pindar's works), ending with the pun that "the Devil's in Paine" — reprinted in *Notes and Queries*, CLXXII (1937), 390.

29. *Monthly Anthology*, IX (1810), 346. Tyler, in his later proposed preface, said: "The Algerine Captive was reviewed in a Boston Magazine by some one who had the sagacity to discover that it savored of infidelity. The Author was prepared to meet severe criticism on his style; and various other imperfections; but certainly he never imagined it was objectionable on the score of infidelity, or even scepticism. The part objected to, as far as the Author recollects, was written with a view to do away the vulgar prejudices against Islamism. He never thought that in adopting the liberality of the good Sale, the translator of the Koran, he was even jeopardizing the truths of Christianity: for the Author considered then, and now considers, that, after exhibiting Islamism in its best light, the Mahometan imposture will be obvious to those who compare the language, the dogmatic fables, the monstrous absurdities of the Koran, with the sublime doctrines, morals and language of the Gospel Dispensation" (Tyler memoir, pp. 99–100). Cf. *Diary of William Dunlap* (New York, 1930), p. 174.

30. It is customary to find the second volume inferior to the first, but for a discussion of further merits in volume II, see Teut Riese, *Das englische Erbe in der amerikanischen Literatur* (Bochum-Lang-endreer, 1958), pp. 139–149.

31. Alexander Cowie, in *The Rise of the American Novel* (New York, 1948), describes Tyler's "finished prose" as "swift, well-balanced, allusive but comparatively unembellished." He says, "In maturity of observation and in command of language, Tyler was far superior to the average popular novelist" (p. 67). Frederick Tupper compares Tyler's prose to the "plain unvarnished style" of Defoe, in *Proceedings of the Vermont Historical Society*, IV (1928), 84.

VI. *Essayist*

1. See *UVM Notes*, XVII (December 1920), 8.

2. Letter of 22 May 1810, in Tyler memoir (cf. Chapter 1, note 4, above), p. ²80. Pliny H. White, in "Early Poets of Vermont," *Proceedings of the Vermont Historical Society, 1917–1918* (1920), p. 119, says that four quarto pages of the dictionary were printed.

3. Letter of 14 February 1800, in Tyler memoir, p. 119.

4. The agreement between Tyler and Ide is preserved at The New-York Historical Society; there is a reproduction of it in the Tyler Papers at the Vermont Historical Society. The document goes on to say that if Tyler does finish the work, Ide will pay him $24 for the copyright. The title was entered by Ide for copyright on 26 April 1817. The 36-page copy of the book was once in the library of the University of Vermont, but no trace of it can now be found. The work was listed as Tyler's in M. D. Gilman's *Bibliography of Vermont* (Burlington, 1897), pp. 282–284; it is also recorded in R. W. G. Vail's list of Ide imprints in Louis W. Flanders and Edith F. Dunbar, *Simeon Ide* (Rutland, Vt., 1931), p. 146.

5. Tyler later hoped to collect these tales and his other unpublished works into a volume with the title "Utile Dulci"; a typed copy of some of the contents is in the Tyler Papers (Box 45, Envelope 35). The proposed title page was to read as follows: "UTILE DULCI / Being / A Collection compiled / from the more Juvenile and unpublish'd / Works / of the Author / embracing Dialogues Sacred Dramas Fables in Prose / and verse, Tales, / &c / Design'd to allure the youth / of both Sexes / To Profitable Studies. / By / Royall Tyler, A.M." (Quoted, with permission, from the Royall Tyler Collection, gift of Helen Tyler Brown.) The surviving fragments include "Five Pumpkins," "Historiette of the Tub Woman," and a poem on Darius' rule by intellect rather than force.

6. Dennie to Tyler, 14 April 1797, in *The Letters of Joseph Dennie*, ed. Laura G. Pedder (Orono, Me.: University of Maine Studies, 2nd series, no. 36, 1936), pp. 155–156. Dennie also refers briefly to "your historical labors," still another project (or perhaps the "Cosmography").

7. Tyler to Nancrede, March 1800, in Tyler memoir, pp. 126–127; it is also quoted, from the memoir, in Henry Burnham, *Brattleboro, Windham County, Vermont* (Brattleboro, 1880), p. 96.

8. These letters are transcribed in the Tyler memoir, pp. 115–127; they are published in G. T. Tanselle, "Author and Publisher in 1800: Letters of Royall Tyler and Joseph Nancrede," *Harvard Library Bulletin*, XV (1967).

9. See Chapter 4, note 5, above. The two men have therefore been referred to as "Damon and Pythias Among Our Early Journalists" by

S. Arthur Bent in *New England Magazine*, n.s. XIV (August 1896), 666–675. Cf. E. C. Coleman, *The Influence of the Addisonian Essay before 1810* (Urbana, Ill., 1936). Further information about the periodicals to which Tyler contributed is found in Chapter 4 above, on Tyler's poetry.

10. This copy is now in the Boston Public Library. One must use even these annotations with caution because some items are marked only with a "T" and others with "Tyler"; some of the "T"'s occur in parts of the book where other pieces are labeled "Thomas," and they could logically stand for "Thomas" as easily as for "Tyler" (see pp. 61–62, 65, 151–158). Brief items labeled either "T" or "Tyler" appear on pp. 53, 55, 56, 57, 58, 59, 61, 65, 151, 153, 188, 252, 253; of the longer "Colon & Spondee" prose pieces, the name "Tyler" is written on the following: pp. 256–258, 266–269, 271–274, 277–281, 286–314. There is a copy of the *Spirit* at the University of Vermont with similar annotations, in pencil; the annotator is not indicated, but the distinction between "T" and "Tyler" exactly follows the Boston copy. Cf. G. T. Tanselle, "Attribution of Authorship in *The Spirit of the Farmers' Museum* (1801)," *Papers of the Bibliographical Society of America*, LIX (1965), 170–176.

11. *Farmer's Weekly Museum*, 11 April 1797, 3 May 1796, 27 May 1799, and 31 July 1797 (reprinted in *Spirit*, pp. 277–281, 288–289, 302–303, 309–310).

12. *Farmer's Weekly Museum*, 18 February 1799 (reprinted in *Spirit*, pp. 271–274).

13. See Randolph C. Randall, "Authors of the *Port Folio* Revealed by the Hall Files," *American Literature*, XI (1940), 379–416.

14. *Port Folio*, I (21 November 1801), 371.

15. In addition to one item (partly prose and partly verse, incorporating the "Mouser" sonnet), reprinted from the *Museum*; see Chapter 4, note 28, above.

16. *Port Folio*, II (21 January, 27 February, 15 May 1802), 9–10, 57–58, 148.

17. In William Duane's Philadelphia *Aurora*, 20 June 1803.

18. This series is identified as Tyler's by Joseph T. Buckingham in his *Personal Memoirs and Recollections of Editorial Life* (Boston, 1852), I, 56. The four "Trash" numbers appeared in the *Polyanthos* for May and June 1806, and April and May 1807 (II, 92–97, 181–184; V, 14–19, 86–89). The third was unsigned, but the others were signed "S."

19. Tyler to Riley, 16 June 1809, in Tyler memoir, pp. 263–64. "Captain Holbrook" was probably a member of the firm of booksellers in Brattleboro, Holbrook & Fessenden — see *Grandmother Tyler's Book* (New York, 1925), p. 298. Tyler also sent the manuscript

of *The Maternal Physician* by Holbrook, and Riley (in a letter of 13 December 1809) mentioned shipping a supply of the *Reports* to Fessenden.

20. Riley to Tyler, 7 October 1809, in Tyler memoir, p. ²66. The book was entered for copyright on 23 September 1809.

21. Tyler to Riley, 22 May 1810, in Tyler memoir, pp. ²79–80.

22. See *Grandmother Tyler's Book*, pp. 294–295, and Tyler memoir, p. ²67.

23. *Grandmother Tyler's Book*, pp. 265, 294.

24. As it had in *The Algerine Captive*.

25. The first by Frederick Tupper in "Royall Tyler, Man of Law and Man of Letters," *Proceedings of the Vermont Historical Society*, IV (1928), 90; the second by Constance Rourke in *The Roots of American Culture* (New York, 1942), p. 123. Miss Rourke says that in *The Yankey in London* the "humor is keen, the style silvery-sharp: the little book is close to being a minor classic." A contrary view is expressed by the contemporary reviewer William Tudor, Jr. (identified in the entries for 24 October 1809 and 16 January 1810 in *Journal of the Proceedings of the Society Which Conducts the Monthly Anthology & Boston Review*, introd. M. A. DeWolfe Howe [Boston, 1910], pp. 209, 220): in the *Monthly Anthology and Boston Review* for January 1810 (VIII, 50–58), he called the book "a very useless addition to the almost innumerable books of travels, which crowd the shelves of libraries" (p. 50). He took the work as an authentic account of a visit to London (and quoted the complete chapter on the House of Commons) but recognized the lack of first-hand observation: "There is a degree of smartness and some humour in this writer, that would induce us to think he might do better. The fault of his work is, that it gives nothing new, nothing but what a man, with some knowledge of English history, and the habit of reading English newspapers and magazines, might write in this country. The account of the English bookseller and the remarks on the House of Lords are really too stale even for a magazine" (pp. 57–58). Whether or not the title was derived from Tyler, David Humphreys' play *The Yankey in England* (1815) makes dramatic use of the conflict of ideas present in Tyler's book and carries on the tradition of *The Contrast*.

26. G. F. Newbrough, "Mary Tyler's Journal," *Vermont Quarterly*, XX (1952), 28.

27. This typescript of "The Bay Boy" is in the Tyler Papers, Box 45, Envelope 29 (and a second copy is in Box 77, Envelope 13); quotations are here made, by permission of the heirs and the Vermont Historical Society, from these papers in the Royall Tyler Collection, gift of Helen Tyler Brown. Of the larger sections, four of them are labeled with the chapter numbers 5, 6, 7, and 9, but the position of the

others is not indicated; all have epigraphs (mainly of Tyler's own composition) except the one which quotes "The Wolf and Wooden Beauty." Of the smaller fragments, one is a preface of two pages (pointing out that the work is "designed not so much for the entertainment of the existing generation" as "for the gratification of their descendants"); two are marked as fragments of chapters 3 (2 pp.) and 4 (3 pp.); and two, unnumbered, deal with Updike's birth (2 pp. and 1 p.). The fragment of the third chapter of "The Bay Boy" consists of part of chapter 5 of *The Algerine Captive*; the sixth incorporates chapter 6, on Updike's education; the seventh consists of chapters 7 and 8, on his teaching and his return home; and the ninth is made up of chapters 9–11, on his early medical study. Though these papers were not available for many years, Bertrand W. Chapman had access to them in writing his 1933 master's thesis at the University of Vermont on "The Nativism of Royall Tyler," and he includes an extensive discussion of "The Bay Boy" on pp. 52–98. It is his belief that "The Bay Boy" contains "many of the elements of a literary masterpiece" (p. 97), and that it could have been "the first realistic work of fiction to be produced in the United States" (p. 98).

28. For a good discussion identifying the historical figures Tyler refers to, see Chapman, "Nativism," esp. pp. 75–80, 92–93.

29. The concrete details can be illustrated by a passage from the description of a Boston street in the evening: "The streets were now almost deserted, nothing was seen except the tardy footsteps of some belated labourer, or the cautious tread of some conscientious beau who was returning from the barber's shop under the shade of the projecting pent house, with his chin smoothly shaved, his toupee nicely craped his side curls neatly bound over leaden wires, and the whole as white as the powder puff and caster could make them. At length the old South Clock struck eight and all was silence." But the language can occasionally partake of all the worst features of Tyler's style: "When the gloom of vexation or the thunder gusts of anger and revenge are rapidly succeeded by the bright beams of hope which reflect their glittering rays on the watery bubbles that hang pendent from every Shrub and Spray in the Youngsters Horizon. . . ."

30. Dennie to Tyler, 14 April and 22 April 1797 respectively, in *Letters*, pp. 156, 157.

31. Dennie to Tyler, 2 October 1795, in *Letters*, p. 151.

Index

Index

Index

Index

Kellogg, Daniel, 241
Kelly, Hugh, 247
Kemble, Charles, 84
Kettell, Samuel, viii
Killheffer, Marie, 248
King, Rufus, 6, 7

La Bruyère, Jean de, 183
Lady's Magazine (London), 146
Langdon, Samuel, 6–7
Lauber, John, 248
Leach, James, 143
Leacock, John, 248
Lewis, Sinclair, 158
Lexington, Mass., 4
Lincoln, Benjamin: quoted, 21, 22; mentioned, 19–20
Lloyd, Robert, 131
Locke, Samuel, 5, 7
Lovell, John, 3
Low, Samuel, 56
Lowell, James Russell: quoted, 226

McGrath, Charles, 243
McKee, Thomas J.: quoted, 58–59, 79; mentioned, x
McKnight, George H., 248
Madison, James, 83
Mallory, R. C.: opinion of RT's *Reports* quoted, 40
Mann, Horace, 25
Markoe, Peter, 142
Mason, Jeremiah: quoted, 8, 114, 257
Massachusetts Magazine, 79
Melville, Herman, 179
Merry, Robert, 121
Mills, Samuel, 43
Mitchell, Donald G.: quoted, 139
Molière (Jean Baptiste Poquelin), 86, 108, 252
Monthly Anthology (Boston): review of *Algerine Captive* quoted, 148; review of *Yankey in London* quoted, 271; mentioned, 172
Monthly Review (London): review of *Algerine Captive* quoted, 147
Morgan, J., 143
Morning Ray (Windsor, Vt.), 111

Morris, Owen, 245
Morse, Katharine, 8, 225–226
Morse, Royal, 8, 225–226
Moses, Montrose, 53
Moyes, Henry, 19, 163

Nancrede, Joseph: RT's correspondence with, 183–184; mentioned, 140, 181, 208
Nethercot, Arthur H., 247
New England Primer, 123
New Lebanon, N.Y., 28
New York City, 22, 23, 27, 30
Newbrough, George Floyd, x, 86
Newhampshire and Vermont Journal (Walpole, N.H.), 114, 126
Newport, R.I., 8–9
Nicholson, Thomas, 143

Odell, George C. D., 56
Otis, James, 2

Paige, Lucius R.: quoted, 226
Paine, Robert Treat, 113
Paine, Thomas, 155, 156, 167, 168, 262, 268
Palmer, Amelia, 25
Palmer, Catherine, 25
Palmer, Edward, 29, 235
Palmer, Elizabeth, 25
Palmer, Hampden, 29
Palmer, Joseph (Mary Palmer Tyler's grandfather): opinion of RT quoted, 228; mentioned, 24–25
Palmer, Joseph Pearse (Mary Palmer Tyler's father), 19, 25, 26, 27, 29, 234, 235
Palmer, Mary Cranch, 24
Palmer, William A.: opinion of RT's *Reports* quoted, 40
Park Street Theatre (New York), 51
Patrat, Joseph, 57
Pattee, F. L.: quoted, 246; mentioned, 59
Patterson, Mrs., 149
Peabody, Andrew: quoted, 53, 257; mentioned, ix
Peabody, Elizabeth Palmer, 25, 47
Peabody, Mary, 25

276

Index

Index

Sullivan, John, 8–9

Tablet (Boston), 114
Tefft, Israel, 241
Thacher, George, 6
Thacher, James: *American Modern Practice* quoted, 32
Theophrastus, 183
Thomas, Isaiah, 30, 36, 79, 114, 249
Tichenor, Isaac, 36
Townsend, Micah, 30, 236
Trent, William P.: quoted, ix
Trowbridge, Edmund, 221
Trumbull, John: quoted, 7; mentioned, 224–225
Trumbull, Jonathan, 245, 249
Tudor, William: review of *Yankey in London* quoted, 271
Tufts, Cotton, 229
Tupper, Frederick: quoted, 54, 96, 205; mentioned, x, xi, xii
Twaits, William, 130–131
Tyler, Abiel Winship (RT's son), 46
Tyler, Amelia Sophia (RT's daughter), 47
Tyler, Andrew (RT's great-uncle), 222
Tyler, Charles [Royall] (RT's son), 47
Tyler, Edward Royall (RT's son), 46
Tyler, George Palmer (RT's son), 47
Tyler, Jane (RT's sister), 3
Tyler, John (RT's great-uncle), 222
Tyler, John Steele (RT's brother): manages Federal Street Theatre (Boston), 30, 83, 84; quoted, 85; mentioned, 3, 6, 8, 12, 27, 129, 224–225, 227, 236
Tyler, John Steele (RT's son), 46, 47
Tyler, Joseph (RT's uncle), 222
Tyler, Joseph Dennie (RT's son), 46, 236
Tyler, Mary (RT's sister), 3, 6
Tyler, Mary Hunt Palmer (RT's wife): courted by RT, 26–28; life with RT in Guilford and Brattleboro, Vt., 29–31; *Maternal Physician*, 31–33, 36, 236, 271; RT's letters to, 44, 240; care of RT in last illness, 47–48; journal quoted, 48; *Grandmother Tyler's Book*, x, 28–29, 228, 232, 234, 235; opinion of RT's oratory quoted, 35; letter to RT quoted, 240; mentioned, 24, 25, 191, 206, 209, 238
Tyler, Mary Steele (RT's mother), 6, 19, 23, 27, 29, 30, 224
Tyler, Mary Whitwell (RT's daughter), 46
Tyler, Royal S. (of Andover, Conn.), 238
Tyler, Royall (RT's father), 1–2, 3, 6, 12, 221–222, 224
Tyler, Royall: childhood, 3–4; juvenilia, 259; Harvard years, 4–7; study of law, 7–8, 9; in Revolution, 8–9; residence in Maine, 9; love affair with Abigail Adams, 10–19; pursuit of Daniel Shays, 19–23; production of *Contrast*, 23, 51–55; production of other plays, 82–85; courtship of Mary Hunt Palmer, 25–28; residence in Guilford, Vt., 27–30; publication of poetry, 109–118; publication of essays, 184–189; publication and reception of *Algerine Captive*, 140–148; residence in Brattleboro, Vt., 30–31, 47; legal career, 13, 28, 34–45, 47; publication of *Yankey in London*, 189–191; unfinished pieces, 181–184, 205–208; cancer, 45, 47–48; obituary, viii, 239

WORKS

"Address," 85
"Address to Della Crusca," 116, 122–123
Algerine Captive, 140–180; publication, 140–143; reception,

278

Index

Index